DECOLONIZING BIBLICAL STUDIES

DECOLONIZING BIBLICAL STUDIES

A View from the Margins

Fernando F. Segovia

ORBIS BOOKS

Maryknoll, New York 10545

The Catholic Foreign Mission Society of America (Maryknoll) recruits and trains people for overseas missionary service. Through Orbis Books, Maryknoll aims to foster the international dialogue that is essential to mission. The books published, however, reflect the opinions of their authors and are not meant to represent the official position of the society.

To obtain more information about Maryknoll and Orbis Books, please visit our website at www.maryknoll.org.

Library of Congress Cataloging-in-Publication Data

Segovia, Fernando F.
    Decolonizing biblical studies : a view from the margins / Fernando F. Segovia.
        p. cm.
    Includes bibliographical references.
    ISBN 1-57075-338-5 (pbk.)
    1. Bible—Criticism, interpretation, etc.—History—20th century. 2. Postcolonialism. I. Title.

BS500.S42 2000
220.6'01—dc21

                                                                00-039983

Contents

PART III
BIBLICAL STUDIES
AND POSTCOLONIAL STUDIES

PART IV
VOICES FROM OUTSIDE

Acknowledgments

For the putting together of this collection of essays, I stand in deep gratitude to three individuals in particular: first and foremost, to Robert Ellsberg, editor in chief of Orbis Books, who gave his undivided support to the project from the first; second, to the Rev. Tan Yak-Hwee, a student in the Graduate Department of Religion at Vanderbilt University, who undertook the arduous task of preparing for publication a variety of essays extracted from different venues and published in quite different formats and who did so with a wonderful mixture of amiability, patience, and excellence; finally, to Dr. H. Jackson Forstman, Acting Dean of the Divinity School at Vanderbilt University, who kindly approved funding for the editorial task. I stand deeply indebted as well to the entire staff of Orbis Books, and in particular to Catherine Costello, who oversaw with its usual care and acumen the process of publication.

Grateful acknowledgment is made for permission to reprint the following previously published material:

"'And They Began to Speak in Other Tongues': Competing Modes of Discourse in Contemporary Biblical Criticism," in *Reading from This Place*. Volume 1: *Social Location and Biblical Interpretation in the United States*, ed. F. F. Segovia and M. A. Tolbert (Minneapolis: Fortress Press, 1995).

"Cultural Studies and Contemporary Biblical Criticism: Ideological Criticism as Mode of Discourse," in *Reading from This Place*. Volume 2: *Social Location and Biblical Interpretation in Global Perspective*, ed. F. F. Segovia and M. A. Tolbert (Minneapolis: Fortress Press, 1995).

"Pedagogical Discourse and Practices in Contemporary Biblical Criticism," in *Teaching the Bible: The Discourses and Politics of Biblical Pedagogy*, ed. F. F. Segovia and M. A. Tolbert (Maryknoll, N.Y.: Orbis Books, 1998).

"Pedagogical Discourse and Practices in Cultural Studies: Toward a Contextual Biblical Pedagogy," in *Teaching the Bible: The Discourses and Politics of Biblical Pedagogy*, ed. F. F. Segovia and M. A. Tolbert (Maryknoll, N.Y.: Orbis Books, 1998).

"Biblical Criticism and Postcolonial Studies: Toward a Postcolonial Optic," in *The Postcolonial Bible*, ed. R. S. Sugirtharajah, The Bible and Postcolonialism 1 (Sheffield: Sheffield Academic Press, 1998).

"Notes toward Refining the Postcolonial Optic," *Journal for the Study of the New Testament* 75 (1999): 103-14.

"My Personal Voice: The Making of a Postcolonial Critic," in *The Personal Voice in Biblical Studies*, ed. I. R. Kitzberger (London: Routledge, 1998).

"Racial and Ethnic Minorities in Biblical Studies," in *Ethnicity and the Bible*, ed. M. G. Brett, Biblical Interpretation Series 19 (Leiden; New York; Köln: Brill, 1996).

Introduction

The present volume brings together eight essays of mine written over the course of the last five years or so. As a genre, collections of essays can range from the loosely to the tightly knit. There is truly no ideal in this regard; it all depends on the context and aims of the project in question. The present volume, I should think, falls very much at the latter end of this spectrum. A word of explanation regarding both context and aims is in order, therefore.

I began my professional and scholarly career in biblical studies in the academic year of 1977-78. It was a time when traditional historical criticism still held sway in the discipline; it was also a time when the first voices of dissent had begun to be registered from within the discipline itself. I was but vaguely aware of such voices and would remain so for a few years still. In the more than twenty years that have elapsed since that first academic appointment of mine, I have witnessed radical changes in the conception, practice, and teaching of biblical criticism. Such changes have demanded considerable retooling on my part, involving long and wide reading in a number of other academic fields as well as considerable rethinking of the grounds and aims of that very discipline I had come to call my own.

Some years ago I decided to come to terms with these changes in both the discipline and myself by undertaking an account of the path of biblical criticism, not by way of major figures and pursuits but rather by way of major models of interpretation, their underlying principles of interpretation as well as their relationship to one another in terms of method and theory. It gradually dawned on me, as I attempted to conceptualize and articulate such a plotting of the discipline, that what I had witnessed was a veritable process of decolonization and liberation. The use of such concepts was by no means fortuitous. At that time I was also becoming increasingly aware of my own context and perspective as a child of both the non-Western world and the non-Western diaspora in the West.

At the outset of my career I was one of a handful of biblical scholars from either Latin America, the place of my birth and the context of my primary socialization, or an ethnic/racial group in the United States, the place of my exile and the context of my secondary socialization. In fact, it was not long before that theological discourse from the non-Western world had begun to make itself heard by way of liberation theology in Latin

America. Since that time, radical changes have taken place as well across the whole spectrum of Christian studies, including biblical studies: not only have more and more individuals from the non-Western world joined the ranks of biblical criticism and the rest of the theological disciplines, but also more and more members of ethnic and racial minorities in the United States. Indeed, I have witnessed the enormous expansion and diversification of the project of liberation as well as the more recent flowering and spread of the postcolonial program. Such changes, once again, demanded both fundamental retooling and fundamental rethinking on my part, away from the strictly Western critical and theological training I had received and appropriated.

Thus, to repeat, the use of the terms *decolonization* and *liberation* to describe the path of biblical criticism was quite deliberate on my part. In time I began to recount my own path in the discipline from such a perspective and to entertain the intersection between biblical studies and postcolonial studies. The present volume brings together the fruits of such labor by way of eight essays.

The first four I had originally intended—along with two others not included here, one on the hermeneutics of the diaspora and the other on intercultural criticism—as part of a monograph on the path of biblical criticism. However, my ongoing participation in a number of collaborative projects led me to use them instead in a variety of different venues. To see them together here is thus a source of pleasure for me—the partial fulfillment of an original project. I say partial because of the two pieces left out; these, however, I have set apart for inclusion in another collection of essays, where, I believe, they will find an even better fit. The last four, all the results of further collaborative projects, represent logical extensions of the first four, insofar as they pursue, in sundry ways, lines of thought introduced in the course of the first group. Thus, in the first two pieces I reflect in more sustained fashion on the relationship between biblical criticism and the global process of decolonization and liberation, while in the last two I explore in more detailed fashion the status and role of voices from outside the West in the discipline and the profession. To see them alongside the first group of essays proves a source of revelation for me—an insight into the path of my own development as a critic over the last few years. Their fit here, I thus find, is quite good.

These eight essays I have arranged in four parts: Part I contains studies in which I set out to trace the recent path of biblical criticism as a discipline—"Grand Models and Strategies of Interpretation"; Part II brings together studies in which I examine the pedagogical discourses and practices at work in such a development—"Grand Models and Strategies of Pedagogy"; Part III consists of essays in which I proceed to explore the intersection between biblical criticism and postcolonial studies—"Biblical Studies and Postcolonial Studies"; Part IV contains essays in which I address the question of "the other" in biblical criticism, both in personal and general terms—"Voices from Outside."

Needless to say, despite the fit that I perceive in the collection as a whole, a certain amount of repetition is inevitable in all projects of this kind, and the present volume is no exception. I have tried to keep such duplication to a minimum, without inflicting damage on the structure and coherence of any one piece. For whatever repetition remains I can only beg the kind indulgence of the reader. This means, to be sure, that the essays as presented here are not to be found exactly as they were published in their original versions. Nevertheless, I hasten to point out, the editorial hand at work has been, on the whole, rather minimal, confined for the most part to the following sorts of alterations: the use of a common bibliographical format, the updating of some materials and references, and the omission of some material for the sake of avoiding duplication.

For the title of the collection I have chosen *Decolonizing Biblical Studies: A View from the Margins*. The title proper reflects a theme that can be found in each and every one of these essays, and that I have highlighted above—the argument that the discipline of biblical criticism has witnessed, over the last quarter of a century, a process of decolonization and liberation by way of both theoretical/methodological diversity and sociocultural diversity. The subtitle conveys the perspective from which the argument is mounted and thus the postmodernist stance of the collection as a whole—this is my view, my own construction and plotting, of recent developments in the discipline.

A final comment is in order. For some time now I have been urged by many individuals to gather together in one volume material that is presently to be found in a broad variety of sources. The present collection represents a first effort on my part to do so, motivated as well, as specified above, by the desire to see an original conception for a monograph come true, although now, as it turns out, with different components in mind, and the realization that the essays thus assembled do represent an expanding project of mine over the last few years. For all such requests, given the results, I am most grateful.

PART I

GRAND MODELS AND STRATEGIES OF INTERPRETATION

1

"And They Began to Speak
in Other Tongues"

Competing Modes of Discourse
in Contemporary Biblical Criticism

The world of biblical criticism today is very different from that of the world of the mid-1970s. In the last few decades the field has undergone a fundamental and radical shift of such magnitude and consequences that it cannot be reasonably compared to any other in the twentieth century. This shift, moreover, is by no means over; in fact, its impact has only just begun. Among its manifold and far-reaching consequences, it has allowed for incredible diversity in models of interpretation as well as for a thoroughgoing reformulation of the role of culture and experience in the task of criticism, two issues with which I shall be specifically concerned in this study. The shift to which I am referring concerns the long dominance and swift demise of the historical-critical model of interpretation, in unquestioned control for the first three-quarters of the twentieth century but in broad retreat during its last quarter.[1] In what follows I will set forth my own overview of this change and hence of the overall course of biblical criticism throughout the twentieth century. I undertake such a seemingly grandiose project for a variety of reasons, all of which I regard as ultimately interrelated and interdependent.

---

[1] The first notes of concern or warning began to appear in the 1970s. In the United States, for example, N. R. Petersen spoke of "a process of potentially revolutionary change" with the future of the method as a "lively question" (*Literary Criticism for New Testament Critics*, Guides to Biblical Scholarship [Philadelphia: Fortress Press, 1978], 9-10). Similarly, in Germany, P. Stuhlmacher spoke of the method as "involved in a war on many fronts," with its "relevance . . . in part subject to serious doubt in theological and ecclesiastical circles" (*Historical Criticism and Theological Interpretation of Scripture: Toward a Hermeneutic of Consent* [Philadelphia: Fortress Press, 1977; German original, Göttingen: Vandenhoeck und Ruprecht, 1975], 19-21).

First, I find the shift is thoroughly intertwined with my own life as a critic, with autobiography and discipline going hand in hand. In effect, I have experienced the shift firsthand, having moved myself through the various interpretive paradigms of historical criticism, beginning just as redaction criticism was about to change into composition criticism; literary criticism, as it gradually ran the course of the interpretive spectrum from text-dominant to reader-dominant approaches; and cultural criticism, which has shifted from sociological to anthropological models, increasingly addressing the question of the reader's sociocultural context and stance. Such experience yields the benefit of analysis from within, from the point of view of the insider and practitioner—highly informed and self-critical. Such experience also yields the advantage of analysis from without, from the point of view of the outsider and former adherent— profoundly aware of social location in terms of intellectual currents of thought and hence of oneself as forming part, as reader and critic, of much wider modes of discourse involving different reading strategies and underlying theoretical orientations. This is not to say, of course, that such experience confers on the proposed overview any sort of privileged or unassailable status, for it is and remains, as with any such analysis, a construction on my part and from my perspective; such experience, however, does lend the overview a certain sense of commitment and authenticity. To recount the course of the discipline represents for me, therefore, a coming to terms with my own socioeducational life.

Second, for me the proposed overview of both shift and discipline is also closely linked to the ending of the twentieth century. There is something about the end of certain time periods—such as a year, a decade, or a century—whereby they become inevitably laden with profound significance and symbolism, despite the fact that such time delimitations are ultimately as arbitrary as any other.[2] Such periods elicit, in effect, a greater than usual desire for order and coherence, as a searching and reflective glance is cast backward as well as forward. Such periods thus call for the imposition of a plot on what would otherwise remain a totally unwieldy

---

[2] For similar ruminations and a similar analysis of a discipline in terms of a time period, see the use of the decade by N. K. Miller in approaching feminist criticism from a personal perspective ("Decades," in *Writing Cultural Criticism*, ed. M. Torgovnick, *The South Atlantic Quarterly* 91 [1992]: 65-86). On the power of the concept of an ending century, witness the number of sociopolitical studies appearing in the 1990s: Z. Brzezinski, *Out of Control: Global Turmoil on the Eve of the Twenty-first Century* (New York: Scribner's, 1993); P. Kennedy, *Preparing for the Twenty-first Century* (New York: Random House, 1993); J. Lukacs, *The End of the Twentieth Century and the End of the Modern Age* (New York: Ticknor & Fields, 1993). From a more popular point of view, see D. Richards, "Counting Down to the Year 2000," *The New York Times*, June 27, 1993, national ed., H5; and F. Haskell, "Art and the Apocalypse," *The New York Review of Books*, July 15, 1993, 25.

and deeply frustrating mass of details. With the close of the century, thoughts of the discipline come readily to mind and call for an account of its recent trajectory and future directions, especially in the light of the profound shift that marks the last quarter of the century. For me, therefore, to recount the course of the discipline means also to come to terms with my own sociohistorical context.

Third, I find the shift to be closely intertwined with certain global developments in the sociopolitical arena, developments within which I have found myself inextricably implicated from birth. Indeed, in my own case this yearning for order and organization is directly propelled by the conviction, pointedly reinforced by the recent implosion and collapse of the Soviet Empire, that a predominant characteristic of the twentieth century was the gradual but steady process of liberation and decolonization in the world at large as the colonial powers of the Northern Hemisphere have lost their sociopolitical grip—though by no means their socioeconomic grip—on the colonized peoples of the Southern Hemisphere. This is a process that I presently see as reaching a climactic stage, as the voices of the colonized come increasingly to the fore. It is also a discourse in which I find myself, as a subject of a number of layers of colonialism,[3] *arrojado* ("thrown"), with not much choice regarding participation or abstention.[4] As I reflect on the sociopolitical course of the twentieth century and the outlook for the future, I find it impossible not to see an analogous process at work in the classical theological disciplines, including biblical criticism, and hence not to use the same categories of analysis in the formulation of the proposed overview—a process of decolonization and liberation at work in and through the shift. For me,

---

[3] Indeed, I come from a country (Cuba) that has lived under three very different colonial powers in the course of the twentieth century and still finds itself, with but a few years to go to the centenary of its independence, under the aegis of one such power, even when the imperial center itself has collapsed—the ultimate irony of the colonized mentality! To wit: Spanish colonialism, from the very first year of the era of conquest through the conclusion of the long War of Independence at the turn of the century (1492-1898); American colonialism and neocolonialism, encompassing respectively the period of the occupation (1898-1902) and the period of the republic, at least in name (1902-59); and Soviet colonialism (1959–), covering not only the emergence of a Socialist-Leninist state in alliance with the Warsaw Pact (1959-90) but also its present continuation as a committed outpost or redoubt of Socialism-Leninism even after the demise and breakup of the center itself (1990–).

[4] The Indian critic G. C. Spivak describes the space she occupies as having been "written" for her by history and thus as ineluctable; see, for example, her "The Post-Colonial Critic," in *The Post-Colonial Critic: Interviews, Strategies, Dialogues*, ed. S. Harasym (New York: Routledge, 1990), 67-74, esp. 68. I much prefer the Spanish term, *arrojar* (to be thrown), as reflecting the unpredictable and turbulent nature of the discourse imposed by colonization; indeed, I find the further connotation of the term ("to be vomited") not altogether out of place.

therefore, to recount the course of the discipline means to come to terms with my own sociocultural context as well.

Finally, this shift is directly responsible as well for my ongoing critical project. I believe that such an overview of the discipline will serve as a proper introduction to this project, which reflects and addresses in a variety of ways the state of anomie—permanent anomie, perhaps—that has come to characterize the discipline at this critical though enormously creative juncture in its life.[5] Central to this project has been a focus on the relationship between biblical interpretation and the social location of the interpreter. Such a focus on real readers and communities of readers is one that remained submerged for most of the twentieth century but is now beginning to come to the forefront of the discussion, pressed as it is by those who had remained in the margins for most of the century but who are now beginning to enter the ranks of the discipline in ever greater numbers. Indeed, it is at this point, when the shift in the discipline has reached a certain level of methodological and theoretical maturity, that such a question can be properly raised and pursued from an informed and sophisticated point of view. Finally, therefore, for me to recount the course of the discipline is to account for the present tenor and direction of my own socioacademic project.

The title I have chosen for this chapter—"And They Began to Speak in Other Tongues"—is meant to reflect the proposed course of the discipline; in so doing, however, it also gives away the main lines of the plot. One day as I reflected upon the present situation of the discipline, on the verge of becoming truly global for the first time, this particular statement from the Lukan scene of Pentecost (Acts 2) came suddenly to mind. It is certainly not my intention to produce an elaborate allegorical reading of this narrative event in the light of the developments in question nor to claim any sort of spiritual guidance or sanction from above for such developments; all I wish to do is to engage in a bit of constructive intertextual encounter.

Indeed, while the present state of the discipline does remind me of a number of elements from the Lukan scene, it also requires a fundamental revisioning of that scene. What I have in mind is a "speaking in other tongues," to be sure, but of a very different kind. Thus, it is not that one and the same group now speaks in other tongues to the multitudes at large—in fact, a rather accurate description of the situation up to this point—but rather that the multitudes at large have begun to speak in other tongues, their own tongues. Given such a revisioning of the scene, a number of analogous observations are in order (2:4-5): "Men [men and women, readers and critics] from every nation under heaven [from all corners of the world and all configurations of social location in the world]

---

[5] I borrow such a description of the discipline from the article by S. Ortner in which she describes the present state of anthropological theory in such terms ("Theory in Anthropology since the Sixties," *Comparative Studies in Society and History* 26 [1984]: 126-66, esp. 126-27).

began to speak in their own tongues [to read and interpret the biblical texts out of their own contexts, addressing not only one another but also the world at large]." The result of such "speaking in tongues" is no longer a discourse controlled by the center, as the Lukan narrative would have it (though in effect any translation of such a discourse would immediately serve to decenter the center), but a discourse with no center or with many centers, hence the reason for my subtitle, "Competing Modes of Discourse in Contemporary Biblical Criticism." Such, in my opinion, is where the discipline presently stands, with a beginning moment in the shift involving methodological and theoretical diversity now giving way to a second moment involving sociocultural diversity as well. I argue, therefore, that what is occurring is actually the reverse of the Lukan agenda: not at all a movement from "Jerusalem" out to the world at large, but rather one decentered from "Jerusalem" (for "Jerusalem" no longer exists) and in the world at large. I see it as a process of liberation and decolonization, away from the Eurocentric moorings and concerns of the discipline, not in complete abandonment of such discourse but in search of other discourses heretofore bypassed and ignored. I begin my overview of this process with an exposition of the main structural components to be used in the construction and deployment of its plot.

COMPETING MODES OF DISCOURSE IN BIBLICAL CRITICISM

In the plotting of the shift in the discipline that follows, I have recourse to three structural principles: first, I argue that the process has so far involved three distinct paradigms or umbrella models of interpretation, each involving a variety of interpretive approaches; second, I describe such a process in terms of liberation and decolonization, although for different reasons at different times; finally, I argue that, at this point in the process, these three paradigms need not be seen as mutually exclusive but rather as subject to creative interaction.

Competing Interpretive Paradigms

As the discipline has shifted, three different and competing paradigms in contemporary biblical criticism have emerged, each involving a different and distinctive mode of discourse.[6] First, there is traditional historical

---

[6] By "paradigm" or "umbrella model of interpretation" I mean a certain sharing of values and practices, of theory and criticism. I do not mean to imply uniformity or close agreement among the different practitioners, nor do I wish to create hard-and-fast distinctions. Indeed, differences and variations are not only the norm but also quite profound within each proposed paradigm; similarly, the different paradigms advanced also reveal a variety of features in common. Nevertheless, at a certain level of abstraction a grouping of values and practices is helpful in critical analysis. On this point, see A. Easthope, *Literary into Cultural Studies* (New York: Routledge, 1991), 3-21.

criticism broadly conceived, the dominant type of criticism through the mid-1970s, encompassing such different methodological approaches or strategies as literary or source criticism, history-of-religions criticism, tradition criticism, form criticism, redaction criticism, and composition criticism. As an umbrella model or paradigm, historical criticism may be summarized in terms of the medium or text as means, with an emphasis on the signified—the text as a means to the author who composed it or the world in which it was composed. From the point of view of culture and experience, the model calls for a radical contextualization of the text but for universality and objectivity on the part of the reader.

Second, there is literary criticism broadly conceived, the umbrella type of criticism that first began to dislodge traditional historical criticism from its position of dominance in the 1970s, rapidly establishing itself as a solid alternative in the discipline through the 1980s and into the 1990s. It includes such different approaches as narrative criticism, structuralism, rhetorical criticism, psychological criticism, reader-response criticism, and deconstructionism. As a paradigm or umbrella model, literary criticism may be described in terms of the medium or text as medium, with an emphasis on the signifier—the text as a message from author to readers, with an emphasis on the principles governing the formal aspects of this communication. It is a development that reflects, rather belatedly, the modernist impulse. In terms of culture and experience, the emphasis on the contextuality of the text may or may not diminish, depending on the specific approach in question; however, even when such emphasis continues, its course of direction does undergo a fundamental change. On the one hand, such emphasis tends to disappear considerably when the text is approached as a self-standing and independent object, divorced from world/author and reader. On the other hand, such emphasis shifts direction when contextuality is pursued from a mostly aesthetic or formalist perspective, along the lines, for example, of generic studies or literary history. At the same time, universality and objectivity clearly remain the order of the day with regard to the reader of the text.

Finally, there is cultural criticism broadly conceived, an umbrella type of criticism that arose alongside literary criticism in the mid-1970s and played a major role as well in the dislodging of historical criticism from its entrenched position in the discipline, firmly establishing itself as a viable alternative through the 1980s and into the 1990s. It encompasses such different lines of inquiry as socioeconomic and ideological analysis along neo-Marxist lines; sociological approaches, mostly informed by the sociology of religion, as with millenarian theory and sectarian theory, but also involving such other approaches as cognitive dissonance, the sociology of knowledge, and the analysis of social dynamics and roles; and anthropological approaches, informed in large measure by cultural anthropology, as in the case of Mediterranean studies, crosscultural analysis of purity codes, and comparative societal studies in terms of group and grid. As a paradigm, cultural criticism may be summarized in terms of the medium or text as both medium and means, but with a much greater emphasis on the signified than on the signifier—the text as a message from author to readers within a given context, with an emphasis on the codes or principles governing the sociocultural aspects of such communication; hence, the text as a means to that world in which it was produced. As such, it is a development that continues the traditionalist impulse, with its focus on the text as a period construction and remnant. From the point of view of culture and experience, the model calls for an even more radical contextualization of the text; it may also call, though not necessarily, for a contextualization of the reader, as in the case of neo-Marxist approaches and less so in the case of anthropological approaches.

Even a cursory look at the discipline in action, in any of its institutionalized channels—such as annual meetings, faculty composition, book reviewing, and the like—readily shows the presence of all three modes of discourse at work, both in terms of practice and theory.[7] However, while historical criticism may be said to be on the decline, both literary and cultural criticism are clearly on the ascendancy.[8]

---

[7] On a similar use of paradigms, see, from the point of view of literary theory, T. Eagleton, *Literary Theory: An Introduction* (Minneapolis: University of Minnesota Press, 1983), 74; from the point of view of biblical criticism, E. Schüssler Fiorenza, "'For the Sake of Our Salvation . . . ' Biblical Interpretation and the Community of Faith," in *Bread Not Stone: The Challenge of Feminist Biblical Interpretation* (Boston: Beacon Press, 1984), 23-42.

[8] Indeed, the historical-critical model may even be described as defunct from a theoretical point of view but not from a practical point of view. From a theoretical perspective, the method is so defunct that it has been unable to mount a serious and informed defense of its own methodological principles or reading strategy and underlying theoretical orientation. From a practical perspective, the method is alive, though at various stages of health: while its grasp in the United States has slipped considerably, its dominance in Europe is still very much in evidence, though with dangerous cracks beginning to appear here and there as well. For example, the recent launching of a new journal, *Biblical Interpretation: A Journal of Contemporary Approaches*, by such a publisher as E. J. Brill is quite telling. Indeed, the first paragraph of its "Editorial Statement," as published in its first issue (1 [1993]: i-ii), provides, subtly but surely, a thoroughly political rationale for its appearance: "The recent burgeoning of new and sometimes competing approaches to textual interpretation is only sporadically reflected, and reflected upon, in the leading journals of historical, biblical criticism. The need for an international vehicle for both modes of study, practical and theoretical, is acute." In effect, the rationale argues—with recourse even to the liberation language of center and margins—that control of the leading journals in the field by historical critics has prevented the publication of manuscripts reflecting the newer interpretative currents, making a new outlet for such voices imperative.

A Process of Liberation and Decolonization

I regard the emergence of these models of interpretation as a gradual process of liberation and decolonization. On the one hand, one finds that the stranglehold of one particular and institutionalized model of interpretation, historical criticism, has been broken. For a long time all biblical critics were trained in this model, with all faculties eventually dominated by its adherents and representatives. Consequently, its grip on both the academy and the church was close to total.[9] On the other hand, this change has not led to the enthronement of any one model of interpretation but has given rise instead to enormous diversity—not only two other interpretive paradigms but also each with a wide repertoire of interpretive approaches much more diverse among themselves than the different methodologies of historical criticism ever were.[10] At first, with the advent of literary criticism and cultural criticism, such diversity was largely methodological and theoretical, with a focus on texts and models for the reading of such texts. More recently, with certain developments in literary criticism and cultural criticism, such diversity has become sociocultural as well, with a focus on readers and their models for reading. Such a process can be appropriately described in terms of liberation and decolonization: first, in the sense of self-determination regarding the choice of interpretive model; second, in the sense of calling into question the myth of objectivity and universality required of the critic.

---

[9] One must be careful to observe in this regard that, from a socioreligious or ecclesiastical point of view, there were many religious bodies for which historical criticism was never an option, let alone the dominant type of biblical criticism; for others, moreover, such as the Roman Catholic Church, historical criticism did become, with time, an option and eventually the dominant method but only after a period of considerable struggle. The grip I am talking about has to do primarily with the so-called mainline churches, including Roman Catholicism by this time, and their institutions of higher learning.

[10] It would not be at all difficult for a historical critic to shift, say, from a form-critical to a redaction-critical perspective or from redaction criticism to composition criticism; in the end, the overall mode of discourse remained very, very similar. It would be much harder, however, for a literary critic to go from narrative analysis to psychological criticism or deconstruction, or for a cultural critic to go from neo-Marxist criticism to anthropological or sociological criticism. In both instances, while the mode of discourse does possess a certain undeniable common character, the body of theory underlying each particular approach within the given mode of discourse is quite different, extensive, and demanding.

Creative Interaction

Finally, from the particular position I occupy, working out of a postmodernist context, I do not regard these three competing modes of discourse as mutually exclusive. I believe that they can and should be used creatively. First, the historical impulse of traditional criticism—its sense of the distance of the text—should not be bypassed. In many ways these texts represent an "other" to us. Second, the formalist impulse of literary criticism—its regard for the principles of narrative—should also not be ignored. These texts do follow certain conventions that are foreign to us. Third, the hermeneutical impulse of cultural criticism—its regard for the context of both text and reader—should be greatly enhanced. To be sure, these texts constitute an "other" to us and follow principles and conventions of another time and culture; at the same time, such "otherness" is always apprehended through our own lenses as readers, socially and historically located as we are. As such, from a postmodernist perspective, reading and interpretation always involve construction on the part of the reader, and the reader proceeds to engage in such a construction knowing that it is in the end a construction. Thus, both the historical and the formalist impulse are followed and put to good use, but in so doing one is always aware that the reconstruction of history and the reconstruction of the text are constructions, also dependent on the social context of the readers.

With these three structural principles fully in mind, I can now proceed with the plotting of the shift in the discipline, following the three interpretive paradigms outlined above.

HISTORICAL CRITICISM: THE TEXT AS MEANS

Though the general sequence as well as the aims and tools of the various methodological movements within historical criticism are well-known, its basic strategy for reading and underlying theoretical orientation are not, since the paradigm itself did not require much theoretical sophistication of its adherents, only practical expertise. In other words, the model had little critical self-consciousness, either of itself as a paradigm or of its relationship as model to other modes of interpretation. Though clearly a form of literary criticism, involving the criticism of ancient texts, historical criticism did not require an informed and thorough grounding in the wider world of literary theory, whether European or American. Thus, how this particular approach to texts stood within the history of literary theory or how it conformed to or differed from other contemporary approaches was never considered a subject of interest or discussion; as a result, the question of why it did what it did in the way that it did was never addressed explicitly, much less in a critically comparative fashion.[11] An overview of the basic principles underlying the model and its strategy for reading a text is therefore in order and will serve in turn as a basis for comparison with the two paradigms that emanated from it.[12]

Basic Principles

1. The historical-critical model approached the biblical text primarily as a means, as historical evidence from and for the time of composition. As such, the text was to be read and analyzed within its own historical context and regarded as a direct means for reconstructing the historical situation that it presupposed, reflected, and addressed. Such a task was broadly conceived, involving extensive knowledge of the period and area under consideration, for example, historical framework, social institutions, cultural conventions, forms of religious expression, and literary production and forms. Within this overall historical conception of the text, its character as a religious document was especially emphasized, with a corresponding focus on its theological content and message.

For the model, therefore, the meaning of the text resided either in the world represented by it, in the intention of the author, or both.[13] Consequently, an analysis of the text as text never really formed part of its methodological repertoire until the very end, and then the entire model began to collapse. In addition, an analysis of the world or the author behind the text, learned and detailed as it was, never availed itself consistently of any type of social or cultural theory, remaining throughout at a rather impressionistic

---

[11] Such theoretical myopia had inevitable consequences. For example, its concentration on acquiring the basic methodological tools for interpretation allowed it to think of itself, quite unreflectively and uncritically, as *the* method, as the one view of criticism shared by all, without any realization of its own theoretical and ideological foundations. Likewise, its failure to enter into critical exchange with other interpretive models, varied as they were during the course of the twentieth century, not only reinforced this provincial view of itself as *the* method but also prevented it from responding satisfactorily to the theoretical challenges that eventually emerged, adding thereby to the consternation and frustration of its practitioners. Its focus on the wherewithal of exegesis rendered any concern for its theoretical rationale unnecessary, and, as such, devoid of theoretical sophistication, it was left basically defenseless.

[12] For an overview of its historical development, its main figures and concerns, see R. F. Collins, *Introduction to the New Testament* (Garden City, N.Y.: Doubleday, 1983), 41-69 (chap. 2: "Historical-Critical Methodology"); and Stuhlmacher, *Historical Criticism*, 22-60.

[13] In terms of M. H. Abrams's still-useful typology of critical theories, historical criticism would qualify as a combination of mimetic and expressive theory; see M. H. Abrams, *The Mirror and the Lamp: Romantic Theory and the Critical Tradition* (New York: Oxford University Press, 1953), 3-29; and also "Types and Orientations of Critical Theories," in *Doing Things with Texts: Essays in Criticism and Critical Theory* (New York: W. W. Norton, 1989), 3-30.

level. Finally, only the intended readers of the text, usually conceived in terms of the rather loose concept of "community," were of any interest; the task of contemporary readers was to search and recover the original audience of the text, along with its original message and intention.

2. Since the model did not regard the biblical text as an artistic, rhetorical, and ideological production in its own right, there was little conception of the text as a literary, strategic, and ideological whole. In fact, as it presently stood, the text was often regarded as quite problematic and even unintelligible, full of *aporias*—textual unevennesses, difficulties, or contradictions—of a stylistic, logical, or theological sort. The presence of such *aporias* led to a view of the text as the result of a long process of accretion and redaction and an analysis of such a text in terms of an excavative reading involving the separation and reconstruction of its constitutive literary layers, often in conflict with one another. In fact, it was the juxtaposition of such layers that created the *aporias*, which served in turn as guideposts for the process of composition and analysis.[14] The reading involved was, therefore, a reading from the ground up rather than from beginning to end.[15]

3. The model had a strong positivistic foundation and orientation. The meaning of the text was regarded as univocal and objective, and thus it could be retrieved if the proper methodology, scientific in nature, was rigorously applied. Further, since the text presupposed, reflected, and addressed a historical situation, the path of history itself, likewise univocal and objective in nature, could be scientifically reconstructed as well. To be sure, disagreements in such retrievals and reconstructions were constant and profound, leading to criticism of works other than one's own as somehow defective in conception or application. Intrinsic to historical criticism was the methodological exposé or demolition of previous scholarship, usually carried out at the beginning of any work in a section known as the *status quaestionis*, the history of scholarship. Scholarship

---

[14] For a sophisticated exposition of this procedure in the area of gospel studies, see R. T. Fortna, *The Fourth Gospel and Its Predecessor: From Narrative Source to Present Gospel* (Minneapolis: Fortress Press, 1988), 1-11. Interestingly enough, this technical term of historical criticism becomes very important as well for deconstruction, with *aporia* as that point where the self-contradictory meanings of the text can no longer be resolved. While in historical criticism the *aporia* leads to earlier versions of the text, with varying degrees of reconstruction, in deconstruction the *aporia* leads to a view of the meaning of the text as undecidable.

[15] For the evolutionary theory of literature underlying the model, see Petersen, *Literary Criticism*, 11-20. I believe this reading was informed from the ground up by an operative though implicit theological principle to the effect that what comes earlier is better. In other words, the separation and reconstruction of layers were undertaken not only as a critical exercise but also as a theological imperative, with an underlying view of the earlier layers or traditions as somehow closer to the source, whether that source was Jesus himself or earliest Christianity, and hence more historically secure or accurate.

was thus seen as ultimately progressive and evolutionary in principle, though subject to serious deviations and aberrations, rather than in terms of different strategies of reading with their corresponding theoretical orientations.

4. Given its proposed scientific basis and approach, the model called for a very specific kind of reader—the reader as a universal and informed critic. The biblical critic assumed a position of neutrality and impartiality with regard to the text through a careful application of the proper methodological tools of the discipline; as a result, the critic brought nothing to the text in the process of interpretation. Thus, in order to recover the objective meaning of the text, the critic assumed an air of objectivity, involving a complete divestiture of all presuppositions, whether theological or sociocultural. It was the function of such a disinterested critic to approximate the meaning of the text, unpack it, and make it available to untrained readers. In the process, to be sure, the position of the critic emerged as highly authoritative and powerful, within a hierarchical system consisting of text-critic-readers.

5. The model was profoundly theological in orientation. Given its overriding concern, as noted above, for the religious content and message of the texts, it pursued a decidedly idealistic approach to them with a strong emphasis on biblical theology and on the theological positions, conflicts, and developments of the early Christian movement. Despite its claims to scientific distance, the model also possessed a strong underlying theological stance, with two distinct variations. On the one hand, interpretation could be regarded as radically divorced from theology, as an exercise in the history of religion yielding facts or data for the theologians to work with in their respective contexts. On the other hand, Christian doctrine and life could be seen as ultimately subject to the guidance and judgment of the Word of God, a "word," however, that could only be appropriated indirectly, via historical criticism itself, rather than directly, as in traditional dogmatic theology. While for both variations the task of theology was independent of the task of historical reconstruction, in the first variation reconstruction was regarded as an exercise in itself, while for the second variation reconstruction became a propaedeutic. Both positions were highly theological but not regarded—much less analyzed—as such.

Since for historical criticism the text as means possessed a univocal and objective meaning and since this could be retrieved via a properly informed and conducted scientific inquiry, the meaning uncovered was for all times and cultures. Consequently, a proper hermeneutical appropriation and application of the text could ultimately be based on such a meaning and interpretation of it. In other words, the original meaning of the text, properly secured and established, could dictate and govern the overall boundaries or parameters of the Christian life everywhere and at all times.

6. The model presupposed and entailed a very specific and universal pedagogical model: all readers, regardless of theological persuasion or sociocultural moorings, could become such informed and universal critics if the right methodological tools were properly disseminated and acquired.

This was a pedagogical model of learned impartation and passive reception, highly hierarchical and authoritative in character, with strong emphasis on academic pedigree (who studied under whom) and schools of thought (proper versus improper approximations to the text). Readers had to learn how to read texts correctly but did not have to read themselves, except of course for a mandatory surfacing of theological presuppositions so that these could be duly obviated. Not surprisingly, such an educational model closely paralleled the interpretive model, with students/readers dependent on teachers/critics for an account of the text and its meaning.

Concluding Comments

In terms of theory and methodology, the historical paradigm was remarkably inbred and thoroughly hegemonic. The theoretical discussion, such as it was, consisted mostly of an in-house affair conducted within certain well-established parameters: acquaintance with the various stages of historical criticism, and a reading of previous exegesis on the area of research in question. Dialogue with other critical models and disciplines was largely nonexistent. As regards experience and culture, the model was mixed: while it took into account the social location of the work under analysis, it deliberately bracketed the social location of those who read and interpreted the work. Thus, while the culture and experience underlying the texts themselves were regarded as essential for sound scholarship and proper interpretation, as something to be avidly pursued, the culture and experience informing the readers of these texts were looked upon as intrusive and unscholarly, as something to be avoided at all cost so as not to vitiate or contaminate the whole process of interpretation. The proper task of the critic was to engage in *exegesis*, not *eisegesis*—a reading of the text, not a reading into the text, allowing the text to speak on its own terms rather than inserting one's words into the text.[16]

---

[16] See in this regard the introduction to a recent handbook on biblical exegesis for the American student, J. R. Hayes and C. R. Holladay, *Biblical Exegesis: A Beginner's Handbook* (Atlanta: John Knox, 1982), 5-29. Here the language of exegesis/eisegesis, proper scientific tools, and meaning of the text still predominate. The authors do specify that the meaning of the text is virtually inexhaustible and hence only partially available to any particular kind of exegesis; at the same time, the role of the reader as reader is almost completely bypassed. In the end, eisegesis is described in terms of either asking the wrong questions of the text or answering the right questions wrongly. See also the beginning remarks to an introduction to New Testament exegesis meant originally for the German student, H. Conzelmann and A. Lindemann, *Interpreting the New Testament: An Introduction to the Principles and Methods of N.T. Exegesis* (Peabody, Mass.: Hendrickson, 1988), 1-5. Once again, the language of exegesis/eisegesis, scientific study and criteria, and proper understanding of the text are very much in evidence. The authors do point out that exegetes must be aware of their own presuppositions, conceived in purely theological terms; however, such awareness is seen as necessary in order to avoid reading such presuppositions in and into the text. A focus on the reader as reader, therefore, remains at a very minimal level indeed.

In the end, historical criticism collapsed from within when its methodological development was no longer able to address the emerging new
questions, concerns, and challenges. On the one hand, with the change
from redaction criticism to composition criticism in the 1970s, a turn to
literary theory became inevitable.[17] Once a consideration of the role of
the author shifted from an analysis of the changes introduced into the
received tradition (the heart of redaction criticism) to an examination of
the finished product in terms of its overall (theological) arrangement and
development (the goal of composition criticism), the need for literary theory
soon became obvious. It no longer proved sufficient to see the composition of the text as text in terms of overall sequence or its meaning in terms
of the author as theologian. On the other hand, with the pronounced
interest of both redaction and composition criticism on the community
and context behind the text, a turn to social theory—of whatever sort,
whether economic, sociological, anthropological—became imperative as
well. It was no longer sufficient to address the text as a social construct in
an impressionistic fashion; the need for a theoretical framework became
evident. The traditional tools of the discipline were simply no longer able
to address such challenges satisfactorily; new tools were very much in
order, and they began to be imported en masse into the discussion. Out of
historical criticism, then, emerged literary criticism and cultural criticism,
although for many historical criticism remained the operative model of
interpretation.

LITERARY CRITICISM: THE TEXT AS MEDIUM

When a prevailing interpretive paradigm begins to collapse in a discipline, there is usually a concomitant and vigorous turn to theory—a turn
to first principles, as it were. Biblical criticism in the last quarter of the
twentieth century was no exception in this regard. As the absence of and
disregard for theory became emblematic of traditional historical criticism,
reflecting its longstanding and institutionalized entrenchment, so did a
pronounced and sophisticated theoretical discussion mark the rise of the
"new" literary criticism (as opposed to the "old" literary criticism or source
criticism), likewise reflecting its character as a movement from the margins of the discipline with a serious challenge to the established center.

---

[17] Redaction criticism began in the 1950s, solidified in the 1960s, and began to
yield to composition criticism in the 1970s. For a brief account of redaction criticism, see Collins, *Introduction*, 196-230; N. Perrin, *What Is Redaction Criticism?*,
Guides to Biblical Scholarship (Philadelphia: Fortress Press, 1969). For composition criticism, see Perrin, "The Evangelist as Author: Reflections on Method in
the Study and Interpretation of the Synoptic Gospels and Acts," *Biblical Research*
17 (1972): 5-18.

Moreover, such theoretical reflection turned directly outward for grounding and inspiration—away from the traditional in-house discussion and theological moorings of the discipline toward a variety of other fields in the humanities, such as literature and psychology; its dialogue partners thus became literary theory, psychoanalytic theory, structuralist theory, and rhetorical theory.[18]

In effect, a new mode of discourse was beginning to emerge: armed with its own tools of analysis and corresponding terminology; by no means monolithic but rather highly diverse and highly dependent on the particular theoretical grounding in question. As a result, any discussion between historical critics and literary critics became well-nigh impossible, despite the cautious stance of the latter at first, grounded as they were in traditional historicism. From a theoretical point of view, historical critics proved no match for literary critics. A new umbrella model of interpretation was gradually coming into being, demanding of its practitioners a very different type of reading and practice.

Basic Principles

1. The literary model envisioned the biblical text primarily as a medium, as a message or communication between a sender and a receiver, an author and a reader. As a result, the text as text began to receive an attention it had never garnered before, now gradually emerging as a literary and rhetorical product in its own right. The main focus of inquiry was no longer on the world behind the text or on the author who conceived it, but rather on the aesthetic or artistic character of the text, with a corresponding emphasis on its formal features. Such analysis encompassed, for example, questions of genre and generic theory; questions of structure and architecture, whether at the surface or a deep level; and questions of anatomy and texture, ranging from the study of ancient rhetoric to modern narratology. Consequently, for literary criticism the artistic features of the text drew far more attention than its religious or theological aspects. In turn, while the analysis of author and reader focused on the concepts of implied author and implied reader (on the author and reader as derived from the text as a whole) rather than real authors and real readers, the analysis of the world centered on such concepts as levels of

---

[18] For examples of such early work and concern with theory, see D. O. Via, *The Parables: Their Literary and Existential Dimension* (Philadelphia: Fortress Press, 1967); idem, *Kerygma and Comedy in the New Testament: A Structuralist Approach to Hermeneutic* (Philadelphia: Fortress Press, 1975); D. Patte, *What Is Structural Exegesis?*, Guides to Biblical Scholarship (Philadelphia: Fortress Press, 1976); Petersen, *Literary Criticism*; and M. A. Tolbert, *Perspectives on the Parables: An Approach to Multiple Interpretations* (Philadelphia: Fortress Press, 1979).

narration, characterization, and above all point of view—on the world as depicted in and through the text.[19]

In retrospect, such a turn in biblical studies was quite logical and not at all surprising. It followed rather closely, in fact, a pattern already set in the wider realm of critical theory, though approximately forty years later. Just as the stranglehold of historicism in literary studies in the early part of the twentieth century eventually gave way to the roughly contemporary though largely independent movements of new criticism in the United States and formalism in Europe, with their similar emphasis on the text as an independent aesthetic object, so was historical criticism in biblical studies replaced in part by the new literary criticism in all of its various forms: the text, submerged as it had been under the critical focus on world and author, had now come fully to the surface.[20] This is not to say, however, that critical attention to the world and author behind the text was now altogether abandoned; rather, such analysis now perceived the text, as medium, as a primary and unavoidable filter in any such inquiry.

With the benefit provided by twenty years of hindsight, it is now possible to trace the overall course of literary criticism. In an interpretive spectrum ranging from a text-dominant pole to a reader-dominant pole, the path of analysis gradually wound its way from the former to the latter, from a focus on the text as text to a focus on the reader of the text, that is, from textual analysis in the form of narrative or rhetorical analysis to reader-response criticism.

2. With the new literary criticism, the highly atomistic approach of historical criticism, with its sustained emphasis on textual ruptures, gave way to an analysis that viewed the text as a literary and rhetorical whole. Instead of regarding the text as suffused with all types of *aporias*, the text was increasingly seen as a unified and coherent whole, a harmony and unity often ascribed to authorial intention itself, with such expressions as "carefully prepared" or "consciously crafted" much in vogue. As a result, the vertical reading of historicism, that inevitable sifting and reconstruction of literary layers necessary for a proper reading of the text from the ground up, began to yield to a horizontal reading, a reading from beginning to end, for which development and temporality became of the essence. The *aporias* of the past, over which there had never been much

---

[19] Within Abrams's typology, literary criticism would represent an example of an objective critical theory, with an increasingly pronounced though always subordinate expressive emphasis as it began to shower more and more attention on the reader; see n. 13 above. For a concise contrast with literary criticism in biblical studies, see M. A. Powell, *What Is Narrative Criticism?*, Guides to Biblical Scholarship (Minneapolis: Fortress Press, 1990), 1-10.

[20] On the character and context of formalism in literary theory, see Eagleton, *Literary Theory*, 17-53; V. B. Leitch, *American Literary Criticism from the Thirties to the Eighties* (New York: Columbia University Press, 1988), 24-59.

agreement, were now either altogether dismissed, disregarded from a methodological point of view, or ironically revisioned as examples of literary techniques. Even if excavative work was granted in principle, as it often was, the age of the *aporia* had basically come to an end.

3. The age of positivism or empiricism, however, had by no means ended. For literary criticism, above all in its text-dominant varieties but also in many of its reader-dominant expressions, the meaning of the text still tended to be regarded as univocal and objective and hence as retrievable on the basis of a rigorous application of proper and scientific methodology, now derived from literary or psychoanalytic theory. By and large, the literary and rhetorical features of the text, the concepts of implied author and implied reader, and the view of the world advanced by the text were regarded as present in the text and rather passively received or activated by the reader. With time, such objectivism began to recede in the light of other theoretical developments. For example, as regards the text, the polysemic nature of all signs, including language, was increasingly acknowledged, giving rise to the concept of a plurality of interpretations based on the text itself; no one interpretation, it was now argued, could exhaust the meaning of the text. Similarly, a much more active role was gradually assigned to the reader in the production of meaning, insofar as the text began to be seen as replete with gaps or lacunae that were to be filled in by the reader. Again, the notion of a plurality of interpretations, now grounded in the reader, began to come to the fore, insofar as different readers would supplement such gaps in different ways. In the end, however, the principle of a plurality of interpretations was always fairly circumscribed, with a view of such interpretations as ultimately subject to the constraints imposed by the text.

On the whole, therefore, disagreements over the identification and interpretation of the literary or rhetorical features of a text were still common and sharp, with criticism of works other than one's own perceived as somehow deficient in grounding or application. At the same time, the methodological exposé of the *status questionis* within historical criticism was replaced by a beginning section with a dual thrust: on the one hand, the sense of demolition still prevailed, though now with a twofold focus on the methodological shortcomings of historical criticism and the radical difference entailed by the new literary approach to be adopted; on the other, a sense of pedagogy entered the scene, as the theory that was to underpin the particular approach in question was paraphrased at great length and without much critical acumen. As such, scholarship was still basically regarded as progressive and evolutionary in principle, with the light of literary criticism leaving behind the darkness of historical criticism. Only with time, and to a rather limited extent, did the possibility of different readings begin to be granted within the literary model, but the consequences of such a position were left largely undeveloped.

4. It is fair to say that for the new literary criticism the reader remained faceless, even when the reading process became in and of itself a focus of attention—the reader as a universal and informed critic. In its text-dominant expressions, the biblical critic was called upon to master a specific body of theory, so that it could be applied correctly, from a technical point of view, to the biblical text and yield the desired results: this was a reader whose voice remained largely in the background. In its reader-dominant expressions, the biblical critic was also called upon to become self-conscious about the various strategies available for reading (for example, a recourse to the implied reader; the assumption of a naive, first-time reading; the assumption of a sophisticated reader, with the advantage of multiple readings; any combination thereof) and proceed accordingly: this was a reader whose voice was duly foregrounded, with constant references to such expressions as "now the reader does this" and "then the reader does that." In either case the identity of the reader in question remained of little interest: this was a technically proficient reader devoid of all presuppositions, theological or sociocultural. Even when most active, therefore, such a reader remained fundamentally neutral and impartial. In the end, the basic function of such a reader consisted in activating the meaning of the text, whether in a mostly passive way or more actively so, and making it available to uninformed and untrained readers. The position of the critic thus remained highly authoritative and powerful, maintaining that important mediating role within the text-critic-reader hierarchy.

5. As literary criticism veered away from the traditional moorings of historicism, its theological concerns and underlying theological stance shifted accordingly. On the one hand, following a course of action not unlike that adopted by those historical critics who saw their task as radically divorced from the larger theological enterprise, there was a move to focus on the newly highlighted literary and rhetorical features of the text to the detriment of that religious or theological dimension that had been so dear to historical criticism. Interpretation could be seen thereby as an exercise in literary formalism or even literary history, providing data for the theologians to apply in their respective situations. On the other hand, akin to those historical critics who did see in their work a necessary foundation for a proper hermeneutical appropriation and application of the Word of God, such a newfound interest in the formal features of the text could also be invested with a more explicit theological function. It could be argued that by bringing such features to the surface, literary criticism made possible not only a better appreciation of the craft and beauty of the Word of God but also a better feel for its power and hold upon readers. Again, both positions were theological to the core, but neither was regarded nor analyzed as such.

Since for literary criticism the meaning of the text resided by and large in the text as medium, it could be argued that a more enlightened approach to the text—an approach with due sensitivity to its literary features—would ultimately bring such meaning with greater clarity and force to the surface. In turn, such a meaning—a meaning for all readers and hence for all times and cultures—could still dictate and govern, in a far more effective way, the overall boundaries and parameters of the Christian life.

6. The pedagogical implications of literary criticism were, at least to begin with, not all that different from those of historical criticism: all readers, regardless of their respective sociocultural contexts or theological positions, could become informed and universal critics, if the right theoretical and methodological apparatuses were properly learned and propagated. In this regard the model was still, by and large, one of sophisticated impartation and passive acquisition. The model continued to be highly authoritative and hierarchical as well, with a strong emphasis now on theory (position within the interpretive spectrum) and theoretician (external authority to be read). Even when readers began to read themselves, they did so only in a highly formalistic way; the real readers remained strangely absent. As in historical criticism, therefore, the pedagogical model closely followed the interpretive model, with students/readers still ultimately dependent on teachers/critics for an account of the text and its meaning. To be sure, such a position gradually weakened; once the concept of a plurality of interpretations found its way into the discussion, no matter how constrained or circumscribed, the question of authority and hierarchy became problematic.

Concluding Comments

From the point of view of theory and methodology, the literary paradigm represented a profound liberating step in biblical studies. Not only did it break with historicism, which had had a stranglehold on critical practice, exposing along the way the largely unspoken and seemingly natural assumptions of the historical model, but it also, in critical theory, opened the way for a new direction of research involving an enormous diversity of interpretive approaches and hence a myriad of new ways in which to read and interpret the biblical texts. What had been, despite the differences in methodologies, a rather tight common discourse was now replaced by a variety of different discourses—related, to be sure, but quite distinct nonetheless. In terms of experience and culture, the model was also a mixed model, though with less emphasis than the historical model on the context of the text. While attention continued to be bestowed on the social location of the text, such attention was now largely literary or formalist, with much less regard for the sociocultural dimensions of the text. In addition, while attention did focus on the reader for a change and the notion of a plurality of interpretations gradually entered the discussion, such attention also remained largely formalist in tone, with little if any regard for the social location of the reader. For the model, therefore, the identity of the reader was of no importance whatsoever, totally unrelated to the analysis and interpretation of the biblical texts, even if the language of *exegesis* and *eisegesis* was no longer employed.

In more recent times, however, as the model has expanded into the reader-dominant pole of the interpretive spectrum, from an analysis of the features of the text to an analysis of the role of the reader in the production of meaning, and as the notion of a plurality of interpretations has been increasingly contemplated, whether based primarily on the text or on the reader, an encounter with the fundamental issue of flesh-and-blood readers has become inevitable. In other words, literary criticism must come to terms with the fact that lying behind the identification and interpretation of the formal features of a text in text-dominant approaches and lying behind the different reading strategies in reader-dominant approaches is always the real reader—the flesh-and-blood reader, historically and culturally conditioned, with a field of vision fundamentally informed and circumscribed by such a social location. It is such a reader, out of such social locations, who engages in the reading and interpretation of texts, arguing for certain literary and rhetorical reconstructions of the text and employing in the process a variety of interpretive model-constructs.

CULTURAL CRITICISM: THE TEXT AS MEANS AND MEDIUM

The explosion of theory that served to mark the breakdown of the historical-critical paradigm was actually twofold in nature, though with not much interaction between these two different currents even to this day. Alongside literary criticism there emerged another line of inquiry variously characterized by its own practitioners as sociological, social-world, or social-scientific criticism—what I prefer to call cultural criticism.[21] As in the case of literary criticism, its vigorous and sophisticated turn to theory was indicative of both its marginal beginnings in the discipline and its profound challenge to the established center. Like literary criticism, moreover, such theoretical activity turned outward for grounding and

---

[21] See, for example, H. C. Kee, *Christian Origins in Sociological Perspective* (Philadelphia: Westminster, 1980); R. Scroggs, "The Sociological Interpretation of the New Testament: The Present State of Research," *New Testament Studies* 26 (1980): 164-79; J. G. Gager, *Kingdom and Community: The Social World of Early Christianity* (Englewood Cliffs, N.J.: Prentice-Hall, 1975); J. H. Neyrey, ed., *The Social World of Luke-Acts: Models for Interpretation* (Peabody, Mass.: Hendrickson, 1991); J. H. Elliott, ed., *Social Scientific Criticism of the New Testament and Its Social World, Semeia* 35 (Decatur, Ga.: Scholars Press, 1986); B. J. Malina and R. L. Rohrbaugh, *Social-Science Commentary on the Synoptic Gospels* (Minneapolis: Fortress Press, 1992).

inspiration, away from the in-house, largely theological discussion of the discipline toward other fields in the humanities, like economics, sociology, and anthropology; its partners in conversation became neo-Marxist theory, sociological theory with an emphasis on the sociology of religion, and anthropological theory with a focus on cultural anthropology.[22]

A new mode of discourse was again in the offing: while possessing once again its own analytical apparatus and accompanying vocabulary, the movement was not at all uniform but quite wide-ranging, since such vocabulary and apparatus were directly dependent as well on the specific theoretical basis employed. For the discipline the result was the same: dialogue between cultural critics and historical critics proved largely futile, again despite the cautious positions of the cultural critics at first, trained as they had been in historical criticism. From a theoretical point of view, historical critics were again at a deep disadvantage. At the same time, dialogue between literary critics and cultural critics proved to be largely nonexistent, with each movement going in its own direction. For the literary critics, the cultural critics remained mired in a different form of historicism, with little sense for the character of the text as text; for the cultural critics, the literary critics remained hopelessly immersed in an ahistorical exercise in aestheticism, with a disembodied view of the text as text. Neither set of critics engaged in metatheory, despite the fact that their own supporting disciplines were fast becoming at this time increasingly interrelated and interdependent.[23] As a result, yet another umbrella model of interpretation was gradually coming into being, requiring of its adherents a very different type of orientation and application.

---

[22] For examples of such early work and involvement with theory, see, from a neo-Marxist perspective: J. P. Miranda, *Marx and the Bible: A Critique of the Philosophy of Oppression* (Maryknoll, N.Y.: Orbis Books, 1977) and also *Being and the Messiah: The Message of St. John* (Maryknoll, N.Y.: Orbis Books, 1977), as well as F. Belo, *A Materialist Reading of the Gospel of Mark* (Maryknoll, N.Y.: Orbis Books, 1981); from a sociological perspective, Gager, *Kingdom and Community,* and G. Theissen, *The First Followers of Jesus: A Sociological Analysis of Early Palestinian Christianity* (Philadelphia: Fortress Press, 1978); from an anthropological perspective, B. J. Malina, *The New Testament World: Insights from Cultural Anthropology* (Atlanta: John Knox, 1981).

[23] See, for example, J. Culler, *On Deconstruction: Theory and Criticism after Structuralism* (Ithaca, N.Y.: Cornell University Press, 1982); C. Geertz, "Blurred Genres: The Refiguration of Social Thought," in *Local Knowledge: Further Essays in Interpretive Anthropology* (New York: Basic Books, 1983); J. Clifford, "Introduction: Partial Truths," in *Writing Culture: The Poetics and Politics of Ethnography,* ed. J. Clifford and G. E. Marcus (Berkeley and Los Angeles: University of California Press, 1986), 1-26; and R. Rosaldo, "The Erosion of Classical Norms," in *Culture and Truth: The Remaking of Social Analysis* (Boston: Beacon Press, 1989), 25-45.

Basic Principles

1. With regard to the location of meaning, the cultural model was much closer in spirit to historical criticism than to literary criticism. Despite a view of the text as medium somewhat similar to that of literary criticism—a message or communication between a sender and a receiver, an author and a reader—the primary focus of cultural criticism lay not on the text as text, as medium or message, but on the text as means, as evidence from and for the time of composition. Such evidence, however, was now approached not so much in terms of its historical uniqueness or specificity, as in historical criticism, but rather in terms of its broader social and cultural dimensions. The emphasis was on the text as a product and reflection of its context or world, with specific social and cultural codes inscribed, and hence as a means for reconstructing the sociocultural situation presupposed, reflected, and addressed. Such analysis involved, for example, questions of social class and class conflict—applicable across time and cultures and hence addressed from a broad comparative perspective; questions of social institutions, roles, and behavior—again widely ranging across time and cultures and thus analyzed from a similarly broad comparative position; and questions of cultural matrix and values—deliberately culture-specific in orientation and hence examined from a more self-conscious crosscultural perspective. For cultural criticism, therefore, the economic, social, or cultural dimensions of the biblical text proved far more attractive than its theological or religious character. The meaning of the text was seen as residing primarily in the world behind it, with analysis of text, author, and readers undertaken in terms of their relationship to and participation in that world.[24]

In retrospect, this second turn in biblical studies was also quite understandable and to be expected. Indeed, a similar pattern can again be discerned in the wider field of literary theory with the breakdown of historicism: alongside the rise of formalism, one witnesses as well the emergence of cultural criticism, whether in the form of neo-Marxist criticism, with its emphasis on the socioeconomic context of the text and on the text as an ideological product, or along the lines of either the New York Intellectuals movement or myth criticism, with a view of the text as a broad cultural phenomenon.[25] Thus, the impressionistic approach of historical criticism to the world behind the text gave way as well to a much more

---

[24] From the point of view of Abrams's fourfold typology, cultural criticism should be seen as a mimetic type of theory, though with some expressive as well as objective elements here and there; see nn. 13 and 19 above.

[25] On the emergence and development of Marxist criticism, see T. Eagleton, *Marxism and Literary Criticism* (Berkeley and Los Angeles: University of California Press, 1976); Leitch, *American Literary Criticism*, 1-23; on the rise of cultural criticism, see Leitch, *American Literary Criticism*, 81-147.

rigorous and systematic analysis of that world. Forty years later, the same development could be observed in biblical studies.

With two decades of hindsight, it becomes possible here also to trace the overall course of cultural criticism: a gradual movement away from sociological models to anthropological models, with a persistent neo-Marxist emphasis on economics and ideology throughout; that is to say, a movement away from more universal to more culture-specific models, with a continuing concern throughout for the socioeconomic and ideological dimensions of the text.

2. From a practical point of view, the discussion between a reading founded in *aporias* and a holistic reading, a vertical reading and a horizontal reading, proved largely inconsequential for cultural criticism, with examples of both approaches in evidence within the model. The emphasis was neither on the need for a diachronic reading of the text, with a view of the text as consisting of different and conflicting literary layers, nor on the need for a synchronic reading, with a view of the text as a unified and coherent whole. What now mattered above all was the proper decoding of the economic, social, or cultural codes contained in the text, whether such codes were approached diachronically or synchronically. By and large, however, cultural criticism did tend to work with the text as a whole, as a sociocultural entity within a larger sociocultural context, but not so much as a matter of principle and thus without the same reverence for the formalist canons of anatomy, development, and temporality so dear to literary criticism. One way of describing the difference between the two models is to say that whereas literary criticism emphasized plotting and texture (the text as a literary and rhetorical whole), cultural criticism focused on story and codes (the text as an ideological whole). In any case, though excavative work was indeed pursued from time to time, the age of the *aporia* had once again, for all practical purposes, come to an end.

3. The same could not be said, however, for the age of positivism and empiricism. For cultural criticism as a whole, regardless of its specific variation, the meaning of the text was still seen as largely univocal and objective and, as such, retrievable. Indeed, cultural criticism saw in the borrowing of models from the social sciences a much more scientific and rigorous way of approaching and recovering the meaning of the biblical text in the fullness of its context, going far beyond the simplistic and unstructured impressionism of historical criticism. In fact, the principles of historical criticism were turned directly against it: without a proper and informed theoretical foundation, historical criticism had been engaging in *eisegesis*. The goal of cultural criticism was true *exegesis*, objectivity in approach and results. Thus, the codes of the world behind the text, no longer in use or even understood, were regarded as preserved in the text, as if in a repository or time capsule; such codes could, moreover, be properly decoded through the use of appropriate models.

Sharp debate ensued as to which models constituted the right models: models that found their point of departure in a world very different from that of the ancient Mediterranean basin and did not reflect self-consciously on the gulf created by such profound differences, as in the case of neo-Marxist analysis or the sociology of religion; or models that attempted to take seriously into account the crosstemporal and crosscultural character of any such enterprise, as with cultural anthropology. The result, once again, was sharp disagreement regarding the reconstruction of the world that lay behind and informed the text, with opposing critics charging that one another's works were flawed in grounding. In terms of composition, the *status questionis* of historical criticism was replaced by the same two-fold thrust of demolition and pedagogy observed in literary criticism: a beginning exposé of the profound methodological inadequacies of historical criticism alongside praise for the benefits of the new approach, followed by an extensive and largely uncritical exposition of the particular model to be adopted. Consequently, scholarship was still looked upon as progressive and evolutionary in principle, even more so than in literary criticism insofar as the possibility of a plurality of interpretations was little entertained; with the light of cultural criticism, the shadows of historical criticism would be left behind.

4. With regard to the readers behind the models, a number of distinctions are in order within cultural criticism. First, within the socioeconomic approach represented by neo-Marxist criticism, the reader did by no means remain faceless. Just as the text was considered an ideological product and hence a site of struggle in the class conflict, so was the critic: the task of criticism was similarly regarded as ideological to the core, a site of struggle. Thus, in effect, only a sophisticated *and* committed critic would be able to perceive and evaluate the socioeconomic, ideological dimension of the text and hence its position within the class struggle—the reader as an informed and interested critic. In a sense, objectivism was now born out of both theoretical sophistication and political commitment: only the properly trained and *engagé* critic could arrive at the deep meaning of the text. At the same time, consideration of all other sociocultural dimensions of the text was regarded as distracting and ultimately apolitical.

Second, within the sociological approach informed by the sociology of religion, the reader did remain faceless—the reader as a universal and informed critic. The new models from the social sciences allowed the biblical critic to assume an even greater position of neutrality and impartiality vis-à-vis the text. No critical analysis of the reader was called for, and none was undertaken. Finally, within the anthropological approach rooted in cultural anthropology, the reader was called upon to become self-conscious with regard to his or her own sociocultural world, so that the world of the text could be more sharply differentiated and its reconstruction more clearly articulated. A combination of such self-awareness and the models in question was regarded as affording a more secure position of neutrality and impartiality with regard to the text—the reader as informed and culture-specific but able to transcend the acknowledged limitations of culture. In other words, when properly accounted for, the sociocultural location of the biblical critic could be not only methodologically obviated but also put to good use in the search for the meaning of the text, insofar as the gulf between text and reader would be properly acknowledged as a point of departure.

In all three variations it remained the function of the reader—interested or disinterested, *engagé* or distant—to search for the meaning inherent in the text, bring it to the surface, and make it available to untrained and unsophisticated readers. As such, the position of the critic remained highly authoritative and powerful, with the hierarchy of text-critic-reader still very much in place.

5. As in the case of literary criticism, the shift of cultural criticism away from the theoretical moorings of historicism brought about a clear change in theological concerns and underlying stance. At this point an important distinction is in order between the socioeconomic approach, on the one hand, and sociological and anthropological approaches, on the other.

From the perspective of neo-Marxist criticism, the view of the text as an ideological product, of the world behind the text as a site of struggle, and of the critic as committed and hence as a further factor in the struggle ultimately led to the belief that proper criticism is criticism on the side of the oppressed and with liberation in mind. Thus, to engage in the recovery of the deep, socioeconomic meaning of the text was to take sides in the struggle for liberation and against oppression; that choice became, in turn, the fundamental theological motivation of the critic, carried out in practice either by rejecting that which is oppressive in the biblical text or adopting that which is liberating. In this case the theological commitment of the critic was neither denied nor bypassed but roundly affirmed, with theology itself conceived not just as worldview but as engagement.

From the point of view of sociological and anthropological criticism, a twofold theological direction may be observed, following the basic pattern outlined in historical criticism and then traced also by literary criticism. On the one hand, criticism was regarded as radically divorced from any type of theologizing, with emphasis placed on the newly highlighted sociocultural dimensions of the text to the detriment of its religious or theological aspects so central to historical criticism. Interpretation could thus be seen as an even more sophisticated exercise in the history of religion, yielding far more rigorous data for the theologians to work with in their respective applications of the text. On the other hand, interpretation could also be seen as laying an even more solid foundation for a proper hermeneutical appropriation and application of the Word of God—the focus on the sociocultural dimensions of the text yielding a much more realistic reading of the Word of God and hence a greater grasp of its flesh and power. Yet again, although both positions were deeply theological, neither was properly regarded or analyzed as such.

Since for cultural criticism the meaning of the text resides in the text as a product of its context, it could readily be argued that a more enlightened approach to the text would bring out such a meaning more securely and forcefully. Such a meaning then—a meaning for all times and cultures—could still be used to dictate and govern, again in a far more effective way, the overall boundaries or parameters of Christian life in the world.

6. The pedagogical implications of cultural criticism were very similar to those of historical criticism: all readers, regardless of their respective theological beliefs or sociocultural contexts, could become informed as well as universal or committed readers if the right methodological tools and theoretical apparatus were properly acquired and taught. Learned impartation and passive reception thus remained the order of the day. Insofar as the untrained reader had to be trained in order to read the biblical text correctly, the model also remained highly authoritative and hierarchical, with a twofold emphasis on which model (what discipline to use) and which authority (whom to read) to follow. Although readers were now reading themselves, such readings either remained quite circumscribed, limited to the question of socioeconomic class, or, even when more broadly pursued, were regarded as somehow separable and distinct from the task of interpretation. As in the other two paradigms, the educational model followed thereby the interpretive model, with students/readers looking to teachers/critics for an account of the text and its meaning.

Concluding Comments

As regards theory and methodology, the cultural paradigm constituted, as in the case of literary criticism, another profound liberating step in biblical studies. In terms of critical practice, the model pointed out certain salient weaknesses of the historical paradigm: not only the lack of a well-informed and articulated theory regarding the study of texts from a very different time and culture, but also the largely idealistic character of the enterprise with its heavy emphasis on theological positions, developments, and conflicts. In terms of critical theory, the model also brought into the discipline a refreshingly wide variety of interpretive approaches, giving rise once again to many new ways of reading and interpreting the biblical texts. In so doing, the stranglehold of historical criticism was further loosened: what had been a fairly compact common discourse yielded once again to a number of different discourses—ultimately related, of course, but also quite distinct in their own right.

With regard to culture and experience, the cultural paradigm was a mixed model as well, though with more emphasis than the historical model on the context of both text and reader. On the one hand, the social location of the text was more radically emphasized, with a systematic and sustained emphasis on its economic, social, and cultural aspects and ramifications. On the other hand, the social location of the reader received varying degrees of attention: from no analysis whatsoever, as in the case of studies employing sociological models; to analysis in terms of socioeconomic and ideological aspects, as with neo-Marxist models of interpretation; to analysis from a broad cultural perspective, as in the case of studies informed by anthropological theory. However, even when the reader was taken into consideration, such analysis still remained quite limited. In the case of neo-Marxist models, for example, since a clear relationship was acknowledged between the ideological commitment of readers and their interpretation of the text, analysis concentrated on the socioeconomic dimensions of the readers to the exclusion of all other sociocultural aspects. Similarly, in the case of anthropological models, the broader sociocultural dimensions of the readers were addressed, but the relationship between context and interpretation was largely bypassed if not altogether denied. In both cases the goal remained the proper retrieval of the meaning of the text, not the vision that social location bestows on the results of such retrievals as well as on the very process of retrieval itself.

More recently, given the persistent focus of neo-Marxist interpretations on readers and readings as ideological products and sites of struggle and the turn toward readers and readings as sociocultural products on the part of anthropological approaches, an encounter with the full complexity of the issue of flesh-and-blood readers has become inevitable. Again, cultural criticism must come to terms with the fact that lying behind the identification and interpretation of the sociocultural codes present in the text, the reconstructions of the world behind the text, and the interpretive models employed in such reconstructions is always the real reader—the flesh-and-blood reader, historically and culturally conditioned, with a field of vision fundamentally informed and circumscribed by such a social location. It is such a reader, immersed in such social locations, who engages in the reading and interpretation of texts, arguing for certain economic, social, and cultural reconstructions of the world of the text and employing in the process a variety of interpretive model-constructs.

CULTURAL STUDIES: THE TEXT AS CONSTRUCTION

The distinct turn toward the real reader observed within both literary and cultural criticism represents, in my opinion, the beginning of another major development within the profound shift affecting biblical criticism since the 1970s. Such a development, I would venture to say, represents the beginning of a fourth paradigm or umbrella model of interpretation, with its own mode of discourse in which historical, formalist, and hermeneutical questions and concerns become closely interrelated and interdependent.

It is a development that calls into question the construct of a neutral and disinterested reader presupposed by historical criticism and followed in large part by both literary and cultural criticism—the universal and informed reader whose different variations can be readily outlined: the reader of historical criticism, steeped in theological presuppositions but able to put them aside in the task of interpretation through proper self-awareness; the reader of literary criticism, forthcoming with regard to reading strategy in the process of interpretation but only at a formalist level; the reader of cultural criticism, whether forthcoming with regard to socioeconomic class and ideological stance, or quite unaware of the processes of socialization and acculturation informing readers and readings, or properly aware of such processes but able to transcend them in the task of interpretation through the use of appropriate comparative and crosscultural models. This new development posits instead a very different construct, the flesh-and-blood reader: always positioned and interested; socially and historically conditioned and unable to transcend such conditions—to attain a sort of asocial and ahistorical nirvana—not only with respect to socioeconomic class but also with regard to the many other factors that make up human identity. As such, it is a development that carries the ongoing process of liberation and decolonization in the discipline a step further, from enormous diversity in the realm of theory and methodology to enormous diversity in the sociocultural realm. It is a development that I describe in terms of "cultural studies"—a joint critical study of texts and readers, perspectives and ideologies—thereby distinguishing it from cultural criticism and at the same time showing its affinity with similar developments in other disciplines and critical practices.

The enduring construct of a universal and informed reader, the reader who would attain to impartiality and objectivity through the adoption of scientific methods and the denial of particularity and contextuality, was a praiseworthy goal but also quite naive and dangerous. It was praiseworthy because it did realize, however faintly, the effects of social location on all reading and interpretation. It was naive because it thought that it could avoid or neutralize such effects by means of an acquired and hard-earned scientific persona. It was dangerous because in the end what were in effect highly personal and social constructions regarding texts and history were advanced as scholarly retrievals and reconstructions, scientifically secured and hence not only methodologically unassailable but also ideologically neutral. Indeed, given the origins and development of such constructions on both sides of the North Atlantic, the construct remained inherently colonialist and imperialistic. It emerged out of a Eurocentric setting and, as such, it was and remained thoroughly Eurocentric at every level of discourse and inquiry.[26] As a result, the construct unreflectively universalized its bracketed identity, expecting on the surface all readers everywhere to become ideal critics, informed and universal, while in actuality requiring all readers to interpret like Eurocentric critics. In fact, the entire discussion, from beginning to end and top to bottom, was characterized and governed by the fundamental concerns, questions, and horizons of this particular group, uncritically disguised as the fundamental questions, horizons, and concerns of the entire Christian world. To become the ideal critic, therefore, was to enter into a specific and contextualized discussion, a Eurocentric discussion.[27]

In retrospect, one may say that the use of such a construct, under the guise of neutrality and impartiality, dehumanized the reader, asking for divestiture of all those identity factors that constitute and characterize the reader as reader—for example, gender, ethnic or racial background, socioeconomic class, sociocultural conventions, educational attainment, and ideological stance. On another level, such divestiture was not a dehumanization at all but a rehumanization, insofar as objectivity and impartiality were cover terms for Europeanization, given the thoroughly Eurocentric contours and orientation of the discipline. Thus, while the experience and culture of readers and critics were seemingly sacrificed in the pursuit of truth, in effect it was the experience and culture of some critics and readers that were sacrificed to the experience and culture of other critics and readers. The result was a classic case of neocolonialism, where the interests of the colonized or margins were sacrificed, subtly but surely, to the interests of the colonizers or the center.

This situation of neocolonialism began to come apart with the emergence and solidification of the literary and cultural paradigms in the mid-

---

[26] This is not to say that there were not profound differences and rivalries among the different Eurocentric traditions. In fact, the discipline was often quite provincial in character, as even a cursory survey of notes and bibliography readily shows. The Germans, the English, and the French dominated the discussion by far and in that order, with each group basically reading and interacting with members of the same group. North American scholars (leaving Mexico out), reflecting that peculiar combination of former colonials/empire builders, were far more eclectic in their reading and dialogue partners but always rather servile in their attitude toward and estimation of their European colleagues.

[27] On this point, with a specific focus on African American students and critics in graduate programs and academic institutions governed by Eurocentric interests, see the interesting essay by W. H. Myers, "The Hermeneutical Dilemma of the African American Biblical Student," in *Stony the Road We Trod: African American Biblical Interpretation,* ed. C. H. Felder (Minneapolis: Fortress Press, 1991), 40-56. See also the beginning remarks by R. S. Sugirtharajah in a volume he edited, *Voices from the Margin: Interpreting the Bible in the Third World* (Maryknoll, N.Y.: Orbis Books, 1991), 1-6 and 434-44.

1970s. Liberation came largely by way of diversity in methodological principles and theoretical orientation. Although in and of itself an important step in the process of liberation and decolonization, the construct of a universal and informed reader still remained largely in place, however. Such neocolonialism now threatens to come apart altogether with the recent developments described above within both cultural and literary criticism. Slowly but surely the foundations behind such a construct have been eroded. Ongoing developments in a wide number of disciplines as well as in theological studies itself, involving a focus on theory as perspective with its own sociocultural and ideological foundations, made any claims for a disinterested objectivity in reading and interpretation increasingly untenable and subject to critical exposé. In large part such developments were the result of outsiders coming into the different disciplines for the first time. In the theological world, for example, the validity and ideology of such claims came under increasing attack from a wide variety of quarters, as more and more silent/silenced voices entered the discipline, both in the North Atlantic world and the Third World, laying claim to their own voices and vision in theology and interpretation. Most prominent among such voices were the liberation theologians from the colonial world, feminist theologians in the First World, and minority theologians residing in the First World.[28]

Thus, with readers now fully foregrounding themselves as flesh-and-blood readers, variously situated and engaged in their own respective social locations, the process of liberation and decolonization moves into the sociocultural domain itself. Different readers see themselves not only as using different interpretive models and reading strategies but also as reading in different ways in the light of the multilevel social groupings they represent and to which they belong. Such a way of reading ultimately looks upon all interpretive models, retrievals of meaning from texts, and reconstructions of history as constructs—formulated and advanced by positioned readers, flesh-and-blood readers reading and interpreting from different and highly complex social locations.[29] It is a reading highly influenced by postmodernist theory, with its ironic realization that all is

---

[28] In fact, it would be very interesting indeed to trace the relationship of these three movements to the paradigms described above, to analyze the different reading strategies and theoretical orientations adopted along the way, but that is a task that lies beyond the scope of the present study.

[29] For different applications of such an approach, see the following works: with regard to Greece and classical antiquity, R. and F. Etienne, *The Search for Ancient Greece*, Discoveries (New York: Harry N. Abrams, 1992); with regard to the Middle Ages, N. F. Cantor, *Inventing the Middle Ages: The Lives, Works, and Ideas of the Great Medievalists of the Twentieth Century* (New York: Morrow, 1991); with regard to tradition, E. Hobsbawm and T. Ranger, eds., *The Invention of Tradition* (Cambridge: Cambridge University Press, 1983).

construction and that one has no choice but to engage in such construction.[30] Such a reading calls for a "speaking in other tongues," in one's own tongue, because otherwise such a "speaking" would be usurped and carried out—as it often has been—by other tongues. Such a reading also calls for critical dialogue among the many tongues, in the course of which the foundations, contours, and ramifications of all such constructs would be addressed and weighed. Such a reading takes competing modes of discourse for granted, renounces the idea of any master narrative as in itself a construct, and looks for a truly global interaction. Such a reading is both the inevitable result and mode of a postcolonial Christian world and a postcolonial biblical criticism.

---

[30] For a fine overview of postmodernism, see C. Jencks, *What Is Post-Modernism?*, 3d ed. (New York: St. Martin's, 1989); for this and other definitions of postmodernism, see L. Hutcheon, *The Poetics of Postmodernism: History, Theory, Fiction* (New York: Routledge, 1988), and idem, *The Politics of Postmodernism*, New Accents (New York: Routledge, 1989); for the ramifications of postmodernist thought, see V. B. Leitch, *Cultural Criticism, Literary Theory, Poststructuralism* (New York: Columbia University Press, 1992).

2

Cultural Studies
and Contemporary Biblical Criticism

Ideological Criticism as Mode of Discourse

I have argued that the development of biblical criticism in the twentieth century can be plotted in terms of four different paradigms or umbrella models of interpretation, each with its own fairly distinctive mode
of discourse and broad spectrum of interpretation.[1] I have further argued
that these four paradigms find themselves at present in competition with
one another within the discipline, in what is perhaps best described as a
state of seemingly stable if not actually permanent anomie.[2] Now, having

---

[1] See chap. 1 in this volume. For a different plotting, with a focus on the
gospel of Mark and the author-role as leitmotif, see J. Capel Anderson and S. D.
Moore, "Introduction: The Lives of Mark," in *Mark and Method: New Approaches
in Biblical Studies*, ed. J. Capel Anderson and S. D. Moore (Minneapolis: Fortress
Press, 1992), 1-22.

[2] This characterization I borrow in part from the parallel plotting of anthropological studies from the 1950s through the early 1980s undertaken by S. B.
Ortner ("Theory in Anthropology since the Sixties," *Comparative Studies in Society and History* 26 [1984]: 126-66). With the 1960s, Ortner observes, the major
paradigms in place in the 1950s gave way to a wide array of theoretical models,
rendering communication itself within the field a forbidding if not altogether impossible enterprise, what she describes as a classic situation of liminality (see, for
example, 372: "The field appears to be a thing of shreds and patches, of individuals and small coteries pursuing disjunctive investigations and talking mainly to
themselves . . . confusion of categories, expressions of chaos and antistructure").
That was not at all unlike what happened in biblical criticism in the 1980s, or
approximately twenty years later. Interestingly enough, Ortner does point to a
new key symbol in anthropological orientation (a focus on "practice" or "praxis"
and the "agent" or "actor") that gave rise to a variety of theories and methods and
that perhaps marked an initial movement in the direction of a new and emerging
consensus. Despite clear similarities between such practice theory and the cultural
[continued]

already focused upon the first three paradigms involved in the plot, I should like to provide in this study an initial, overall characterization of the fourth paradigm in question, which I have chosen to call cultural studies or ideological criticism.[3] By way of introduction a brief recapitulation and further explication of the plot in question will prove most appropriate and useful.

PLOTTING BIBLICAL CRITICISM

The proposed plot as I construct it includes a spatial and poetic dimension as well as a temporal and ideological dimension; further, there are three basic stages involving the largely sequential emergence and development of the critical paradigms in terms of a process of liberation and decolonization at work in the discipline.[4] As such, the plot reveals a fairly classic mold with regard to structure and movement. On the one hand, the plot does have a beginning, a middle, and an end: an existing state of affairs, unruffled and long-lasting, undergoes from within a situation of conflict and tension, ultimately giving way to resolution and a new state of affairs. On the other hand, besides this implicit sense of movement, the plot possesses an explicit sense of progress, whereby the beginning state of affairs is seen as changing throughout *for the better*, as the terms "liberation" and "decolonization" readily imply. At the same time, however, the plot also reveals a more contemporary, ironic mode with respect to content and argumentation. First, the resolution envisioned is quite open-ended and hence a sort of nonresolution: instead of a new consensus, multiplicity reigns. Second, the progress is not so much linear or monolin-

---

studies I envision, I would make no such claims for the latter in biblical criticism. Not only do I not see any developing or forthcoming consensus in sight, but also I must confess that I find anomie neither inherently objectionable nor unattractive. On the impact of the 1960s on the humanities in general, see, for example, V. B. Leitch, *American Literary Criticism from the Thirties to the Eighties* (New York: Columbia University Press, 1988), 366-407; S. Seidman, *Contested Knowledge: Social Theory in the Postmodern Era* (Oxford: Blackwell, 1984), 234-80.

[3] I emphasize the initial or tentative character of this description, insofar as it does not have, unlike the other three, the privilege of years of hindsight. I certainly emphasize as well the constructive and perspectival nature of this description: this is an overview of the paradigm as I see it and practice it from my own vantage point and experience.

[4] The plot involves a rhetorical dimension as well, insofar as it represents an attempt on my part to persuade readers not only of its historical validity and heuristic value but also of the need for and benefits of the paradigm of cultural studies, where I would presently situate myself. Indeed, the study is written not only from the point of view of a practitioner but also in the mode of cultural studies.

gual but rather multidirectional and multilingual: a speaking in many tongues.[5]

The three stages in question proceed as follows. To begin with, a thoroughly entrenched and dominant historical criticism (the first stage)—which had been firmly in place since approximately the middle of the nineteenth century[6]—is rather swiftly displaced, beginning in the mid-1970s, by two different and largely unrelated movements: literary criticism and cultural criticism, each of which rapidly gains strength and sophistication through the 1980s and into the 1990s (the second stage). Subsequently, a number of developments within each of these two paradigms in the late 1980s gradually begins to point the way toward another such paradigm or umbrella model of interpretation, cultural studies or ideological criticism (the third stage), with a specific focus on both texts and readers of texts—real or flesh-and-blood readers.

On the one hand, literary criticism is eventually forced to wrestle with the fundamental issue of real readers on two counts: first, insofar as it gradually moves from an analysis of the formal features or elements of texts (narrative criticism) to an analysis of readers (intratextual readers, that is) and the reading process in the construction of meaning (reader-response criticism); second, insofar as it increasingly entertains the notion of multiple interpretations, whether based primarily on the text (through the polysemy of language) or on the reader (through the filling in of textual gaps).[7] On the other hand, cultural criticism is also brought to con-

---

[5] Thus, while inscribed in the logic and closure of modernism, the plot is also inscribed in the logic and openness of postmodernism, not only insofar as it sees itself in terms of "plotting" and thus admits theoretically and practically of any number of other such plottings, but also insofar as the plot offered does in the end deconstruct itself, so to speak, presenting diversity both as a new and as a positive and welcome state of affairs. On the inescapable relationship of postmodernism to modernism, see especially L. Hutcheon, *The Politics of Postmodernism* (New York: Routledge, 1989).

[6] See, for example, R. F. Collins (*Introduction to the New Testament* [Garden City, N.Y.: Doubleday, 1983], 41-74, esp. 41-45), who attributes the rise of such critical consensus in large part to the work and influence of F. C. Baur (1792-1860) and the success of the Tübingen school. See also in this regard J. Fitzmyer's spirited defense of historical criticism ("Historical Criticism: Its Role in Biblical Interpretation and Church Life," *Theological Studies* 50 [1989]: 244-59), where the relationship between the historical-critical paradigm and the classical philology of the late eighteenth and nineteenth centuries is clearly and directly brought to the surface.

[7] For recent accounts of the path of literary criticism, see E. Struthers Malbon and J. Capel Anderson, "Literary-Critical Methods," in *Searching the Scriptures*, vol. 1: *A Feminist Introduction*, ed. E. Schüssler Fiorenza (New York: Crossroad, 1993), 241-54; D. M. Gunn, "Narrative Criticism," and E. V. McKnight, "Reader-Response Criticism," in *To Each Its Own Meaning: An Introduction to Biblical Criticisms and Their Application*, ed. S. L. McKenzie and S. R. Haynes (Louisville: Westminster/John Knox Press, 1993), 171-95 and 197-219, respectively; E. Struthers Malbon, "Narrative Criticism: How Does the Story Mean?" and R.

[continued]

front this crucial issue of real readers on two counts as well: first, in the light of the persistent emphasis of neo-Marxist interpretations on readers and readings as socioeconomic and ideological products; second, in the light of the turn toward readers and readings as sociocultural products in anthropological approaches.[8]

This gradual turn toward the reader on the part of both literary criticism and cultural criticism eventually brings biblical criticism face to face with the question of real, flesh-and-blood readers, and, in so doing, shifts it into a very different model of interpretation, with its own mode of discourse and theoretical spectrum. The end result, once again, is the existence of four competing paradigms within the discipline at one and the same time: not at all a new consensus replacing the earlier one of historical criticism, but rather a situation of radical plurality (or perhaps a consensus about no consensus).

At the same time, besides such methodological and theoretical developments in the discipline, the proposed plot involves a crucial demographic and sociocultural development as well. Following a pattern at work not only across the entire disciplinary spectrum but also within theological studies itself, biblical criticism, which had remained since its inception largely, if not exclusively, the preserve of Western males—Western male clerics, to be more precise—begins to witness an influx of outsiders, individuals now making their voices heard for the first time: Western women, non-Western theologians and critics, and racial and ethnic minorities from non-Western civilizations in the West.[9]

M. Fowler, "Reader Response Criticism: Figuring Mark's Reader," in Anderson and Moore, *Mark and Method*, 23-49 and 50-83, respectively.

[8] For recent accounts of the path of cultural criticism, see M. A. Tolbert, "Social, Sociological, and Anthropological Methods," in Schüssler Fiorenza, *Searching the Scriptures*, 255-71; D. B. Martin, "Social Scientific Criticism," in McKenzie and Haynes, *To Each Its Own Meaning*, 103-19; D. Rhoads, "Social Criticism: Crossing Boundaries," in *Mark and Method*, 135-61.

[9] By *Western* civilization or culture I mean, following the proposal of S. P. Huntington ("The Clash of Civilizations?" *Foreign Affairs* 72 [summer, 1993]: 22-49; and idem, "If Not Civilizations, What? Paradigms of the Post-Cold War World," *Foreign Affairs* 72 [November/December 1993]: 186-94), all those who view and identify with the West as their highest level of cultural grouping and broadest level of cultural identity. For Huntington, therefore, a civilization or culture encompasses both common objective elements (for example, language, history, religion, customs, institutions) and the subjective self-identification of people. In addition, civilizations may have subcivilizations; for example, the West itself comprises two such variants: Europe and (Anglo/Francophone) North America. To be sure, like any highly abstract category, the concept is not without its problems. For example, an analysis of the construction of "the West"—its narrative elements of plot, characters, events, and so forth—within the West itself would reveal manifold and significant variations. Nevertheless, within the given framework of ideal types for cultures and civilizations, I find that it does have value for purposes of identification and comparison.

Such individuals received their training almost exclusively in the academic institutions of the West, where historical criticism reigned supreme and where they were duly introduced to the fundamentals of the method at the hands of Western male scholars in their role as *Doktorvätern*, master researchers and teachers as well as founders of or links in all-important pedigree lines. These outsiders were very much subject to the powerful centripetal and homogenizing forces of this training, with its emphasis on the classic ideals of the Enlightenment: all knowledge as science; the scientific method as applicable to all areas of inquiry; nature or facts as neutral and knowable; research as a search for truth involving value-free observation and recovery of the facts; and the researcher as a champion of reason who surveys the facts with disinterested eyes. A further, fundamental—though much more implicit—dimension of this socialization, quite in keeping with the cult of modernity emerging from the Enlightenment, should be noted as well: the conviction that such training not only represented progress over against traditional interpretations of the Bible (the triumph of light over darkness and reason over tradition) but also reflected the superiority of the West over against other cultures and civilizations (the hermeneutics of over/against and the white man's burden). In other words, historical criticism was perceived and promoted not only as the proper way to read and interpret the biblical texts but also as the ultimate sign of progress in the discipline, the offer of the (Christian) West to the rest of the (Christian) world and the means by which the backward and ignorant could become modern and educated.[10]

Despite this overwhelming academic socialization, many of these individuals slowly began to question the program and agenda of such biblical criticism, especially the construct of the scientific, objective, and impartial researcher—the universal and informed reader—operative in one form or another not only in historical criticism but also in the other two emerging paradigms. These individuals then also began to raise the radical question of perspective and contextualization in biblical criticism.[11] This grow-

---

[10] A ready analogy can be drawn between the cultural ramifications of this assumption and its ramifications for gender. Just as historical criticism represented progress and superiority vis-à-vis all other cultures, so did it embody the "masculine" traits of reason and objectivity vis-à-vis the "feminine" traits of emotion and subjectivity.

[11] Not surprisingly, the very same phenomenon was taking place in the field of historical studies, a discipline constituted in the aftermath of the French Revolution; biblical criticism turned to historical studies for guidance and inspiration in the first half of the nineteenth century as it sought to come to terms with the Enlightenment, modernity, and the scientific method. On the significance of voices from the outside in historical studies, see the recent overview of historiography by J. Appleby, L. Hunt, and M. Jacob (*Telling the Truth about History* [New York: Norton, 1994], esp. 129-59 and 198-237), as well as the similarly recent overview

[continued]

ing insistence on the situated and interested nature of all reading and interpretation would bring additional, pointed, and unrelenting pressure on biblical criticism to come to terms with the question of flesh-and-blood readers, further pushing the discipline into a quite different model of interpretation, with its own mode of discourse and interpretive spectrum.[12]

Thus, the longstanding project of the Enlightenment, as embodied in historical criticism and its emerging rivals, was ultimately being called into question, as were a number of attendant principles and notions: the character of biblical studies as *science* and the use of the *scientific* method; the nature of *history*; the possibility of *value-free* observation; the role of the *rational, disinterested* researcher; the notion of *progress*. In the process, historical criticism, along with the new competing paradigms, began to be analyzed (like the Enlightenment itself) in terms of perspective and contextualization, agenda and social location, inextricably tied as these were to the gender and origins of its practitioners—Western male clerics. In other words, the thoroughly Western and gendered character of the discipline lying just behind the scientific facade of the universal and informed reader began to be exposed and critiqued. Reading and interpretation were no longer seen as value-free and disinterested, but rather as thoroughly enmeshed in the public arena and thus as irretrievably *political* in character and ramifications, from the point of view of both the

---

of the question of objectivity in historiography by P. Novick (*That Noble Dream: The "Objectivity Question" and the American Historical Profession* [Cambridge: Cambridge University Press, 1988], esp. 469-521). For the impact of outside voices on literary criticism, see V. B. Leitch, *Cultural Criticism, Literary Theory, Poststructuralism* (New York: Columbia University Press, 1992), 83-103. For their impact on social theory in general, see N. B. Dirks, G. Eley, and S. B. Ortner, eds., *Culture/Power/History: A Reader in Contemporary Social Theory* (Princeton: Princeton University Press, 1994), esp. 3-45. For their impact on anthropology, see, for example, T. Asad, ed., *Anthropology and the Colonial Encounter* (New York: Humanities Press, 1973), and R. Rosaldo, *Culture and Truth: The Remaking of Social Analysis* (Boston: Beacon Press, 1989).

[12] See, for example, from the perspective of Western women: E. Schüssler Fiorenza, *Bread Not Stone: The Challenge of Feminist Biblical Interpretation* (Boston: Beacon Press, 1984); E. Schüssler Fiorenza, ed., *Searching the Scriptures*, 2 vols. (New York: Crossroad, 1993-94); C. A. Newsom and S. H. Ringe, eds., *Women's Bible Commentary* (Louisville: Westminster/John Knox Press, 1992); from the perspective of non-Western cultures, see R. S. Sugirtharajah, *Voices from the Margin: Interpreting the Bible in the Third World* (Maryknoll, N.Y.: Orbis Books, 1991); from the perspective of non-Western minorities in the West, see C. H. Felder, ed., *Stony the Road We Trod: African American Biblical Interpretation* (Minneapolis: Fortress Press, 1991). An analysis of the correlation between the raising of such voices and concerns and the critical paradigms available and invoked would prove most valuable and remains a project for the future.

narrower meaning of this term (the realm of politics within the sphere of the sociocultural) and its broader meaning (the realm of power within the sphere of the ideological).

From within and without, therefore, on the basis of internal disciplinary developments as well as external sociocultural developments, biblical criticism was being pushed to take into account not only the texts of ancient Judaism and early Christianity but also the readers and interpreters of such texts—the twofold focus I have advanced as central to the emerging paradigm of cultural studies.[13] Such a plot I have described in terms of liberation and decolonization. This I do on two counts: first, with respect to models and strategies, insofar as a tightly controlling paradigm is displaced by enormous diversity in the theoretical and methodological realm; second, with respect to reader-constructs, insofar as the construct of the scientific and detached ideal reader as well as the faceless and nameless constructs of intratextual readers are displaced by enormous diversity in the sociocultural realm. As a result, the Western and gendered nature of the discipline, operating under the mask of objectivity and impartiality, is unveiled, and the issue of perspective and contextualization is brought to bear as much on the texts as on the real readers and interpreters of the texts. Such a dénouement, I readily confess, represents for me, inscribed as I have been and continue to be in a variety of colonial realities and discourses, a most welcome and attractive situation of liberation and decolonization, whereby other voices can now speak in their own tongues and no center controls the discourse. If the result is a situation of anomie, and I believe that it is, I find that neither regrettable nor deplorable but rather something to be welcomed and embraced.[14]

---

[13] I should explain that by "biblical criticism" I mean not only criticism of the canonical texts, whether of Judaism or Christianity, but also criticism of all other texts surviving from ancient Judaism or early Christianity. I use the term "biblical criticism" throughout merely as a shorthand for such comprehensive studies and for lack of a better inclusive and concise term.

[14] In this regard, quite ironically, my evaluation of the present situation in biblical criticism is further inscribed in the text of modernity and its emphasis on freedom from the past. In other words, just as historical criticism gloried in the élan of freedom from religious tradition and dogmatism and as both literary criticism and cultural criticism rejoiced in the feeling of freedom from a critical stranglehold, so does cultural studies, as I envision it, rejoice and glory in the sense of liberation from the surface dehumanization of readers (the call for objectivity) and of decolonization from the underlying rehumanization of readers (the Westernization of all readers). Of course, the evaluation is also inscribed in the text of postmodernity, insofar as the operative concepts of liberation and decolonization call for a humanization of all readers, whether high or low, in the center or on the periphery, dominant or subaltern.

CULTURAL STUDIES: THE TEXT AS CONSTRUCTION

For this still-emerging paradigm of cultural studies, then, real readers lie behind all models of interpretation and all reading strategies, all recreations of meaning from texts and all reconstructions of history; further, all such models, strategies, recreations, and reconstructions are seen as constructs on the part of flesh-and-blood readers; and all such readers are themselves regarded as variously positioned and engaged in their own respective social locations. Thus, different real readers use different strategies and models in different ways, at different times, and with different results (different readings and interpretations) in the light of their different and highly complex social locations. Consequently, for cultural studies a critical analysis of real readers and their readings (their representations of the ancient texts and the ancient world) becomes as important and necessary as a critical analysis of the ancient texts themselves (the remains of the ancient world), since these two critical foci are seen as ultimately interdependent and interrelated. In other words, all recreations of meaning and all reconstructions of history are in the end regarded as constructs or re-presentations: re-creations and re-constructions.

As such, cultural studies has recourse to a broad variety of theoretical frameworks and modes of discourse, ranging from the more traditional historical and theological discussion of historical criticism, to the more recent dialogue partners of literary criticism and cultural criticism, to the field of cultural studies as such.[15] Cultural studies within biblical criticism thus seeks to integrate, in different ways, the historical, formalist, and sociocultural questions and concerns of the other paradigms on a different key, a hermeneutical key, with the situated and interested reader and interpreter always at its core. As a result, a new mode of discourse, bearing its own analytical wherewithal and corresponding nomenclature, comes into play—a mode of discourse best characterized as *ideological*, given its central focus on contextualization and perspective, social location and agenda, and hence on the political character of all composition and texts as well as reading and interpretation. Such a mode of discourse is by no means monolingual but rather quite varied, profoundly polyglot, given the complex nature of social locations and agendas. In the end, a different model of interpretation begins to take shape, calling yet again for a very different type of reading and application on the part of its subscribers.

---

[15] On cultural studies, see, for example, S. Hall, "Cultural Studies: Two Paradigms," in *Media, Culture, and Society,* 2 vols. (Newbury Park, Calif.: Sage, 1980), 2:57-82; A. Easthope, *Literary into Cultural Studies* (New York: Routledge, 1991); L. Grossberg, C. Nelson, and P. Treichler, *Cultural Studies* (New York: Routledge, 1992); Leitch, *Cultural Criticism*; F. Inglis, *Cultural Studies* (Oxford: Blackwell, 1993).

With this background in mind, I now proceed to an overview—again, I stress, preliminary and tentative, given the absence of precious hindsight—of the basic principles I see as guiding and informing this umbrella model in biblical criticism. In so doing, I follow my earlier analysis of the other paradigms with respect to the categories of comparison employed: location of meaning, reading strategy, theoretical foundations, the role of the reader, theological presuppositions, and pedagogical implications.

Location of Meaning

The cultural studies model approaches the text as a construct, insofar as meaning is taken to reside not in the author of the text or the world behind the text (as postulated by both historical criticism and cultural criticism) or in the text as such (as postulated by literary criticism of the text-dominant variety) but in the encounter or interchange between text and reader. For the model, moreover, the reader in this interaction is seen primarily in terms of real readers rather than intermediate and formalistic reader-constructs (as in literary criticism of the reader-dominant sort), although the latter are not at all ruled out in the process of reading and interpretation.[16] Meaning emerges, therefore, as the result of an encounter between a socially and historically conditioned text and a socially and historically conditioned reader.

From this perspective, the text—no matter how approached, whether as medium or means, or by whom, whether oneself or others—is always looked upon not as an autonomous and unchanging object, as something "out there" with a stable meaning that precedes and guides/controls interpretation, but rather as a "text," as something that is always read and interpreted by real readers.[17] The text, therefore, may be approached and analyzed from a variety of angles.

------

[16] Two points are in order. First, such reader-constructs (see the section below entitled "The Role of the Reader") would be explicitly identified as such, justified in terms of reading strategies, and acknowledged as constructions on the part of real readers, variously positioned and engaged in their respective social locations. Consequently, the readings produced through the use of such intermediate and formalistic reader-constructs, regardless of the goals and purposes adduced for their employment, are not seen as more neutral and objective productions but rather as thoroughly contextualized and ideological productions. Second, real readers themselves would ultimately have to be seen and analyzed in terms of constructs as well.

[17] Such a position need not deny altogether the existence of authorial intention (whether realized or intended), literary or rhetorical elements and features, and sociohistorical context or sociocultural scripts and codes. Self-reflection has taught me in no uncertain ways that, when writing or speaking or acting, I very often do so with certain goals and purposes in mind, which I then proceed to formulate in

[continued]

First, it may be viewed as a medium, as a message between a sender and a receiver, an author and a reader. The focus would then lie on the text, with a corresponding emphasis on its artistic and/or strategic character and an examination of its formal aesthetic and/or persuasive features—the text as a literary and rhetorical creation. Second, it may be approached as a means, as evidence from and for the time of composition. The focus would then rest on the world behind the text (the world presupposed by, reflected in, and addressed by the text), with a corresponding emphasis on contextualization and perspective and an examination of its historical, sociocultural, and political dimensions—the text as a historical, cultural, and ideological creation. Third, it may be understood as a construct, as the result of interaction or negotiation between the text and its reader(s). The focus would then lie on the text as actually read and interpreted, with a corresponding emphasis on its various readings, whether historical or contemporary, and an examination of the contextualization and perspective of such readings—the text as a creation on the part of readers and interpreters.

In the end, however, whether the text is approached directly or indirectly, cultural studies remains keenly aware throughout of the fact that any reading and interpretation—any account of the text, whether in terms of its historical and theological, literary and rhetorical, sociocultural and ideological dimensions, by oneself or by others, in the present or in the past—constitutes a construction or re-presentation on the part of real readers: a re-*creation* of its meaning and re-*construction* of its context on the part of readers who read and interpret from within specific social locations and with specific interests in mind. For cultural studies, therefore, this character of the text as "text" ultimately makes a joint analysis of texts and readings of texts indispensable and imperative. There is never a text out there but many "texts."

Reading Strategy

In principle, in terms of theory, cultural studies would be as interested in layered as in holistic readings of the text. In other words, both the largely vertical reading of historical criticism, that reading that is based

---

certain ways in the light of the context at hand and under the influence of a variety of sociocultural scripts and codes. At the same time, experience has taught me that there are usually many other goals and purposes at work—many other subtexts behind the texts—of which I am not even aware at the time of acting, speaking, or writing. Experience has further taught me that any perception or rendering of such intentions, elements, context, and script of myself and the various "texts" I put forth—and hence of texts as well—always constitutes a reading and interpretation, contextualized and perspectival, that in the end reveal as much about myself and my "texts" (or about texts) as about my readers and interpreters.

on *aporias* and textual ruptures, and the largely horizontal reading of both literary and cultural criticism, that reading that is based on the unity and coherence of the text, are seen in terms of reading strategies and underlying theoretical models on the part of real readers. As such, the presuppositions and ramifications of such strategies and models become a primary focus of attention: Why is it that some readers see disunity in the text to the extent that a reading of it as it presently stands is deemed impossible, proceed to identify the seams and ruptures in question, and engage in an excavative sort of criticism whereby literary layers are sifted out and chronologically arranged for a proper reading of the text? Why do other readers find unity and coherence in the text as it stands, downplay or rule out altogether the presence of ruptures and seams, and opt for a horizontal type of criticism with an emphasis on literary anatomy and flow or social script and codes?

In practice, therefore, in its own approach to texts, cultural studies would neither rule out the presence of textual ruptures nor find it necessary to argue for unity and coherence. Indeed, it could very well argue, along the lines of deconstruction, that there are *aporias* in the text but that such *aporias* point not to conflicting literary layers but rather to a fundamental lack of unity or coherence in the text.[18] Any decision would be made ad hoc, as the occasion were deemed to require. In the end, however, regardless of the particular decision reached and applied with respect to the text in question, the result would be regarded as a "text," a reading and interpretation on the part of real readers, involving and thus calling for an analysis of contextualization and perspective: situated and interested flesh-and-blood readers arguing for disunity and incoherence as evidence for underlying literary strata, unity and coherence, or disunity and incoherence as evidence for ideological contradictions and implosion.

Theoretical Foundations

With cultural studies the spirit of positivism and empiricism—so prevalent in historical, literary, and cultural criticism—draws to a close. To begin with, the meaning of the text is no longer regarded as objective and

---

[18] In other words, a deconstructive approach would also be seen in terms of reading strategies and underlying theoretical orientation on the part of real readers, bringing to the fore thereby, once again, the question of presuppositions and ramifications: Why is it that some readers look for inconsistencies and contradictions in the text so as to emphasize its disunity and incoherence? Further, why is such a strategy presented as a critical move against any and all totalizing ideologies and characterized as liberative? For deconstruction in biblical criticism, see S. D. Moore, *Literary Criticism and the Gospels: The Theoretical Challenge* (New Haven, Conn.: Yale University Press, 1989), 131-78; idem, "Deconstructive Criticism: The Gospel of Mark," in Anderson and Moore, *Mark and Method*, 84-102.

univocal, nor is the critical approach employed in the analysis of the text presented as scientific in the sense of yielding, when rigorously formulated and applied, an accurate retrieval and recreation of such meaning. Similarly, the path of history behind the text also ceases to be regarded as univocal and objective and thus open to scientific retrieval and reconstruction. For cultural studies the text has no meaning and history has no path without a reader or interpreter—without a creation of such a meaning and a construction of such a path from within a contextualized perspective; likewise, there is no critical approach without a critic—without a construction of methods and models out of a contextualized perspective.

Given its location of meaning in the interchange between text and reader (real reader, that is) and its view of the text not as something out there, both preceding and guiding/ controlling interpretation, but as "text," as something that is always read and interpreted, cultural studies accepts a plurality of interpretations not only as a given but also as a point of departure for an analysis of texts and history. As such, it approaches the question of validity in interpretation as a problematic, since even the very criteria used for judgment and evaluation are seen not in essentialist terms, as universally valid and applicable at all times and in all places, across all models and social locations, but as themselves constructions on the part of real readers and hence as emerging from and formulated within specific social locations and agendas. For cultural studies, therefore, the concept of multiple interpretations is, in the end, much less circumscribed and much more open-ended than in literary criticism.

Consequently, cultural studies focuses on the variety of readings and interpretations of texts. As such, scholarship tends to be seen less as evolutionary and progressive, with serious aberrations and deviations along the way, and more as multidirectional and multilingual, reflecting different reading strategies and models at work on the part of real readers, whose contexts and interests call for critical analysis as well.[19] It should be pointed out in this regard that the critical situation envisioned is not necessarily one where "anything goes," since readers and interpreters are always positioned and interested and thus always engaged in evaluation

---

[19] This is not to say that there is no sense of evolution and progress at all. Indeed, I myself have recourse to categories that imply a measure of progress and development: liberation and decolonization. On the one hand, however, such categories are themselves presented as constructions on my part, as my concept of plotting has made amply clear. On the other hand, the evolution and progress envisioned have nothing to do with a final and definitive retrieval and unveiling, almost eschatological in character, of the stable meaning of the text or the given path of history; to the contrary, such progress and evolution are seen in terms of movement toward diversity and multiplicity, with a view of both meaning and history as decentered and polyglot.

and construction: both texts and "texts" are constantly analyzed and engaged, with acceptance or rejection, full or partial, as ever-present and ever-shifting possibilities. At the same time, that sense of sharp competition, of demolition and exposé, that has been at the heart of the discipline for so long (reflecting, no doubt, its primary context in both the male world and the capitalism of the West) yields as well to a realization that no final recreation of meaning or reconstruction of history is possible beyond all perspective and contextualization; that all recreations and reconstructions are productions—creations and constructions—on the part of real readers; that such readers are differently situated and engaged; and that all constructs call for critical analysis and engagement in a spirit of critical dialogue.

The Role of the Reader

It is the role assigned to the reader that, without doubt, most sharply differentiates cultural studies from the other competing paradigms in contemporary biblical criticism. For cultural studies the reader does not and cannot remain faceless. The reader is a real reader whose voice does not and cannot remain in the background, even if so wished and attempted, but is actively and inevitably involved in the production of meaning, of "texts" and history; who does not and cannot make any claims to objectivity and universality but is profoundly aware of the social location and agendas of all readers and readings, including his or her own; and who does not and cannot argue for sophisticated training, of whatever sort, and the creation of corresponding ideal readers as essential for a correct and proper understanding of a text but is keenly aware of the nature of all readings as "texts," whether high or low, academic or popular, trained or untrained.[20] Such a foregrounding of the reader's face and voice has immediate consequences for the critical task.

First, cultural studies calls for critical analysis of reading strategies. On the one hand, strategies are to be identified, with a broad variety of options

---

[20] The argument is not, lest I be misunderstood on this score, that education and scholarship are unnecessary and superfluous. Indeed, I see both scholarship and education as vital for liberation and decolonization. It is no accident that a primary tool of the colonizer is either to deny formal education altogether to the colonized (What would it benefit them?) or to undertake it in such a way as to deny the social location and interests of the colonized (Let us make them in our image and likeness!). The argument, rather, is that education and scholarship—a high socioeducational level—represent no privileged access to the meaning of a text or the path of history but are simply other constitutive factors of human identity affecting all reading and interpretation, and in this sense are no different from any other such factor. It should be clear how such a position is inscribed in both modernism and postmodernism: in the former, insofar as education and scholarship are regarded as most valuable and liberating; in the latter, insofar as they are also seen in terms of social context and ideology.

regarding reader-constructs available: internal readers or readers "inscribed" in the text, such as narratees, implied readers, or implicit readers; external readers of a historical sort, such as original, intended readers and ancient, Mediterranean readers; external readers of a suprahistorical sort, such as first-time, naive readers and sophisticated, ideal readers; external readers of a contemporary sort, whether considered as individuals or as social beings; any combination thereof. On the other hand, since all strategies are regarded as constructs, their use is also to be justified: What goals and purposes are served thereby? What are the presuppositions and ramifications of the approach adopted? Why are different strategies invoked at different times?

Second, cultural studies also calls for critical analysis of real readers—of those who lie behind, opt for, construct, and apply such strategies. Real readers are seen as neither neutral nor impartial but as inextricably positioned and engaged within their own different and complex social locations. For cultural studies, therefore, the contextualization and perspective of readers are seen as impinging, in one way or another, upon their readings and interpretations, thus calling for critical analysis of such social locations and agendas in terms of the various constitutive factors of human identity: sexuality and gender; socioeconomic class; race and ethnicity; sociopolitical status and affiliation; socioeducational background and level; intellectual moorings; socioreligious background and affiliation; ideological stance; and so forth. For cultural studies all these dimensions of human existence must be studied not only with regard to texts, their representation in texts, but also with regard to readers of texts and their readings, their representation in "texts."

Finally, cultural studies calls for critical analysis of all readers and readings, whether located in the academy or not, highly informed or not. In effect, the traditional distinction between high and low is collapsed. The readings of, say, base Christian communities *(comunidades de base)* or marginalized social groups, such as millenarian groups, are considered as worthy of analysis and critique as the readings emerging from prominent scholars following the latest intellectual movements. Thus the position of the critic ultimately emerges as much less powerful and authoritative, at least in principle. On the one hand, the critic ceases to be a necessary intermediary between texts and readers, since the critic also has to acknowledge a particular reading strategy or set of reading strategies based on certain theoretical frameworks as well as certain social contexts and interests. In other words, the critic is no less positioned and interested than any other reader. On the other hand, the critic, given the highly privileged socioeducational training received, is *presumably*—although experience often indicates otherwise—in a better position to articulate not only his or her reading strategy but also those of others. While the former position tends to diminish the highly powerful and authoritative role of the critic, the latter tends to perpetuate it. All in all, however, the open admission of contextualization and perspective does serve, in the end, to relativize and hence subvert the highly privileged education and position of the critic. In this regard a fundamental question regarding the role of the critic in society and the church comes immediately to the fore, a question that lies, however, beyond the scope of the present essay.

Theological Presuppositions

The model of cultural studies is no less theological than any of the other models, but it does call for radical openness in this regard as well. Besides the factors of sexuality and gender (the male nature of the discipline) and sociopolitical status and affiliation (the Western character of the discipline), a third factor has been highly influential as well in biblical criticism: socioreligious background and affiliation. In fact, the socioreligious matrix or ambit of the critic—his or her institutional, religious, and theological moorings—has been more explicit or evident than any other factor as regards the re-creation of meaning from texts, the reconstruction of history behind texts, and the use of critical methodologies in relation to texts. Even when a critic pretended to the highest levels of objectivity and impartiality, his or her socioreligious identity proved inconcealable and undeniable in reading and interpretation, with the representation of ancient texts and communities bearing the unmistakable stamp of the world of that critic.

For cultural studies the socioreligious factor—the question of belief systems, their discourses and practices, and their relationship to ideological worldview and stance—is not and cannot be denied or put aside but rather must be brought out into the open and critically analyzed, not only in texts but also in the reading of texts. In other words, all recreations of meaning from texts, all reconstructions of history behind texts, and all critical models and methods used to approach texts are seen as profoundly religious, whether by way of affirmation or negation, reflecting once again the contextuality and perspective of critics and readers.

On the one hand, therefore, cultural studies is interested in the deeply socioreligious character of texts: both the theological positions, conflicts, and developments present in texts and a comparative analysis of these in the light of other socioreligious traditions are seen as worth pursuing from a critical point of view, as an important dimension of the text's meaning and history. At the same time, on the other hand, cultural studies is also interested in the socioreligious matrix of real readers and hence in the relationship of interpretation to theology, howsoever conceived or articulated: as an exercise in the history of religions, divorced from the wider theological enterprise and yielding facts or data for the theologians to deal with in their respective contexts; as an exercise leading to a greater understanding of the text in its original setting—whether conceived along historical, literary, or cultural lines—and thus ultimately to a more informed hermeneutical appropriation of the text as the "Word of God" in the contemporary religious community; or as an exercise on the side of the oppressed and with liberation in mind, sifting from the text what is liberating and putting aside what is oppressive.

For cultural studies, therefore, all readers and critics are theologians, implicitly or explicitly, by way of negation or affirmation, and all approaches to the text are theological in one respect or another. It is, then, this socioreligious dimension of reading and interpretation that needs to be surfaced and examined, in terms both of belief systems and of their ramifications for ideological worldviews and stances. For cultural studies there is simply no escape from the socioreligious dimension. Moreover, given its fundamental conception of texts as constructs or "texts," there is not and cannot be *a* meaning for all readers at all times and in all cultures. No meaning can dictate and govern the overall boundaries and parameters of Christian life; in effect, such boundaries and parameters are radically problematized thereby.

Pedagogical Implications

The educational implications of cultural studies are radically different from those of the other three paradigms. A number of factors call for a complete rethinking and reformulation of biblical pedagogy, its discourse and practice, within theological education: the broad variety of interpretive models; the conception of all readings as constructions on the part of real readers; the emphasis on social location and perspective with regard to real readers; the view of the critic as being as contextualized and perspectival as any other reader of the text. Certain consequences of such a revisioning are immediately clear.

First, there can no longer be a demand for a common methodological approach and theoretical apparatus on the part of all readers, regardless of theological moorings or sociocultural contexts, in order to become informed critics. Diversity in methods and models has rendered such a call not only unworkable in practice but also and above all groundless in theory. Indeed, one could very well argue that what is now necessary to become an informed reader or critic is metatheory, a grasp of theory and its history, not only within the discipline itself but also across the disciplinary spectrum. Second, informed readings can no longer be perceived as hermeneutically privileged and hence inherently superior to uninformed or "popular" readings, since both modes of readings involve, in their own respective ways, contextualization and perspective on the part of real readers. In this regard the call for readers to become informed, to become critics, has to be reconceptualized as well. Finally, readers can no longer be called upon to put aside their "faces" and voices in order to become informed but rather must be called upon to become self-conscious and self-critical regarding these in the process of reading and interpretation, that is, learn how to read not only texts but also themselves and their readings.

In the end, the long-established model of learned impartation and passive reception, carried on within a seemingly ahistorical and asocial vacuum, must yield to a model of self-conscious, highly critical, and global dialogue involving constant and ever-shifting impartation and reception. In so doing, the pedagogical model would follow closely upon the interpretive model, becoming in the process highly decentered (or multicentered) and multilingual.

CONCLUDING COMMENTS

Such, then, are the basic principles that inform and guide the paradigm of cultural studies. Following this overview of the model, I should like to conclude, as I did in the case of the other three paradigms, with some remarks on the consequences of this new paradigm for theory and methodology as well as culture and experience in the task of biblical criticism. In so doing, I make use once again of the fundamental themes of liberation and decolonization invoked and deployed in my plotting of the discipline—its past, its present, and its future.

First, from a methodological and theoretical point of view, cultural studies represents a further and profound liberating step in biblical criticism, insofar as it allows for a diversity of reading strategies and theoretical models while calling for critical awareness and engagement regarding the grounding, application, and ramifications of all such models and strategies. Cultural studies does not argue for any one strategy or framework as the sole and proper entry into the text to the exclusion of all others, for a totalizing narrative as it were; it contemplates instead a creative use of historical, literary, and cultural perspectives and concerns. In so doing, cultural studies finds itself in conversation with a wide variety of disciplines and critical frameworks. It does regard, however, all strategies and models as constructs on the part of real readers and thus calls on all readers to be quite open regarding their reading strategies and theoretical frameworks as well as their social locations and agendas.

Second, from a historical and cultural point of view, cultural studies represents an even more profound and liberating step in biblical criticism, insofar as it moves well beyond diversity in the methodological and theoretical realm into diversity in the sociocultural realm. Cultural studies is interested in analyzing not only the social location and agendas of texts but also the social location and agendas of flesh-and-blood readers and "texts," their readings of texts. Since all reading strategies and "texts" are regarded as constructs on the part of real readers, the task of criticism is seen as encompassing both an analysis of culture and experience vis-à-vis texts and an analysis of culture and experience vis-à-vis their readers, in the fullness of their diversity. For cultural studies, therefore, all *exegesis* is ultimately *eisegesis;* that is, interpretation and hermeneutics go hand in hand.

Through such a joint analysis of texts and "texts," readers and their readings, cultural studies moves well beyond the implicit and dominant Western moorings and concerns of the discipline to embrace the concerns and moorings of readers throughout the rest of the world, to let everyone speak in his or her own tongue and from his or her own place. With cultural studies, therefore, the process of liberation and decolonization in biblical criticism takes a crucial step. What happens when the inculturation of the critic as gendered and Western ceases? What happens, in effect, is what can be presently witnessed in the discipline and what takes place whenever any process of liberation and decolonization begins to prove successful: a situation of simultaneous celebration, wailing, and conflict. First, the outsiders rejoice over their newfound identity and history on the periphery. Second, the insiders wail over the decline of standards and "scholarship" represented by the center. Third, there is conflict: on the one hand, sharp and inevitable criticism of the center, of its discourse and practice (the what-have-you-done-to-us syndrome), by the outsiders; on the other hand, ready dismissal of the periphery, of its discourse and practice (the after-all-we-have-done-for-you syndrome), by the center.

At the same time, beyond the celebration, lamentation, and conflict, new and fundamental problems arise. To mention but a few: If no master narrative is to be posited or desired, how does one deal with the continued abuse of the oppressed by the oppressor, the weak by the strong, the subaltern by the dominant? If the ideal of the master teacher is to be put aside, how does one carry on the task of biblical pedagogy and theological education? If the critic is neither objective nor disinterested, what then becomes the role of the critic in society and religion? If biblical criticism is not to be regarded as scientific, nontheological, and nonreligious at heart, what then should be its relationship vis-à-vis the other classical theological disciplines and the so-called fields of religious studies? Anomie, to be sure, does have its price. A consideration of such issues must, however, wait for another occasion.

A final comment is in order. I have argued that cultural studies calls for and demands dialogue, critical dialogue. I also argue, however, that there should be no romantic illusions whatsoever about such dialogue. Were one to plot the discourse and practice of dialogue along an interpretive spectrum, the following three positions would readily come to mind: toward one end, the totalitarian position, whether of the left or the right, of no dialogue whatsoever, with dialogue seen as profoundly subversive; in the center, the liberal-humanist position of genteel dialogue—perhaps the most common position in both professional and graduate theological programs—in which the political questions of power and ideology are distinctly frowned upon and actively skirted as disruptive and politicizing, as undoing or not building "community"; toward the other end, the democratic and liberative position of critical dialogue, according to which all voices have a right to speak up, loud and clear, and no subject remains untouched, including that of power and ideology. I see cultural studies as fully ensconced at this latter end of the spectrum and thus as both a progeny of conflict and a progenitor of conflict; such dialogue is born out of conflict and engenders conflict. Such is also the inevitable result and mode of a postcolonial world and a postcolonial biblical criticism.

PART II

GRAND MODELS
AND STRATEGIES
OF PEDAGOGY

3

Pedagogical Discourse and Practices in Contemporary Biblical Criticism

In the previous analyses of the course of biblical criticism in the twentieth century, I have portrayed the world of contemporary biblical criticism as consisting of four main and competing paradigms or umbrella models of interpretation, each with its own distinctive mode of discourse and broad spectrum of interpretive positions. These four paradigms I have identified as follows: historical criticism, literary criticism, cultural criticism, and cultural studies.[1]

I have also argued that these umbrella models of interpretation presently find themselves, at the turn of the century, at different levels of competitiveness in the public arena of the discipline as a result of the particular path of development or "plot" I have charted for the discipline as a whole. Such varying states of readiness I have described as follows: First, a much-weakened historical criticism (as *traditionally* conceived and practiced), thoroughly displaced from its former position of near-absolute hegemony and left rather at a loss, still, for a vigorous and informed defense regarding its own methodological strategies and theoretical grounds.[2] Second, the two original would-be pretenders to the throne, literary criticism

---

[1] For other ways of looking at the recent path and present state of the discipline, see, e.g., E. Schüssler Fiorenza, "'For the Sake of Our Salvation . . . ,' Biblical Interpretation and the Community of Faith," in *Bread Not Stone: The Challenge of Feminist Biblical Interpretation* (Boston: Beacon Press, 1984), 23-42; A. C. Thiselton, "New Testament Interpretation in Historical Perspective," in *Hearing the New Testament: Strategies for Interpretation,* ed. J. B. Green (Grand Rapids, Mich.: William B. Eerdmans, 1995), 10-36; The Bible and Culture Collective, "Introduction," in *The Postmodern Bible* (New Haven, Conn.: Yale University Press, 1995), 1-19.

[2] I always insist on describing this first umbrella model in terms of *traditional* historical criticism, and I do so not only to refer to that particular approach to texts that governed the discipline for so long and according to which so many generations were trained—and indeed continue to be trained—but also to high-

[continued]

and cultural criticism, which have become, since their sharp and success-ful challenge to historical criticism, quite entrenched in the discipline, quite sophisticated in method and theory, and quite vibrant in interdisciplinary dialogue and exchange. Finally, the still-nascent cultural studies, essen-tially a child of mixed parentage—on the one hand, a product of the pro-found methodological and theoretical shifts introduced into the discipline by both literary and cultural criticism; on the other hand, and above all, the result of certain crucial demographic and sociocultural changes at work in the discipline, as in all other classical theological disciplines, that is, an ever-growing presence of outsiders (Western women; non-Western critics and theologians; and non-Western minorities residing in the West) in the discipline, who have entered what had been a thoroughly clerical, male, and Western domain.[3] I should specify that such an evaluation of the competitive dynamics among these four paradigms reflects more ac-curately the situation in Western North America than in Europe; indeed, in many ways, though with some outstanding exceptions here and there, the "Old World" is only now beginning to struggle with issues that many in the United States have already engaged and moved beyond.[4]

I have further undertaken to surface and unpack a number of funda-mental presuppositions at work in the construction and employment of each umbrella model of interpretation by means of a comparative analy-sis of six basic elements or principles operative, in one way or another, in all four paradigms: location of meaning, reading strategy, theoretical foun-dations, role of the reader, theological presuppositions, and pedagogical implications. A principal aim of such an exercise in metatheory is to out-line as starkly as possible the manifold options and choices facing, at every step of the way, contemporary professional practitioners of the dis-cipline today—choices and options, it should go without saying, that sig-nal immediate and inevitable consequences for any critic's conception and practice of the discipline.

---

light the fact that, as a paradigm, such criticism failed to establish any sort of sustained critical dialogue with developing currents within the field of historiog-raphy itself, its home base since the nineteenth century. In other words, I use the adjective "traditional" to signify both a particular historical phenomenon in the discipline and a particular theoretical stance within historiography. From my point of view, such lack of dialogue with historiography and such inability to mount a proper defense on its own behalf are closely related.

[3] On the nature and ramifications of this development, see chap. 8 in this volume.

[4] In my opinion two factors have played a significant role in this regard: (1) the persistent character of biblical criticism in Europe as thoroughly clerical, male, and Western; and (2) an evident lack of interdisciplinary dialogue with the hu-manities, in itself highly ironic given the riches available in poststructuralist and postmodernist currents and movements within Europe itself.

In effect, as I have further argued, the situation has become radically different now from what it was in the mid-1970s. To wit, methodological diversity within a dominant paradigm (historical criticism), involving over-all consensus regarding the same basic mode of discourse, has yielded to (1) diversity of paradigms, with widely different modes of discourse; (2) diversity of methods and theories within each paradigm, of a sort far more difficult to manage and transcend than that present in the previously dominant paradigm; and (3) ever-increasing diversity of interpreters, bringing to the fore issues of ideology across all paradigms. Quite aside from the question of whether such a shift has been beneficial or harmful to the discipline—in the end, a highly personal and contextualized judgment—the fact remains that its implications and ramifications impinge upon all critics at every step of the way. As a result, such questions as the following now call for explicit and sustained consideration:

- How are ancient texts—indeed "antiquity" itself—to be approached and why?
- What is precisely the role of the biblical critic as critic?
- What is the relationship of biblical criticism to the other theological disciplines as well as to other disciplines in the humanities and the social sciences?
- What is the relationship of the biblical critic not only to the church but also to other religious traditions and their own forms of criticism regarding such traditions?
- What is the relationship of the biblical critic to the broader society as well as to the world at large?
- What are the ethical, social, and ideological responsibilities of biblical interpretation?
- How is the teaching of the discipline to be undertaken in this day and age?

For any critic who wishes to reflect on these matters, there is really no choice but to proceed step by step, question by question, given the magnitude and significance of each question. In this study, therefore, I should like to focus on the last question—the question of pedagogy—and hence on the last of the six basic principles mentioned above, which I have already surfaced and unpacked in all four critical paradigms. I shall do so in two stages.

First, I shall examine in a more sustained and systematic fashion the pedagogical discourse and practices proper to each of the first three paradigms: historical criticism, literary criticism, and cultural criticism. It should be made clear from the start that the proposed analysis faces a significant though not insurmountable obstacle: the question of pedagogy has rarely, if ever, been raised, much less addressed explicitly, in any of these three paradigms. This means, of course, that the proposed analysis can only proceed by rendering explicit what has remained largely implicit throughout, that is to say, by bringing to the surface the pedagogical discourse and practices presupposed within each paradigm. At the same time, however, such analysis is not entirely an exercise in deduction; it is also an exercise in recollection. In other words, I approach this question neither as a complete stranger nor as a participant observer, but as a cognizant insider—as someone who, given the coincidence between such disciplinary developments and my own engagement with the discipline, has both resided in and worked from within each of the paradigms in question.

I shall pursue this mixture of deduction and recollection by means of a conversation with a number of individuals who not only embody in a very distinctive way the ideals and goals of each paradigm, but who also have captured in writing such ideals and goals in a very precise way—individuals whom I regard as both key representatives of and outstanding spokespersons for their respective crafts. In so doing, I emphasize, my aim is not to engage in scorched-earth tactics, slashing and burning, tearing down and destroying—a regrettable and still much-too-common dimension of our discipline, I am afraid, due in large part to its emergence alongside Western capitalism and expansionism, with its credo of a ruthless "virile" competition; my aim, rather, is to engage in critical dialogue with a number of individuals from whom I have learned a great deal and with whose work I happen to be thoroughly familiar.

Second, I shall then proceed to examine, in a similar type of conversation, a number of voices that have, in recent times and within the ambit of the cultural studies paradigm, begun to call for new directions in the teaching of the discipline, with specific reference to its expanding methodological and theoretical apparatus and, above all, the growing phenomenon of globalization at work within it. My aim in such an exercise is to analyze the various diagnoses offered for the discipline—the overall perception of its present state of affairs—as well as any corresponding prescriptions for change.

Such a twofold analysis and engagement, in itself a central component of intercultural criticism as I have defined it,[5] has two basic purposes: to reveal the direction and tenor of the pedagogical discussion in the discipline in the face of a new century, and to set the stage for a

---

[5] See my "Toward a Hermeneutics of the Diaspora: A Hermeneutics of Otherness and Engagement," in *Reading from This Place*, vol. 1: *Social Location and Biblical Interpretation in the United States*, ed. F. F. Segovia and M. A. Tolbert (Minneapolis: Fortress Press, 1995), 57-73; and "Toward Intercultural Criticism: A Reading Strategy from the Diaspora," in *Reading from This Place*, vol. 2: *Social Location and Biblical Interpretation in Global Perspective*, ed. F. F. Segovia and M. A. Tolbert (Minneapolis: Fortress Press, 1995), 303-30.

constructive pedagogical proposal of my own from the perspective of cultural studies.

PEDAGOGICAL DISCOURSE AND PRACTICES IN HISTORICAL, LITERARY, AND CULTURAL CRITICISM

Historical Criticism

In chapter 1, in my initial assessment of the pedagogical model underlying historical criticism, I made a number of observations with regard to its basic principles and implications: First, the model involved learned impartation and passive reception. In keeping with its corresponding demand for a universal and informed reader-construct, the model argued that the proper dissemination and acquisition of the right methodological tools could turn students/readers, regardless of sociocultural moorings or theological persuasion, into informed and universal teachers/critics. Second, given such emphasis on learned impartation, the model was at heart highly pyramidal and authoritative, quintessentially patriarchal, with competing claims to honor advanced in terms of academic genealogy (who begat whom: where one studied and with whom) and critical sociolect (proper *vs.* improper approximations to the text). Third, quite in keeping once again with the universal and informed reader-construct, the model further entailed a process of dehumanization as a key component in its rite of initiation for all would-be practitioners and devotees. Student/readers would become teacher/critics by learning how not to read themselves as readers, except for the purpose of surfacing theological presuppositions so that these could be properly identified and duly obviated. In the end, I concluded, this was a model for which students/readers remained dependent on teacher/critics for an account of the text and its meaning. Only the voice of reason, properly activated and cultivated through a concomitant acquisition of scientific tools and divestment of sociocultural vagaries, could speak *ex cathedra* on matters interpretive.

As interlocutor in historical criticism, I turn to the work of Joseph A. Fitzmyer, S.J., by way of an article on historical criticism that he contributed some years ago to a special issue of *Theological Studies* devoted to the question of contemporary biblical criticism.[6] The study represents a

---

[6] J. A. Fitzmyer, "Historical Criticism: Its Role in Biblical Interpretation and Church Life," *Theological Studies* 50 (1989): 244-59. The venue is a Roman Catholic journal of theology published by the theological faculties of the Society of Jesus in the United States. The issue included articles on U.S. Catholic biblical scholarship, the social sciences, feminist hermeneutics, narrative criticism, New Testament theology, and contemporary translations of scripture into English.

succinct, pointed, and spirited defense of historical criticism[7] in the light of four perceived challenges: (1) integrism within Roman Catholic circles: the method is captive to modernism and underplays the character of the Bible as "Word of God"; (2) liberalism within Roman Catholic circles: the method represents the end of traditional, folk catholicism; (3) theological criticism: the method shows no concern for the final text—its literary features, canonical setting, and theological meaning; (4) fundamentalism within Protestant circles: the method forsakes the fundamentals of Christian doctrine by bypassing the inspiration of the text and the authority of the written Word. Interestingly enough, however, despite the date in question (1989), no challenge from within the tradition of academic criticism is entertained.[8]

The defense itself is broadly mounted, touching upon such various facets of the method as historical trajectory, reading strategy, ideological presuppositions, and ecclesiological role. It is further undertaken from the perspective of the critic as historian of religion and Christian theologian—a perspective that includes a view of criticism as involving both historical reconstruction and theological propaedeutics (Bible as ancient record and Word of God) and thus a view of Christian doctrine and life as subject to the guidance and judgment of the Word of God and of this Word as accessible only through the channel of historical criticism. The defense also makes a fundamental distinction between method and presuppositions.

The method itself, which is said to consist of a basic core and subsequent refinements, is characterized as "neutral," that is to say, as without

---

[7] For other recent presentations of historical criticism, see J. Reumann, "After Historical Criticism, What? Trends in Biblical Interpretation and Ecumenical, Interfaith Dialogues," *Journal of Ecumenical Studies* 29 (1992): 55-86; M. Fander, "Historical-Critical Methods," in *Searching the Scriptures,* vol. 1: *A Feminist Introduction,* ed. E. Schüssler Fiorenza (New York: Crossroad, 1993), 205-24; J. M. Miller, "Reading the Bible Historically: The Historian's Approach," in *To Each Its Own Meaning: An Introduction to Biblical Criticisms and Their Application,* ed. S. L. McKenzie and S. R. Haynes (Louisville: Westminster/John Knox Press, 1993), 11-28; J. D. Levenson, "The Hebrew Bible, the Old Testament, and Historical Criticism" and "Historical Criticism and the Fate of the Enlightenment Project," in J. D. Levenson, *The Hebrew Bible, the Old Testament, and Historical Criticism: Jews and Christians in Biblical Studies* (Minneapolis: Fortress Press, 1993), 1-32 and 106-26, respectively.

[8] The reason is clear. For Fitzmyer ("Historical Criticism," 255) "new modes" of interpretation can only serve to correct or refine the "basic" method of historical criticism; they can neither substitute for nor be allowed to replace this "fundamental" approach. In other words, traditional historical criticism is represented as theoretically unassailable: it may be refined but it cannot be contested. As a result, the metatheoretical character of the disciplinary discussion already at work at the time of composition is altogether bypassed, if not dismissed in principle.

"presuppositions."[9] Classical philology constitutes the core; at the heart of the method, therefore, lie questions of both a textual (the establishment of the text) and a historical nature (authenticity, integrity, date and place, content, occasion or purpose of writing, background).[10] Beyond this core one finds a series of refinements that, strictly speaking, do not form part of historical criticism but that have become associated with it over time: literary criticism (structure, style, form), source criticism, form criticism, and redaction criticism. From the point of view of historical criticism as philology, therefore, the Bible represents an ancient record and, as such, must be approached and analyzed like any other ancient record—paying close attention to the different historical backgrounds, contemporary contexts, and original languages of the texts in question—if one is to arrive at the meaning intended by the authors themselves.

Given its neutral character, the method can be pursued with different presuppositions in mind: while some are said to "taint" the method unduly (for example, the rationalistic analysis or challenges of the nineteenth century; the demythologizing, existentialist approach of Rudolf Bultmann), one in particular is described as "exegesis" proper, what Fitzmyer calls "philology plus."[11] Such exegesis—defined from the perspective of the Roman Catholic Church—calls for a view of the Bible, of the ancient

---

[9] This "neutral" method reveals, however, all sorts of unspoken and unexamined theoretical presuppositions, such as the following: (a) critical objectivity—the method itself has no presuppositions and thus practitioners can lay claim to impartiality in research; (b) objectivist understanding of meaning—meaning is contained in the texts themselves; (c) authorial intention—such meaning represents what the author intended to write; (d) texts as sociohistorical capsules—such meaning further reflects the world of the text; (e) a hermeneutics of discovery—meaning and reality are out there, beyond readers, and can be properly retrieved through the use of the right scientific methods; (f) exclusive validity—meaning can be retrieved only by way of this method and none other.

[10] On the origins, development, and presuppositions of classical philology, see M. Olender, *The Languages of Paradise: Race, Religion, and Philology in the Nineteenth Century* (Cambridge: Harvard University Press, 1992). On the origins, development, and presuppositions of archaeology, see B. Kurlick, *Puritans in Babylon: The Ancient Near East and American Intellectual Life, 1880-1930* (Cambridge: Harvard University Press, 1996).

[11] The theoretical edifice comes close to collapse at this point. If the historical method is indeed neutral, as claimed, then it should follow that all those who employ it should come to the same historical conclusions, regardless of the "presuppositions" at work in its use or application. The admission that the soundness of the results varies according to the presuppositions of different practitioners should serve as a warning signal that something is very much amiss, that the proposed fundamental division between "method" and "presuppositions" has to be thoroughly reexamined.

record, as the Word of God set forth in human words, a position that entails a number of further presuppositions as well: composed under the guidance of the Spirit, authoritative for the Jewish-Christian heritage, given by God to God's people for edification and salvation, properly expounded only within the context of the tradition that has emerged from it "within the communal faith-life" of the people. From the point of view of historical criticism as exegesis, therefore, God has spoken historically and uniquely in the Bible, and thus it takes a combination of historical criticism and faith presuppositions to ascertain its proper and correct meaning as Word of God in human words.

In the end, Fitzmyer hints at the pedagogical implications of this approach: While the method does impose a "heavy burden" on readers, it alone allows, as suggested by the Bible itself (2 Pt 3:15-17 and Acts 8), for proper reading and interpretation to take place. The pedagogical model at work is thus unmistakable and confirms all the preliminary observations listed above:

First, student/readers need to master the principles of classical philology and the techniques of its later refinements in order to become critic/teachers; further, student/readers also need to possess the proper faith presuppositions to become exegetes. On the one hand, therefore, student/readers must acquire an extensive knowledge of the period and area under consideration, an expertise involving original languages, contemporary contexts, and historical backgrounds. On the other hand, student/readers must also possess extensive familiarity with regard to the exegetical tradition as such, the various presuppositions at work in such a tradition, and the faith presuppositions of proper exegesis.

Second, given their mastery of such principles and techniques and their possession of such knowledge and expertise, teacher/critics hold the key to the meaning of the Bible as an ancient record; likewise, given their familiarity with presuppositions and their grounding in faith presuppositions, teacher/exegetes also hold the key to the meaning of the Bible as Word of God.

Third, such mastery and such learning render critics objective and impartial in their research, lifting them above social location and ideology and allowing them to recover the original meaning of the text (the ancient record) intended by the authors; similarly, such familiarity and such grounding give proper direction to their historical research, placing it within a sound context and agenda and rendering them able to retrieve the full meaning of the text (the Word of God) intended by the sacred authors.

What emerges thereby is a pedagogical model that is highly pyramidal, patriarchal, and authoritative: a model where the teacher/critic, as the voice of reason, collects and disseminates the historical mysteries of the text as ancient record to student/readers, and the teacher/exegete, as the voice of faith, unveils and discloses the theological mysteries of the text as Word of God to student/readers; a model where teacher/critics rise above social location and ideology to arrive at the meaning of the text and where teacher/exegetes locate themselves within a specific context and agenda to arrive at the full meaning of that text.

Literary Criticism

With respect to the pedagogical model underlying literary criticism, I noted in chapter 1 that its basic principles and implications were not unlike those of historical criticism. First, the model again involved sophisticated impartation and passive acquisition. Given its call at first for a universal and informed reader-construct and later for a more specific and formal reader-construct, the model took it for granted that all student/readers, regardless of sociocultural moorings or theological persuasion, could become teacher/critics, provided that the right theoretical and methodological apparatuses were properly propagated and learned. Second, given the continued emphasis on sophisticated impartation, the model remained at heart highly pyramidal and authoritative, typically patriarchal, with competing claims to honor now offered in terms of literary sociolect (which particular critical stance to follow) and external authority (which critics to read). Third, regardless of the reader-construct at work, whether that of the universal and informed reader or that of the specific and formal reader, the model continued to abstain, in its rite of initiation for all would-be practitioners and devotees, from any reading of real readers. The model clearly clung thereby to the ideal of dehumanization: real student/readers would become teacher/critics by learning how not to read themselves. I concluded by stating that this was a model in which student/readers continued to be ultimately dependent on teacher/critics for an account of the text and its meaning, although, to be sure, such a position gradually eroded as more and more attention was placed on the possibility of multiple interpretations and the role of the reader in the act of reading.

As interlocutor in literary criticism, I shall have recourse to the work of Mark Allan Powell, in particular the introductory volume on narrative criticism that he authored for the Guides to Biblical Scholarship Series published by Fortress Press.[12] This is a work that sets out to explain the ways, aims, and consequences of one particular strand of literary criticism—narrative criticism—in the light of both historical criticism and other

---

[12] M. A. Powell, *What Is Narrative Criticism?*, Guides to Biblical Scholarship: New Testament Series (Minneapolis: Fortress Press, 1991). See also his "Narrative Criticism," in Green, *Hearing the New Testament*, 239-55.

approaches within literary criticism itself.[13] In so doing, the work adopts a tone of comparative exposition rather than formal apologia, no doubt due to the fact that, by the time of composition (1990), literary criticism—and certainly narrative criticism—had already become well entrenched in the discipline. As such, its primary aim is not justification but differentiation.[14] This exercise in differentiation is further undertaken from the perspective of the critic as both historian of religion and Christian theologian—a perspective that includes a view of criticism as involving both literary analysis and theological propaedeutics (the Bible as literature and Word of God).

Powell begins by distinguishing literary criticism from traditional criticism. While historical criticism sought to explain the texts in terms of historical circumstances, literary criticism focuses on the literary qualities of the texts as such.[15] As a result, a number of basic differences between the two approaches can be readily outlined. Literary criticism (1) concentrates on the present text in its finished form—rather than on its process of formation; (2) emphasizes the unity and coherence of the text as a whole—rather than its lack of flow and unintelligibility; (3) views the text as an end in itself—rather than as a means toward some type of historical reconstruction; (4) opts for a communications model of interpretation—rather than for an evolutionary or excavative model. Despite such differences and the different insights they generate regarding the text, Powell argues for a relationship of complementarity rather than opposition between the two approaches: Literary criticism does not question the legitimacy of historical criticism but simply suspends the question of historicity in order to study the text as literature.[16] In fact, Powell goes on to

---

[13] For other recent presentations of literary criticism, see C. C. Black, "Rhetorical Criticism," and K. J. Vanhoozer, "The Reader in New Testament Interpretation," in Green, *Hearing the New Testament*, 256-77 and 301-28, respectively; S. E. Porter, "Literary Approaches to the New Testament: From Formalism to Deconstruction and Back," and D. L. Stamps, "Rhetorical Criticism of the New Testament: Ancient and Modern Evaluations of Argumentation," in *Approaches to New Testament Study*, ed. S. E. Porter and D. Tombs, Journal for the Study of the New Testament Supplementary Series 120 (Sheffield: Sheffield Academic Press, 1995), 77-128 and 129-69, respectively. For a more developed summary of rhetorical criticism, see B. L. Mack, *Rhetoric and the New Testament*, Guides to Biblical Scholarship: New Testament Series (Minneapolis: Fortress Press, 1990).

[14] It should be noted, however, that no such differentiation is undertaken with regard to cultural criticism in any of its various formations, a critical movement well on the way by this time as well.

[15] Powell, "Scripture as Story," in *What Is Narrative Criticism?*, 1-10.

[16] This irenic view of the relationship between the two approaches is quite problematic—despite Powell's protestations to the contrary (ibid., 92)—in the light of the basic opposition posited with respect to the present status of the text.

[continued]

argue, narrative criticism must have knowledge of the social and historical circumstances assumed by the narrative in order to be truly effective. One could say, therefore, that for Powell literary criticism functions as a sort of climax to historical criticism, insofar as it brings the final text to the fore for analysis.

Powell then proceeds to distinguish narrative criticism from other "ways of reading" within literary criticism itself—structuralism, rhetorical criticism, and reader-response criticism.[17] It is the aim of narrative criticism to read the text in terms of its "implied" reader—the reader presupposed by, present in, and reconstructed from the text. As such, narrative criticism can be readily distinguished from the other strands of literary criticism: (1) structuralism argues for a "competent" reader—a reader who understands the deep structures and codes undergirding the text; (2) rhetorical criticism opts for the "intended" reader—the reader to whom the text was first addressed; (3) reader-response criticism favors a first-time reader— a reader who encounters the text in sequential order. Again, despite such differences and the different insights generated with regard to the text, Powell tacitly argues for a relationship of complementarity rather than opposition among the various approaches: While clearly favoring the reading offered by way of the "implied" reader, narrative criticism does not call into question the modes of reading at work in the other approaches.[18] One could add, therefore, that for Powell, once the final text is brought to the fore for analysis, it can be subjected to a number of different "ways of reading."

In other words, how can the perception of unity and coherence in the text favored by literary criticism be reconciled with the view of lack of flow and unintelligibility in the text espoused by historical criticism? There has to be a point of no return, a point at which the perceived unevennesses of the text can no longer be subsumed under the principles of unity and coherence . . . unless, of course, one takes the road of deconstruction.

[17] Powell, "Ways of Reading," in *What Is Narrative Criticism?*, 11-21.

[18] This irenic view of the relationship among the various approaches within literary criticism is severely called into question by Powell's own reference (ibid., 20-21) to the critique of the implied reader of narrative criticism advanced by certain reader-response critics. The critique is presented as twofold: (1) from a formalist perspective, it is argued that no reader is able to grasp all the complex interrelationships that occur within a text, as called for by the concept of the implied reader; (2) from a hermeneutical perspective, it is argued that the concept of the implied reader will differ according to the particular interests and contexts of real readers. In response, Powell deals only with the formalist dimension of the critique: While the goal of reading "as the implied reader" may be unattainable, it remains a worthy goal nonetheless. The hermeneutical challenge, however, is much more fundamental and remains unanswered: How can the perception of the implied reader in the text as favored by narrative criticism be reconciled with a view of the implied reader as reflecting the interests and contexts of the real readers as advocated by a number of reader-response critics?

It is clear from both exercises in differentiation that literary criticism, including narrative criticism, involves a set of presuppositions as well as a method.[19] Its key methodological principle is clear: to read the text as the implied reader would. Such a mode of reading may be further described as follows. First, the implied reader—the reader constructed and addressed by the implied author—is reconstructed from the text on the basis of clues provided by the text itself.[20] Second, such reading requires that the reader know everything that the text assumes the reader to know, while bypassing everything that the text does not assume the reader to know. In other words, such reading pursues only those questions that the text assumes its reader will ask and no others. Third, such reading does not necessarily require a first-time reader but may actually call for a multiple reader of the text. Finally, such reading must follow the various narrative devices deployed in the text by the implied author. These devices have to do with story or the content of the narrative (events, characters, settings, plot) as well as discourse or the rhetoric of the narrative (point of view, levels of narration, symbolism and irony, narrative patterns). Consequently, the aim of such reading is to understand the story as presented by the implied author in and through the text. In the end, therefore, the concept of the implied reader does set definite criteria for interpretation: Any proposed reading of a text must be justified in terms of the dictates and expectations to be found within the text itself.

---

[19] In addition to the theoretical presuppositions identified, a number of others remain unacknowledged: (a) critical objectivity—the method allows for the literary features of the text to surface and thus allows for impartiality and accuracy in research; (b) objectivist understanding of text and meaning—the literary features are in the text, come from the hand of the implied author, and serve as a guide to a proper understanding of the text and its meaning; (c) authorial intention—such meaning represents what the implied author actually wrote; (d) hermeneutics of discovery—the literary features and the meaning of the text are out there, beyond readers, and can be properly retrieved through the use of the right methods; (e) privileged validity—despite the argument for the complementarity of different approaches, it is clear that, through its dependence on the concept of the implied reader, narrative criticism does provide criteria for interpretation, insofar as it deals with what is in the text itself. To be quite fair to Powell, however, one should point out that he does acknowledge a measure of ambiguity throughout in narrative criticism: Within the parameters set by the text itself, there may be differences in interpretation.

[20] The implied author is also reconstructed by the reader from the text, constitutes the perspective from which the text must be interpreted, and thus serves as the interpretive key to the text. In other words, to read as the implied reader would read is to read according to the dictates and expectations of the implied author.

Given Powell's view of the Bible as both literature and Word of God, such reading has a further aim: to read the text as Scripture in story form.[21] In so doing, the benefits of narrative criticism for believers are clear. First, such reading remains focused throughout on the Bible itself—not on its history or prehistory. Second, such reading also remains focused thereby on the canonical text, the authoritative text for Christian communities—not on sources and traditions. Third, such reading is very much in line as well with the Christian doctrine of the Spirit, insofar as it allows for revelation to take place not just in the past but also in the present, in the process of engaging the story of the text. Finally, through this focus on story, such reading opens the door to personal and social transformation. Consequently, in shedding light on the literary features of the text, narrative criticism activates as well the socioreligious and spiritual dimensions of the text—its revelatory and transformative character as Scripture.

On the whole, Powell shows only intermittent, limited concern with the pedagogical implications of this approach. Still, the pedagogical model at work is not at all difficult to unravel and confirms the various preliminary observations noted above:

First, although the method is said at one point to bring professional and nonprofessional readers closer together, in the end there is no question that student/readers not only need to master the principles and techniques of literary criticism, and narrative criticism in particular, in order to become teacher/critics, but they also need to acquire extensive knowledge of the social and historical circumstances assumed by the texts. At the same time, there is no need for student/readers to possess a faith stance in order to become teacher/critics, although for those who do, the method is described as most beneficial. Thus, while in a certain sense the method may be said to be much more effective for those who look upon the Bible as both literature and Word of God, it is clear that, in order to read the Bible as literature, one need not regard it as Scripture.

Second, given their mastery of the principles and techniques of narrative criticism as well as their familiarity with the social and historical circumstances presupposed by the texts, teacher/critics do retain the key—allowing for a certain measure of ambiguity present within the text itself—to the meaning of the Bible, whether perceived as a work of literature or as the Word of God. Through such mastery and such familiarity, teacher/critics are able to follow the devices and intentions of the implied author and attain thereby a proper understanding of the text—again, allowing for a certain range of meaning within the parameters set by the text itself.

Third, the combination of such mastery and such familiarity allows for objectivity and impartiality in research, placing teacher/critics beyond all

---

[21] Powell, "Story as Scripture," in *What Is Narrative Criticism?*, 85-101.

consideration of social location and ideology and allowing them to re-cover—within the measure of ambiguity introduced by the text itself—the original meaning of the text intended by its implied author. At the same time, for those operating out of a faith stance, such research also bears immediate fruit from both a socioreligious and a spiritual angle: In the extended process of engaging the story of the text and deciphering the meaning intended by the implied author, there is ample opportunity for the revelation of the Spirit as well as for personal and social transformation.

The result is a pedagogical model that is, once again, highly pyramidal, patriarchal, and authoritative: a model where the teacher/critic, as the voice of the informed and universal (implied) reader, grasps the literary mysteries of the text and discloses them to student/readers, mysteries that also have profound spiritual as well as socioreligious consequences for members of faith communities; a model where teacher/critics move beyond social location and ideology to arrive at the original meaning of the text.

Cultural Criticism

In chapter 1, in my initial assessment of the pedagogical model under-lying cultural criticism, I pointed out that its basic principles and implications were quite similar to those of historical criticism. First, the model involved, once again, learned impartation and passive reception. In the light of its call for either an informed and universal reader-construct or an informed and committed reader-construct, the model argued that all student/readers, regardless of sociocultural location or theological persuasion, could become teacher/critics, if the right methodological tools and theoretical apparatus were properly taught and acquired. Second, given the abiding emphasis on learned impartation, the model was likewise highly pyramidal and authoritative, patriarchal to the core, with competing claims to honor advanced in terms of disciplinary sociolect (which particular discipline to follow) and external authority (which writers or tradition) to read. Third, as part of its rite of initiation for would-be practitioners and devotees, the model, depending on the dominant reader-construct at work, either continued to abstain from any reading of real readers, engaged in a broad reading of real readers (but only for the purpose of surfacing and obviating sociocultural presuppositions and establishing crosscultural communication), or called for a circumscribed reading of real readers in terms of social class. Aside from this last option, dehumanization still prevailed as an ideal: student/readers were still expected to become teacher/critics by learning how not to read themselves, except for the purpose of bringing to the fore sociocultural presuppositions. Within the last option, all student/readers would have to learn how to read themselves, but only according to the categories of oppressors and oppressed. In the end, I concluded, this was yet another model in which student/readers looked to teacher/critics for an account of the text and its meaning, although with some erosion of the position due to the increasing focus placed on sociocultural as well as socioeconomic characteristics.

As partner in dialogue with respect to cultural criticism, I turn to the work of Bruce J. Malina. More specifically, I have in mind a study of his that served as an introduction to his first major venture into what he eventually would come to call social scientific criticism.[22] This early study amounts to a formal apologia for the introduction of cultural anthropology into biblical criticism in the light of the traditional questions brought by historical criticism to the texts—the sort of questions outlined by Joseph Fitzmyer in his own defense of historical criticism years later.[23] Although questions of a "literary" sort are mentioned, it is clear that what Malina has in mind in this regard—despite the time of writing (1981)—are the traditional questions of historical criticism regarding literary forms and style, not the more recent questions introduced by literary criticism, by then very much on the rise.[24]

---

[22] B. J. Malina, "Bible Study and Cultural Anthropology," in *The New Testament World: Insights from Cultural Anthropology* (Atlanta: John Knox Press, 1981), 1-24. In the second edition of this volume (*The New Testament World: Insights from Cultural Anthropology*, rev. ed. [Louisville: Westminster/John Knox Press, 1993], 1-17) this chapter was reproduced with only minor variations, including the addition of a subtitle: "Bible Study and Cultural Anthropology: Interpreting Texts Fairly." (References will be to this second edition.) In the intervening years between these two editions, a number of the basic ideas contained in this study were taken up again and expanded in B. J. Malina, "Reading Theory Perspective: Reading Luke-Acts," in *The Social World of Luke-Acts*, ed. J. H. Neyrey (Peabody, Mass.: Hendrickson Publishers, 1991), 3-23.

[23] For other recent presentations of cultural criticism, see S. C. Barton, "Historical Criticism and Social-Scientific Perspectives in New Testament Study," in Green, *Hearing the New Testament*, 10-36; P. F. Esler, "Social Worlds, Social Sciences and the New Testament," in *The First Christians in Their Social Worlds: Social-Scientific Approaches to New Testament Interpretation* (Minneapolis: Fortress Press, 1990), 1-19; P. F. Esler, "Introduction: Models, Context, and Kerygma in New Testament Interpretation," in *Modelling Early Christianity: Social-Scientific Studies of the New Testament in Its Context*, ed. P. F. Esler (London-New York: Routledge, 1995), 1-20; B. Holmberg, "Sociology and New Testament Studies," in *Sociology and the New Testament: An Appraisal* (Minneapolis: Fortress Press, 1990), 1-20. For a more developed summary, see J. B. Elliott, *What Is Social-Scientific Criticism?*, Guides to Biblical Scholarship (Minneapolis: Fortress Press, 1992).

[24] It should be noted that in his later reformulation of this apologia ("Reading Theory Perspective"), literary criticism has replaced historical criticism as the main point of reference. This reorientation is clear from the start, as Malina argues

[continued]

The thrust of the apologia is not that the concepts and models of cultural anthropology have much to offer biblical studies but rather that the basic question raised by cultural anthropology constitutes not only the climax but also the sine qua non of the discipline. While traditional criticism pursues the important questions of what, who, when, where, historical how, and literary how, cultural anthropology addresses the question of why: the fundamental question of meaning in culture. Without this particular perspective provided by cultural anthropology, therefore, traditional criticism can only deal with this question in highly impressionistic fashion and thus remains constantly exposed to the twin perils of ethnocentrism and anachronism. The apologia itself is undertaken from the perspective of the biblical critic as historian of religion, not as Christian theologian. What is sought is a more sophisticated exercise in the history of religion by way of a focus on the sociocultural dimensions of the texts. Thus, the main concern is not with the Bible as Word of God but with the Bible as a cultural record of antiquity. Consequently, the goal of the exercise is to allow for a more accurate understanding of these texts as "foreign" texts from "a distant place and a distant time." For Malina, therefore, biblical criticism represents, first and foremost, an exercise in crosscultural understanding, and such understanding proves impossible without recourse to cultural anthropology.[25] In the end, it would be quite proper to describe the proposed undertaking as an attempt to perfect historical criticism.

---

against any view of meaning as residing in language, in "wording," rather than in the social systems embodied in and conveyed by language, in "meanings" (3-8). The remainder of the article confirms this shift. All reading, Malina declares, involves an intrapersonal or individual dimension, best explored by psycholinguistics, as well as an interpersonal or social dimension, best explored by sociolinguistics (8-12). With regard to the former, Malina argues (12-17), the model employed by literary criticism in general—the propositional model (the text as "a sort of supersentence") at work in "contemporary structural, semiotic, deconstructionist, 'Marxist,' and aesthetic literary criticism"—is completely off target, insofar as it is unverifiable by actual research into reading. With regard to the latter, Malina continues (17-22), the model followed by most of literary criticism—decontextualized reading (from "the print itself") as in the case of "the effort to read the Bible as literature" and "much of the reader-response approach to literature"—is neither fair nor just, since it dismisses the social dimensions of author, original audience, and text in question.

[25] Malina does address, briefly, the importance and relevance of cultural anthropology for Christian believers, for all those who accept the Bible as the Word of God ("Bible Study and Cultural Anthropology," 17-18). First, the incarnation of the Word of God signifies the inculturation of God's word. In other words, the life of the Word of God and the written accounts of or reflection on that life cannot but follow the cultural story of the period in question. Second, as a result,

[continued]

The desired crosscultural understanding involves presuppositions—not all of which are properly recognized as such[26]—as well as a method. The line of argumentation may be traced as follows. First, an accurate understanding of the texts "on their own terms" is possible. Contemporary readers can cross the cultural and historical divide between the world of today and the world of antiquity. Second, the meaning of a text as embodied in its wording is derived from the social system out of which the text emerges. Consequently, an accurate understanding of texts requires an understanding of the social system behind the texts. Third, in order to understand the social system behind these texts it is necessary to understand the cultural story—the cultural scripts, cues, and models—at work in such a world, the world of the first-century Mediterranean Basin. Fourth, to understand this cultural story across the cultural and historical divide,

---

the only way to understand the Word of God today is to do so from within the context of that cultural story of the past—the cultural story of first-century Palestinian and Mediterranean culture. At the same time, Malina adds (25), such understanding yields a cultural story that is radically different from that of contemporary readers. Indeed, the following hermeneutical principle is offered: An accurate interpretation of these texts is more likely to be one in which the "differences" between the world of the reader and the world of the text are too great, the "variance" between moral judgments too disturbing, and the "focus" between religious concerns too distant. What Malina does not do, however, is to address himself to the implications and ramifications of such profound differences for the theological task of believing Christians. In the end, he remains the historian of religion.

[26] Among those not recognized as such are the following: (a) critical objectivity—the method allows for sociocultural presuppositions to come to the fore and thus for impartiality and accuracy in research; (b) objectivist understanding of meaning—meaning is contained in the texts themselves; (c) texts as sociohistorical capsules—the meaning contained in the texts derives from the world of the text; (d) a hermeneutics of discovery—meaning and reality are out there, beyond readers, and can be properly retrieved through the use of the right scientific methods; (e) exclusive validity—accurate meaning can only be had through the use of this particular approach. A number of other presuppositions are not mentioned at all: (a) Social systems or cultures as monolithic—a view of meanings as universally imparted, shared, and utilized: in other words, there is one cultural story, and all individuals and texts reflect that story, whether in the past or in the present; (b) social systems or cultures as all-encompassing: it is possible to speak, for example, of first-century Mediterranean culture; (c) social systems or cultures as fixed and unchanging: it is possible to use models derived from contemporary anthropological research on Mediterranean culture to apply to first-century Mediterranean culture; (d) models as neutral: the question of the ideological orientation of the models and their creators is never raised; (e) communication within social systems or cultures as unproblematic: meanings are readily conveyed and received across all segments of society.

it is necessary to have recourse to crosscultural models of interpretation. Such models make it possible for the differences between cultural stories to be sharply outlined and differentiated, so that one can avoid reading one's own cultural story into that of the biblical text and thus read the cultural story of the biblical texts "on their own terms." Lastly, human beings are capable of constructing such models as a result of several factors: (1) their ability to think abstractly, to make models of experience, and to compare the various models in question; (2) their awareness that they themselves change; and (3) their ability to take on the role of another empathetically.[27] In sum, only cultural anthropology can supply such crosscultural models for biblical studies, and thus only cultural anthropology can provide the key for an accurate understanding of these texts.

Throughout, Malina is concerned with the pedagogical implications of social scientific criticism. Indeed, the driving question here is how to make it possible for contemporary student/readers to achieve an accurate and fair reading and interpretation of these "foreign" texts and of the "foreigners" behind them. The resultant pedagogical model is quite clear and follows the initial observations listed above:

First, student/readers need not only master the principles and techniques of historical criticism, so that they can continue to ask all of the important questions characteristic of traditional criticism, but also must familiarize themselves thoroughly with concepts and models of cultural anthropology—especially those derived from the study of contemporary Mediterranean society or other similar societies—so that they can proceed to raise the fundamental question of meaning: the why question. Student/readers need not, however, possess a correct faith stance to become teacher/critics. In effect, whether they look upon these texts as Scripture or as cultural remains of the past, student/readers must develop extensive expertise

---

[27] For Malina, therefore, the models of cultural anthropology are indispensable insofar as they are both scientific and crosscultural. On the one hand, as "abstract, simplified representations of more complex real-world objects and interactions," such models allow for "adequate" understanding insofar as they are subject to a scientific process of validation ("Bible Study and Cultural Anthropology," 19-20). Once formulated, the models can be tested against the "real world" experience to which they relate and are either validated or modified in the case of any errors of omission or commission detected in the process of testing. On the other hand, such models allow for "adequate" understanding of other cultures insofar as they deploy a comparative perspective (that of the text and that of the reader) and call upon the cultural trait of empathetic understanding of the other. Malina's vision (25) for the use of cultural anthropology in biblical criticism, therefore, is to borrow crosscultural models from anthropological research on either Mediterranean society or other societies "similar" to those reflected in the biblical texts and to test these models against the evidence of the texts themselves. If a fit exists between model and data, then the model is validated and adequate understanding—accurate understanding—of the "foreign" biblical texts results.

in both the study of first-century Mediterranean society and the anthropological study of contemporary Mediterranean society and other cultural analogues. Only then will they be able to test the crosscultural models of cultural anthropology against the reality of the ancient texts, to establish a fit between data and models, and to attain fair and adequate understanding of these texts.

Second, given their mastery of the principles and techniques of historical criticism as well as their familiarity with the concepts and models of cultural anthropology, teacher/critics still retain the key to the meaning of the Bible, whether perceived as the word of God or as a record of antiquity. Through such mastery and familiarity, teacher/critics attain an accurate and fair understanding of the texts as well as of the social system and cultural story behind the texts.

Third, this combined grasp of historical criticism and cultural anthropology allows teacher/critics to read themselves in terms of their own social system and cultural story, rescues them from the mire of ethnocentrism and anachronism, and renders them objective and impartial in their own understanding—across the historical and cultural divide—of the texts as well as of the social system and cultural story behind these texts. In effect, the humanization of student/readers may be said to serve as a tool for dehumanization: by surfacing and bracketing their own social system and cultural story, student/readers become teacher/critics, beyond social location and ideology, able to read "foreigners" in both present and past, accurately and empathetically.

The result is a pedagogical model that is, yet again, highly pyramidal, patriarchal, and authoritative: a model where the teacher/critic, as the voice of the informed, universal, and self-enlightened reader, captures the sociocultural mysteries of the text and mediates them to student/readers; a model where teacher/critics rise above social location and ideology through self-knowledge to arrive at the meaning of the text.

RECENT CALLS FOR CHANGE: CULTURAL STUDIES

Such then are the pedagogical implications of historical criticism, literary criticism, and cultural criticism for the discipline. I should now like to turn to a number of studies published in the last few years that argue—from a variety of different perspectives—for fundamental changes in such practices and discourses. Given the already extensive and constantly expanding volume of the literature in question, one must of necessity be selective with respect to the voices chosen for analysis and dialogue. In what follows, therefore, I have opted for a series of representative studies that assess the discipline in general in the light of recent developments, especially of the sociocultural sort, and with a strong focus on teaching and education. Furthermore, given my own situation of diaspora in the

West, I have concentrated by and large on the emerging discussion within the United States, although such a discussion could be easily expanded into a conversation of global dimensions.[28] Finally, I have arranged the studies in question in chronological fashion, so as to provide a sense of the evolving discussion.

African Americans and the Academy—W. H. Myers (1991)

Pride of place in this regard should go, without a doubt, to William Myers's analysis of the hermeneutical dilemma confronting African Americans in biblical studies, in itself part of a comprehensive and highly successful volume dealing with the question of African American interpretation of the Bible.[29] The diagnosis is laid out from the start: Biblical interpretation—and Myers has historical criticism specifically in mind—is profoundly Eurocentric, whether in terms of the hermeneutical motifs chosen, the methodological concerns pursued, or the events highlighted in the history of interpretation. Such Eurocentrism has immediate consequences: the exaltation of a particular worldview above all others; the confining of the task of interpretation by and large to the past, while the burning issues of the day remain unaffected; the exclusion of other traditions of

---

[28] For an overview, see R. S. Sugirtharajah, "The Margin as a Site of Creative Revisioning" and "Cultures, Texts and Margins: A Hermeneutical Odyssey," in *Voices from the Margin: Interpreting the Bible in the Third World*, ed. R. S. Sugirtharajah, rev. ed. (Maryknoll, N.Y.: Orbis Books, 1995), 1-8 and 457-75, respectively. For works from the Two-Thirds World in general, see (a) from an African perspective: C. S. Banana, "The Case for a New Bible," in *"Rewriting" the Bible: The Real Issues*, ed. J. L. Cox, I. Mukonyora and F. J. Verstraelen (Gweru: Mambo Press, 1993), 17-32; I. J. Mosala, "The Use of the Bible in Black Theology," in *Biblical Hermeneutics and Black Theology in South Africa* (Grand Rapids, Mich.: William B. Eerdmans, 1989), 13-42; (b) from an Asian perspective: G. Soares-Prabhu, "The Historical Critical Method: Reflections on Its Relevance for the Study of the Gospels in India Today," in *Theologizing in India*, ed. M. Amaladoss (Bangalore: Theological Publications in India, 1981), 214-49; R. S. Sugirtharajah, "Introduction, and Some Thoughts on Asian Biblical Hermeneutics," in *Biblical Interpretation* 2 (1994): 251-63; Kwok Pui-lan, *Discovering the Bible in the Non-Biblical World* (Maryknoll, N.Y.: Orbis Books, 1995); (c) from a Latin American perspective: J. S. Croatto, "Biblical Hermeneutics in the Theologies of Liberation," in *Irruption of the Third World: Challenge to Theology*, ed. V. Fabella and S. Torres (Maryknoll, N.Y.: Orbis Books, 1983), 140-68; P. Richard, "The Hermeneutics of Liberation: Theoretical Orientation for a Communitarian Reading of the Bible," in *Teaching the Bible: The Discourses and Politics of Biblical Pedagogy*, ed. F. F. Segovia and M. A. Tolbert (Maryknoll, N.Y.: Orbis Books, 1998), 272-82.

[29] W. H. Myers, "The Hermeneutical Dilemma of the African American Biblical Student," in *Stony the Road We Trod: African American Biblical Interpretation*, ed. C. H. Felder (Minneapolis: Fortress Press, 1991), 40-56.

interpretation from consideration. This Eurocentric hold on the Bible and its interpretation further reflects the broader Eurocentric control exercised over the political, economic, and social systems of a culture, including its charter documents and the norms for their interpretation.

From the point of view of the African American critic, therefore, to enter the world of biblical interpretation is to enter not only a foreign world, a world of Eurocentric questions and concerns, but also a world that does not see itself as foreign, a world that presents itself as normative and hence without cultural bias. The result is a fundamental dilemma. Anchored in a very different tradition of interpretation altogether, a tradition not considered valid within the discipline as such, the critic is at a loss: wondering, on the one hand, about the relevance of such an approach for the African American community—an oppressed community in need of liberation, for which the Bible has functioned as a traditional and powerful tool in this regard; acquiring, on the other hand, a certain measure of appreciation for the contributions of the Eurocentric approach to the interpretive task.

This dilemma, Myers continues, is accentuated by the Eurocentric character of theological education in general, characterized as it is by the predominance of Eurocentric curricula, a paucity of African American colleagues, the lack of alternative models and sources, a thorough resistance to change, and the profound identification of a tradition with an interpretive approach. The dilemma extends outside African American circles as well. Indeed, from the point of view of the Third World and minorities in the First World, the traditional approach can only be regarded as inadequate, insofar as it fails to take into account how other peoples interpret the texts.[30] For all those outside Eurocentric boundaries, therefore, the diagnosis amounts to an ongoing dilemma.

For Myers, the remedy to be prescribed is not yet altogether clear at this point, given the differences of opinion among African Americans themselves with regard to proper strategies for change. In the end Myers limits himself to a few guiding principles: The solution (1) must come from within the ranks of African American scholars; (2) will probably represent a combination of contextual research and interdisciplinary accord; (3) will probably entail the adoption of a variety of methodologies held in balanced tension; (4) should include dialogue with critics from Europe, Euro-America, and the Third World; and (5) must involve a restructuring of pedagogical content and academic venues.

---

[30] Myers (ibid., 45-47) sees the Eurocentric approach as under challenge from a number of different quarters, not only outside but also inside the West. The discussion, however, is far more cultural than methodological in character, developed almost exclusively from the point of view of groups alien to the Eurocentric perspective.

More specifically, Myers calls for a broader conception of canon, not so much in terms of its final form but rather of the process and functions of the final form,[31] so that the notion of canon can be extended to include the approaches to it of different believing communities—such as sermons, spirituals, testimonials, conversion narratives, and call narratives among African Americans. In this way, he argues, the Eurocentric grip on texts and their interpretation as well as the hermeneutical dilemma faced by all outsiders to Eurocentrism will begin to give way, slowly but surely.

Biblical Studies in the Third World—P. J. Hartin (1992)

This study, which appeared a year later, deals with the challenges that the Third World, as seen through the particular optic of South Africa (a South Africa still engaged at the time of writing in the process of dismantling the system of apartheid), brings to bear on the teaching of biblical studies, specifically within the context of a large state university with a vast majority of black students as its primary constituency.[32] Diagnosis and remedy are immediately identified: A discipline that has been taught in undifferentiated fashion throughout the world, including South Africa, must now begin to take into account the needs and contexts of the students in

---

[31] At this point Myers is drawing on the discussion regarding canonical criticism between Brevard Childs (*Biblical Theology in Crisis* [Philadelphia: Westminster Press, 1970]; *Introduction to the Old Testament as Scripture* [Philadelphia: Fortress Press, 1979]; *The New Testament as Canon* [Philadelphia: Fortress Press, 1985]; *Biblical Theology of the Old and New Testaments* [Minneapolis: Fortress Press, 1993]), with its focus on final form; and James Sanders (*Torah and Canon* [Philadelphia: Fortress Press, 1972]; *Canon and Community* [Philadelphia: Fortress Press, 1984]; *From Sacred Story to Sacred Text* [Philadelphia: Fortress Press, 1987]), with its focus on the functions of the final form. For a recent overview of canonical criticism, see R. W. Wall, "Reading the New Testament in Canonical Context," in Green, *Hearing the New Testament*, 370-93.

[32] P. J. Hartin, *Third World Challenges in the Teaching of Biblical Studies: Occasional Papers* 25 (Claremont, Calif.: The Institute for Antiquity and Christianity, 1992). From a geopolitical point of view, Hartin describes South Africa as a "Third-World country" insofar as it fulfills the various characteristics common to such countries: survival on the basis of external help; exploitation of resources by foreign nations; almost complete lack of infrastructure; absence of basic services for large segments of the population; poverty and illiteracy. From a socioeducational point of view, Hartin describes the University of South Africa, which carries out its mission through distance education and comprises around 120,000 students, as a secular institution. Within such a context he further describes instruction in biblical studies as follows: It is not in the service of the church, much less any particular Christian church; it approaches the Bible as literature, as a classic; and, in so doing, it has recourse to a variety of scientific approaches.

question, which, in the case of South Africa, involves the reality of a multicultural and multireligious society.

Such a reality calls for a type of instruction that is twofold in nature. On the one hand, instead of focusing on the dissemination and absorption of information about the Bible, it calls for the Bible to speak to the lives of students; on the other hand, instead of imposing a particular approach or cultural understanding on the biblical text, it calls for allowing the text to speak for itself. Its goal is to produce students who are "competent" or "responsible" students of the Bible. Such competency has two distinct foci, therefore: students and texts. First, from the point of view of students, competency requires a knowledge of African traditional religions, given their influence upon the students. Second, from the point of view of texts, competency demands the acquisition of tools and methods proper to the sciences used to analyze the texts. Third, from the point of view of both students and texts, competency calls for a commitment to postmodernism, with its view of reality as highly fragmented. Such adherence to postmodernism serves a variety of purposes. With regard to students, it is meant to rule out the dogmatizing of any one cultural understanding of the Bible, to underline the difficult nature of understanding across different perspectives, and to yield respect for the viewpoints of other peoples and cultures. With regard to the texts, it is meant, once again, to rule out the dogmatizing of any one approach to the Bible.

Such competency, moreover, is to be imparted and acquired by means of a "hands-on" approach to the biblical text. Thus, the focus of instruction throughout is the biblical text, which is used as a point of entry into the various areas of inquiry within the discipline. These areas of study are organized in turn around the major components of the standard model in communications theory: from a horizontal perspective, the sequence of author (production), text, and reader (reception); from a vertical perspective, the relationship of text and reference. The sequence of instruction proceeds as follows: (1) a beginning focus on the student as reader—a close reading of the text from the student's own context; (2) a focus on the text, both in terms of production and reference; (3) a focus on the reception of the text by other readers, in the past or in the present. In the end, the result should be the production of a "competent" reading alongside other such readings from both past and present, but now from the perspective of the students' own lives within a multicultural and multireligious society.

The ultimate aim behind such competency is socioreligious as well as sociopolitical. To begin with, competency allows the Bible to inspire the imagination—that is, allows students to recontextualize the images and stories of the Bible within their own cultures and contexts—so that events in their own lives and worlds are formulated and communicated through the terms, stories, and narratives of the Bible.[33] The result should be a similar imaginative retelling on the part of a broad variety of different groups and cultures, all of which would have recourse to the same language and message but express it in a variety of ways.[34] In so doing, therefore, competency further uses the Bible as a way of bringing together different peoples and cultures by way of certain common values—human dignity, justice, and peace. For Hartin, such a situation would represent a possible and much-desired solution for the travails of South Africa.

Feminism and Colonialism—K. O'Brien Wicker (1993)

This study, though brief, is important, insofar as it raises the question of culture—of class, ethnicity, and race—from within the context of the feminist movement; published a year later, it forms part of the landmark two-volume feminist introduction to and commentary on the Bible.[35] The diagnosis of the discipline here is actually twofold, as the study looks backward and forward at the same time.

A first level is presupposed: a view of the discipline as profoundly patriarchal, both in terms of the texts studied and the history of the interpretation of these texts. The prescription, already in effect as well, calls for a pedagogical strategy that reflects the broader scholarly discourse of

---

[33] Needless to say, despite the emphasis on the secular character of biblical studies at the university and the approach to the Bible as a classic of literature within such a setting, one finds a very high theological conception of the Bible at work in this pedagogical program, best expressed perhaps in Hartin's concluding hopes (ibid., 19) for the future of South Africa: the use of the Bible in problem-solving, specifically with regard to the future of South Africa, with the Bible "as a means by which different cultures are able to share their understandings," yielding in the end "an even richer culture illuminated by the possible worlds opened up by the Bible."

[34] In formulating this view of biblical instruction, Hartin relies heavily on the work of Paul Ricoeur (ibid., 10-13), with its well-known threefold sequence of (a) naive understanding—a guess at the meaning of the text; (b) explanation—validation of the guess by attention to the text as a written inscription, now distanced from the life of its author and leading a life of its own; and (c) understanding by appropriation—making the text (the direction opened up by it, the imagination of new possible worlds) one's own. It is this final dimension of interpretation, therefore, that should be the goal of biblical studies: to allow the text to speak "on its own" to the lives of students, wherever they find themselves.

[35] K. O'Brien Wicker, "Teaching Feminist Biblical Studies in a Postcolonial Context," in *Searching the Scriptures*, vol. 1: *A Feminist Introduction*, ed. Elisabeth Schüssler Fiorenza (New York: Crossroad, 1993), 367-80.

women's and feminist studies, with a specific emphasis on women in the biblical texts and women's or gendered readings of the biblical texts. A second level, newly awakened by means of a sojourn in Zimbabwe, is envisioned: a view of the discipline as profoundly Western, not only in terms of patriarchy but also in terms of feminism itself. The prescription demands the development of a feminist pedagogical strategy that takes into consideration issues of class, ethnicity, and race. In other words, as a result of a crosscultural experience in Africa, O'Brien Wicker comes to realize that the discipline has been profoundly colonialist as well, and that in such colonialism Western women find themselves as thoroughly implicated as Western men. The prescription, therefore, requires a feminism that goes beyond the concerns and issues of middle- or upper-class Western women, a feminism that takes an international perspective to heart, a feminism that is postcolonial in nature.[36]

Such an approach to biblical studies, developed in opposition to the traditional colonial mode of education and biblical studies,[37] adheres to the following principles: (1) rejection of the patriarchal worldview, the claims of the inherent superiority of men over women, and the hegemony of the public over the private sphere; (2) condemnation of Christian anti-Semitism as unwarranted and unjustified; and (3) resistance to other historical expressions of Christian imperialism, such as those at work in the

---

[36] Following the lead of Laura E. Donaldson (*Decolonizing Feminisms: Race, Gender, and Empire-building* [Chapel Hill and London: University of North Carolina Press, 1992]), O'Brien Wicker ("Teaching Feminist Biblical Studies," 368) distinguishes between *historical* colonialism, the historical fact of political and geographic conquest, and *discursive* colonialism, the actualization of metaphors in experience. On the one hand, feminism represents a reaction to the discursive colonization of patriarchy. On the other hand, however, feminism also constitutes a form of discursive colonization, insofar it has attempted to speak in the name of all women, to universalize itself. Consequently, feminism must be decolonized, must become postcolonial.

[37] The colonial model of education is represented in terms of a number of basic strategies: (a) education of the native for a subordinate role; (b) integration of the native into the culture of the colonial power; (c) privileging of males, their thoughts and deeds. Its counterpart in biblical studies is represented in terms of the following assumptions: (a) acceptance of the patriarchal perspective as divinely validated, with corresponding rejection of nonpatriarchal readings; (b) affirmation of the inherent superiority of men over women, the public sphere over the private; (c) a view of Christianity as the only true religion or as superior to all other religious traditions; (d) acceptance of political assertions made in the text; (e) use of the categories of orthodoxy and heresy to invalidate certain interpretations of the tradition; (f) decontextualization of biblical texts in ways that absolutize injunctions addressed to particular situations (see O'Brien Wicker, "Teaching Feminist Biblical Studies," 369, 371-72).

process of colonization.[38] Its fundamental goal, variously exercised, is to see how a text like the Bible can not only prove liberating for women but also promote the full humanity of women and men of all races, ethnic backgrounds, and classes.[39]

For O'Brien Wicker the crucial step taken by feminism remains caught in the Western project of colonization and thus must be taken a step further by going beyond a consideration of gender, of woman as woman, to include a consideration of race, ethnicity, and class. As such, the discipline must acquire a global perspective if it is not to remain fundamentally Western in orientation and practice.

Global Outlook—J. R. Levison and P. Pope-Levison (1995)

Within the context of a volume on method and hermeneutics in New Testament studies, the authors contributed an article on the subject of global hermeneutics.[40] The beginning rationale for the inclusion of such an unusual study in the collection provides a sharp diagnosis of the discipline. This diagnosis is twofold. On the one hand, from the point of view of the First World, the traditional view of the critic—the critic as someone who uncovers the "original meaning" of the Bible by "jettisoning all bias"—has been rendered untenable, insofar as "prejudgments" arising from the critic's own context are now widely accepted as influencing the understanding of any text. On the other hand, from the point of view of the Third World, a rapid shift in the center of gravity of Christianity, not only in terms of numbers but also in terms of vitality, is taking place,

---

[38] More concretely, such an approach reveals the following characteristics (ibid., 374-75): (a) reflection on experiences that relate to the ideas or issues under study, with an emphasis on the diversity of voices and hence on race, ethnicity, and class—as opposed to an assimilation of "truth" without regard for experience; (b) alternative feminist readings of texts—as a way of resisting claims to absolute truth, respecting differences, and rejecting the impulse to create artificial unities; (c) critical reflection on the presuppositions regarding stances toward the revelatory nature of the texts, the implications of such presuppositions, and the feminist claim on the priority of experience in interpretation—as a way of showing that all interpretations are necessarily interpretive.

[39] Ibid., 372-73. It is clear in this regard that O'Brien Wicker adopts a variation of the strategy of suspicion (see "Feminist and Womanist Criticism," in *The Postmodern Bible*, ed. The Bible and Culture Collective [New Haven, Conn.: Yale University Press, 1995], 225-71, esp. 247-51). Rather than abandoning the Bible as a hopelessly patriarchal and colonialist text, therefore, the call is for a variety of strategies of subversion meant to weaken or displace its system of oppression as well as to bring to the fore liberating visions of a different and fully inclusive system.

[40] J. R. Levison and P. Pope-Levison, "Global Perspectives on New Testament Interpretation," in Green, *Hearing the New Testament*, 329-48.

toward the Third World and away from the First World. Given the central importance of context in interpretation, therefore, the discipline must develop a global outlook if it is not to remain woefully inadequate for the present day and age.

The prescription recommended is Western-inspired: the dialectical hermeneutics of Hans-Georg Gadamer, which is seen as having replaced the traditional model described above.[41] The effects and implications of such a move are described as follows. First, instead of focusing on the original meaning of the Bible or the contemporary context of the interpreter, the model emphasizes the conversation between the ancient text and the present-day interpreter, in the course of which the latter brings specific questions to the Bible arising from his or her context. Second, the goal behind such a conversation is to bring about a fusion of two horizons—that of the text and that of the interpreter—in a way that is both true to the past and relevant to the present. Third, given the present spread of Christianity, no first-world interpretation of the Bible can exhaust the meaning of a text, since it ignores contexts that bring their own questions into the process of interpretation; consequently, the conversation with the Bible must proceed on a global scale.

What such a global perspective means for the discipline is immediately made clear: from the point of view of Latin America, a focus on class struggle, integral liberation, and the relationship between politics and religion; from the point of view of Asia, a focus on popular traditions, religious traditions, and economics; from the point of view of Africa, a dominant focus on a hermeneutics of resonance with the Bible. At the same time, a critique of such new third-world contributions is appended: (1) despite the emphasis on the importance of readings from grassroots communities, there are few examples of such popular interpretations available; (2) the fusion of horizons can lead to a collapse of the distinction between text and context; (3) interpretations of the New Testament frequently contain a negative portrayal of Second Temple Judaism, furnishing thereby the seeds for anti-Semitism. The elements of the critique are thus quite varied in nature and import: (1) the first is not a theoretical challenge but a basic call for more research; (2) the second represents a theoretical challenge, but is presented only as a possibility and with a remedy attached—proper use of social-scientific criticism as a way of allowing for parallels while keeping the two horizons properly distinct; (3) the third is also a

---

[41] The authors take their cue from David Tracy's discussion in Part Two of R. M. Grant with D. Tracy, *A Short History of the Interpretation of the Bible* (Minneapolis: Fortress Press, 1984), 153-87. For Gadamer himself, see H.-G. Gadamer, *Truth and Method*, 2d ed. (New York: Crossroad, 1990). On the rise and development of the "new hermeneutics," see V. B. Leitch, "Hermeneutics," in *American Literary Criticism from the Thirties to the Eighties* (New York: Columbia University Press, 1988), 182-210.

theoretical challenge, now based on fact and with a remedy supplied: greater use of research showing the rich diversity of Second Temple Judaism.

For the authors, therefore, the discipline has no option but to become global, in the light of developments within both the First World and the Third World. In this regard the hermeneutics of the West—the fusion of horizons à la Gadamer—is taken as pointing the way and as a correction to any actual or possible deficiencies or excesses present in the biblical interpretation of either world. Indeed, one finds no critique of the conversational model as such.[42]

Center and Margins—B. K. Blount (1995)

This full-fledged proposal by this African American scholar calls for a fundamental reorientation of New Testament criticism along the lines of cultural interpretation—a mode of reading that both takes into account the context of readers with regard to the meaning of texts and admits of a variety of responsible readings.[43] Blount contends that traditional biblical studies—primarily understood in terms of historical criticism—have followed a single interpretive ideology: biblical texts have been interpreted according to the perspective of standard Eurocentric values.[44] As a result, any group outside this normative value system not only finds its own interpretive perspective excluded from consideration as unscientific but also finds itself expected to assimilate the interpretive practices and underlying values of the dominant group. Such a diagnosis of the discipline Blount traces to his own origins and experiences in the black church, where he recalls facing the inability of the traditional methods to bring the text to life in the black community as well as the external criticism of black interpretation as prejudiced. Such a diagnosis, however, could also have come from any group at the margins of the Eurocentric perspective, yielding thereby a center-margins type of discourse.[45]

---

[42] A critique undertaken, in a highly sympathetic vein, by Tracy himself (*Interpretation of the Bible*, 160-66).

[43] B. K. Blount, *Cultural Interpretation: Reorienting New Testament Criticism* (Minneapolis: Fortress Press, 1995), esp. 1-23 (chap. 1: "A Contextual Approach"), 89-96, and 175-94 (chap. 11: "Beyond Interpretative Boundaries").

[44] For Blount, it should be noted, the term "ideology" is pejorative, indicating a restrictive rather than inclusive perspective, whether deployed from the center (as in the case of traditional biblical studies) or from the margins (as in the case of liberation hermeneutics). The goal, therefore, is to develop a "non-ideological" method, that is, a method that takes into account a variety of perspectives, from center and margins alike (see ibid., 3-4).

[45] As such, the discussion proceeds throughout at a much broader level than was the case with William Myers, taking into consideration to be sure—indeed as a point of departure—the African American experience but going beyond it as well to encompass a wide variety of other groups and experiences in the margins.

Two fundamental differences distinguish these two interpretive perspectives. On the one hand, while the center highlights issues of christology and soteriology (the question of religious salvation), the margins emphasize social and political issues (the question of inequity). On the other hand, while the center focuses on textual and conceptual issues in the text (the question of the meaning "back then"), the margins emphasize the issue of interpersonal interaction between text and reader (the question of the meaning "for today"). For Blount, the answer lies not in a reverse enthronement of the marginal optic—a move that would simply yield a different type of single interpretive ideology, ultimately as restrictive as that of Eurocentrism—but rather in a type of reading that brings together the two perspectives, a reading that sees texts as both religious and social, and interpretation as involving all three concerns (the textual, the ideational, and the interpersonal). Only such a reading, with its corresponding view of interpretations as complementary rather than alternative, can yield a fuller picture of the meaning of a text. Blount develops this type of reading, cultural interpretation, on the basis of two theoretical discourses—sociolinguistics of the functionalist type and sociology of the liberationist type.[46]

From functionalist sociolinguistics Blount takes the basic insight that context shapes the creation and use of language—that people in different sociological environments operate with different linguistic forms—and that meaning derived from language is also shaped by context.[47] What is true of language, Blount argues, is also true of reading.[48] From the point

---

[46] With regard to functionalist sociolinguistics, Blount follows the model of M. A. K. Halliday, *Explorations in the Functions of Language* (London: Edward Arnold, 1973); with regard to liberationist sociology, he adopts, with modifications, the model of Enrique Dussel, *Philosophy of Liberation* (Maryknoll, N.Y.: Orbis Books, 1985).

[47] The model entails a number of presuppositions. First, it sees language as oriented toward and structured according to its use in act of communication, so that meaning involves both the internal makeup of language and its use. Second, it has recourse to three categories of text-linguistic inquiry: (1) the textual, which considers language as it functions grammatically—the components of language as structured syntactically to establish meaning; (2) the ideational, which considers the conceptual implications behind lexical terms and phrases—the conceptual references signified by those terms and phrases; (3) the interpersonal, which considers the role played by sociolinguistic factors—the sociocultural environment of the language user. Third, since language is seen as functioning interactively, it argues that the meaning of language can be comprehended only by taking all three variables into account (see Blount, *Cultural Interpretation*, 8-14).

[48] While Halliday's model is elaborated from the perspective of the producer of the text, Blount develops it from the standpoint of the reader of the text, with the latter bringing a new contextual element to the interpersonal phase. By itself, therefore, a text is said to possess "meaning potential"—a range of possible meanings open to individual interpreters and made concrete by readings from different sociolinguistic frameworks (see ibid., 15-16).

of view of biblical studies, therefore, interaction between different sociolinguistic perspectives—such as those of the center and the margins—and the language of a text inevitably yields different understandings of the meaning and power of that text.[49] Thus, if a sociolinguistic perspective is to become more comprehensive, it must attempt to see the text from the other perspective. In the end, however, Blount cautions that functionalist sociolinguistics fails to address the crucial issue of sociopolitical power—the fact that one community's sociolinguistic perspective can dominate and devalue those of other communities.

From liberationist sociology, therefore, Blount borrows the missing sociopolitical dimension: Not only does one's spatial location in life determine what one sees, but also that perspective espoused by those who hold political and numerical superiority emerges as the official one, with all others lacking in power and legitimation. This is true of society and politics as well as of science and scholarship.[50] It is also true, Blount adds, of reading. From the point of view of biblical studies, therefore, the sociolinguistic perspective represented by traditional biblical studies has effectively enthroned itself as the official perspective, looking upon all those outside its boundaries as unacceptable and calling instead for assimilation unto itself. Hence, if one is to avoid such an ideological position, one must recognize the validity of all points of view and analyze texts from a perspective that includes both center and margins.[51] Such a task, however, cannot originate with the center, given the latter's inability to surmount its own ideology to begin with; rather, change must come from the outside, and thus the task lies with the margins.

---

[49] The meaning potential of a text, while vast, is not unlimited, since the textual and ideational factors set parameters for the interpersonal dimension, "unequivocally stating what the material cannot mean." For Blount, therefore, a text cannot be interpreted in any way that a community chooses; rather, readings must be meaningful or responsible, that is, must have "linguistically accurate and contextually appropriate conclusions," conclusions that "fit within this textual-ideational boundary" and "simultaneously interact beyond this boundary with the interpersonal context of the reader." At the same time, meaning is not static but expansive; as the interpersonal dynamics change, so do the meaningful and responsible readings (ibid., 27-28, 84-86, 89-92).

[50] Such a model presupposes a scientific process in which a centrist totality is positioned in dialectical fashion against an exterior totality; adjustments to the center, therefore, are carried out within a totalistic framework that coopts rather than accepts input from the periphery (ibid., 18-20).

[51] Such a model calls for an analectical moment in the scientific process—not just the dialectical recognition by the center of an exterior totality, which it proceeds to meet by way of confrontation, but an effective interchange between totalities, with an analysis of reality from that marginal perspective. Such analysis, moreover, poses a threat to any system upholding a centrist view of the social system, insofar as it recognizes that the opposites may work to create a new whole (ibid., 20-22).

It is precisely this task that Blount sets for himself in his agenda of cultural interpretation: to bring the sociolinguistic perspective from the margins fully into the discussion and hence into contact with the center; and, in so doing, to challenge the entire agenda of biblical studies and force a change in its traditional Eurocentric perspective.[52] The vision that emerges is that of a far more inclusive discipline, where there is no such thing as a final and definitive meaning, where readings must work within the confines of textual and ideational elements, and where all interpreters are similarly influenced by and must come to terms with the interpersonal dimension of interpretation.

CONCLUDING COMMENTS

A summary of how these representative voices look upon the present state of affairs in the discipline and what they call for by way of pedagogical changes and innovations is in order:

1. The diagnoses of the discipline offered prove to be remarkably similar; that is, biblical criticism is described as profoundly Eurocentric or Western. Such Eurocentrism is said to match the patriarchal nature of the discipline and to reflect not only the broader Eurocentric character of theological education in general but also the strong Eurocentric control over culture. Its characteristics are variously identified as follows: (a) confinement of the task of interpretation to the past; (b) focus on the discovery of the original meaning of the text, the meaning "back then"; (c) emphasis on the impartation and absorption of information; (d) insistence on a particular method or cultural understanding; (e) predilection for christological and soteriological questions; (f) a view of instruction as universal and undifferentiated. In the end, such a view of the discipline is regarded as profoundly ironic; a worldview that is highly cultural in nature—Western or Eurocentric—presents itself as without cultural bias and hence as normative, as the center, resulting in the exaltation of a particular worldview above all others.

2. Such a state of affairs is seen as having consequences for all outsiders to Eurocentrism and the West, for those in the margins. The descriptions of

---

[52] It should be noted that Blount (ibid., 177-84) does criticize Dussel's model on two counts: (1) it focuses on only two approaches—the traditional and the Latin American; (2) it sees the analectical moment as yielding a new and complete reference for meaning. For Blount, the full spectrum of meaning in a text can only come about by allowing a multitude of communal interpretations to engage one another analectically; further, this spectrum of meaning is never final or complete, but always expanding, sometimes in explosive fashion. While having recourse to the language of center and margins, therefore, it is clear that Blount also looks upon both center and margins as consisting of a wide array of individual and communal interpretations.

such consequences turn out to be quite similar as well: such individuals and groups find themselves in a foreign world. In other words, the discipline constitutes a world where their own traditions of interpretation are excluded from consideration as inadequate, where their own concerns and contexts are ignored as irrelevant, and where they are expected to conform to the traditions and dictates of the normative position.

3. The remedies prescribed for such a situation represent variations of the same principle: the need to take into account the lives and contexts of "the other." Among such remedies one finds (a) a broader conception of the canon, including not only the biblical texts but also the various approaches to these texts emanating from different communities; (b) a different view of textual meaning, with a twofold focus on both texts and interpreters, the past and the present, the meaning "back then" and the meaning "for today"; (c) taking into account the lives and contexts of communities from around the globe, especially of those in the margins, whether in the West or in the Third World, especially given the shift in Christianity away from the West, both in terms of numbers and vitality; (d) a commitment to a view of reality as fragmented, not only in terms of gender but also in terms of class, ethnicity, and race; (e) recourse to a broad range of methodologies and the recognition of multiple readings, so that no one approach or interpretation is enthroned as a result; (f) a view of texts as both religious and social documents, concerned as much with questions of religious salvation as with questions of inequity.

4. The goals and hopes behind such remedies are in keeping with the fundamental diagnosis advanced: the need for the discipline to become less Eurocentric or Western. Such goals and hopes are variously described as follows: (a) an awareness of Christianity as a global religion and of the different questions brought to the text by different groups and cultures of the world; (b) dialogue among all such groups and cultures, now reading the texts from the point of view of their own contexts and lives; (c) use of the Bible as a point of unity for diverse groups and cultures, with a stress on the values of human dignity, peace, and justice; (d) the liberation of women and men of all classes, races, and ethnicities.

With such diagnoses and prescriptions, such goals and hopes, I argue, the tenor and direction of the pedagogical discussion in the discipline leave behind altogether the parameters observed earlier in historical, literary, and cultural criticism and begin to move instead well within the ambit of the cultural studies paradigm as I conceive it, given the emphasis placed, first and foremost, on the diversity of readers and contexts as well as on the diversity of methods and readings. The implications for the discipline, its pedagogical discourse and practices—though still very much in the making—will no doubt prove enormous, perhaps amounting in the end to a complete reconception and reconfiguration of the discipline in line with the twenty-first century now upon us.

4

Pedagogical Discourse and Practices in Cultural Studies

Toward a Contextual Biblical Pedagogy

I have argued that with the ongoing fundamental shift in the complexion and exercise of biblical criticism, a shift encompassing more or less the final quarter of the twentieth century and resulting in four competing paradigms or umbrella models of interpretation, several crucial questions regarding the discipline have been thrown wide open for discussion and now call for explicit and sustained attention. One such question concerns the critic's vision regarding the handing on of the discipline in this day and age.

I undertook in chapter 3, by way of prelude to the present chapter, a process of critical reflection regarding this question of pedagogy. I have, in effect, already examined the pedagogical discourses and practices at work in the first three paradigms of historical, literary, and cultural criticism. I have further examined a number of recent voices, all within the ambit of the fourth paradigm of cultural studies, that have called for a thorough reconception and reorientation of such discourses and practices in the light of the increasing diversity of interpretive approaches and, above all, the expanding globalization of practitioners at work in the discipline. In the present chapter, therefore, I should like to pursue in a more sustained and systematic way the question of pedagogical discourse and practices within the context of the cultural studies paradigm.

As in the case of the other paradigms, the proposed task is not without difficulties. By way of contrast, however, it should be noted that this umbrella model, unlike the other three, poses no problem whatever with regard to pedagogy. In fact, as the analysis of the recent voices for change shows, the model has consistently turned to and addressed the question of pedagogical discourse and practices, often as a point of departure. In so doing, it has followed recent developments in theological studies,[1] cultural studies,[2] and pedagogical studies.[3] The difficulties in question are thus of a different sort altogether, and two come readily to mind.

First, there is the question of consolidation. This is a model that is still in the process of formation and maturation. The precious benefit of hindsight is simply lacking—twenty-five years in the case of literary criticism and cultural criticism and close to a century and a half in the case of historical criticism. Needless to say, dealing with any phenomenon in the making is not only more daring but also more tentative. Second, there is the question of diversity. Cultural studies is a child of mixed parentage: on the one hand, the heir of methodological and theoretical diversity; on the other, the scion of sociocultural and demographic diversity. As such, the rise of cultural studies is directly related, on the one side, to the ever-expanding options and choices in method and theory facing the critic in the discipline. On the other side, it is directly related as well to the ever-increasing presence of outsiders (Western women, non-Western critics and

---

[1] See, for e.g., C. Foster, ed., *Ethnicity in the Education of the Church* (Nashville: Scarritt Press, 1987); W. A. Lesher and R. J. Schreiter, eds., *Fundamental Issues in Globalization*, special issue of *Theological Education* 26, Supplement 1 (Spring 1990); B. G. Wheeler and E. Farley, *Shifting Boundaries: Contextual Approaches to the Structure of Theological Education* (Louisville: Westminster/John Knox Press, 1991); A. Frazer Evans, R. A. Evans, and D. A. Roozen, eds., *The Globalization of Theological Education* (Maryknoll, N.Y.: Orbis Books, 1993); D. S. Schuller, ed., *Globalization: Tracing the Journey, Charting the Course*, special issue of *Theological Education* 30, Supplement 1 (Autumn 1993).

[2] See, for e.g., S. Aronowitz and H. A. Giroux, *Postmodern Education: Politics, Culture, and Social Criticism* (Minneapolis: University of Minnesota Press, 1991); G. Graff, *Beyond the Culture Wars: How Teaching the Conflicts Can Revitalize American Education* (New York and London: W. W. Norton, 1992); D. J. Gless and B. Herrnstein Smith, *The Politics of Liberal Education* (Durham and London: Duke University Press, 1992); C. McCarthy and W. Crichlow, *Race, Identity, and Representation in Education* (New York: Routledge, 1993); bell hooks, *Teaching to Transgress: Education as the Practice of Freedom* (New York: Routledge, 1994).

[3] See, e.g., D. Schoem et al., eds., *Multicultural Teaching in the University* (New York: Praeger Publishers, 1993); B. P. Bowser, T. Jones, and G. Auletta Young, eds., *Toward the Multicultural University* (New York: Praeger Publishers, 1995); D. A. Harris, ed., *Multiculturalism from the Margins: Non-Dominant Voices on Difference and Diversity* (New York: Bergin & Garvey, 1995); B. Kanpol and P. McLaren, eds., *Critical Multiculturalism: Uncommon Voices in a Common Struggle* (New York: Bergin & Garvey, 1995); R. Ng, P. Staton, and J. Scane, eds., *Anti-Racism, Feminism, and Critical Approaches to Education* (New York: Bergin & Garvey, 1995); B. W. Thompson and S. Tyagi, eds., *Beyond a Dream Preferred: Multicultural Education and the Politics of Excellence* (Minneapolis: University of Minnesota Press, 1995).

theologians, non-Western minorities residing in the West) in a discipline that has been, from its inception, thoroughly male, clerical, and Western. This is a model, therefore, that is global in scope: critiques and proposals issue forth not only from within the heart of the West, but also from every quarter of the world where Western imperialism and colonialism brought the religion of Christianity (or, more accurately, the religions of Christianity) as an essential component of its ideological apparatus. Again, dealing with any phenomenon of global dimensions can prove intimidating if not entirely overwhelming.

At the same time, such difficulties are by no means forbidding. In fact, they can be made to serve as marvelous opportunities for creative and innovative work on the part of the critic, now forced to deal at one and the same time with the task of deploying a new umbrella model of interpretation and the responsibility of so doing by way of engagement with the many voices of the global "others." I would add, moreover, that I come to this question, once again, neither as a complete stranger nor as a participant observer, but as a cognizant and interested insider—as someone who has arrived at cultural studies by means of a professional pilgrimage through the other three paradigms, and thus through the thicket of the methodological and theoretical jungle, and as someone who is a member of a non-Western ethnic minority group at the heart of the West, and hence a child of the colonized among the colonizers.

In what follows I shall proceed in two stages. First, I shall comment, within the context of my own conception of cultural studies as a paradigm, on the various diagnoses and remedies advanced by the recent calls for new directions in teaching and education within the discipline. My aim is to compare my own diagnosis of and corresponding prescription for change in the discipline with those offered by these other voices. The spirit at work in such an exercise is, once again—especially given my own fundamental agreement with the tenor and direction of such calls—not one of scorched-earth tactics but rather one of critical dialogue. Then, in the light of this discussion, I shall go on to advance a pedagogical proposal of my own that is in keeping with my overall project of intercultural criticism.

CULTURAL STUDIES: DIAGNOSES AND PRESCRIPTIONS

I should like to begin by recalling, as I did in the case of the other paradigms, a number of preliminary observations advanced in my earlier description of the pedagogical model envisioned by the fourth paradigm of cultural studies (see chapter 2). First, given the diversity in methodological strategies and theoretical orientations, the model moves beyond any demand for a common methodological and theoretical apparatus on the part of readers who wish to become critics. Second, given its emphasis on the contextualized and perspectival nature of all readers, including critics, the model no longer regards the latter as in any way hermeneutically privileged and intrinsically superior to all other readers. Third, further in keeping with this principle that all reading and interpretation are contextualized and perspectival, the model calls for all would-be critics, indeed for all readers, not to learn how to efface themselves, in itself an impossible task, but, on the contrary, to learn how to read themselves and their readings. In the end, I argued, this is a model that calls for an abandonment of the long-established practice of learned impartation and passive reception in favor of a self-conscious, highly critical, and global dialogue involving unceasing and ever-shifting processes of impartation and reception. For such a model the ideal is no longer that of the voice of reason, rising arduously but triumphantly above the endless vagaries of everyday life, but that of multiple voices, multicentered and multilingual.

It is precisely such voices, like the ones highlighted for analysis in my earlier study, that have begun to call for basic changes in pedagogical discourse and practices within the discipline. These are calls, once again, with which I find myself in fundamental agreement, sharing with them a similar view of the discipline, both by way of diagnosis and prescription. At the same time, I would register some differences with respect to certain concrete aspects of such proposals, not so much in terms of their perception of the present state of affairs, but rather in terms of the prescribed remedies for change. In what follows, therefore, I should like to pursue, by way of critical dialogue, such similarities and differences, following the four points highlighted in my earlier summary of these positions:[4]

1. I argued that all such voices offered a remarkably similar diagnosis of the discipline: a view of biblical criticism as profoundly Western, while pretending to scientific objectivity and distance. Indeed, from the beginning until quite recently, the discipline has had a male, clerical, *and* Western orientation. As such, biblical criticism has confined the task of interpretation to antiquity; has concentrated, within an empiricist view of both text and world, on the original meaning of the text; has insisted on particular approaches to the text and even particular understandings of the text, with a definite penchant for questions of a religious nature; and has viewed instruction as universal and undifferentiated, with enormous emphasis on the passive learning of information.

2. I pointed out that such a state of affairs was deemed to have deleterious consequences for all outsiders to the West. Such individuals and groups find themselves in a foreign world altogether. Ethnic and racial minorities both inside and outside the West find the discipline to be both an

---

[4] For my assessment of the discipline, see, in addition to chapters 1 and 2 above, chapter 8 below: "Racial and Ethnic Minorities in Biblical Studies."

alien and an alienating world. Such individuals find their own traditions of interpretation excluded from consideration as unscientific, their own questions and concerns ignored as irrelevant, and their own selves regarded as biased and hence expected to conform to the traditions, concerns, and leadership of the dominant and normative position, if they are to become scientific, universal, and impartial.

3. With regard to the remedies offered for change, I would distinguish between principle and specific proposals. Thus, I find myself in complete agreement with the basic principle at work: the need to take into account the lives and contexts of "the other." I have argued consistently for what amounts to a variation of this principle: the need to take real readers into consideration—the contextualized and perspectival character of all flesh-and-blood readers. I also find myself in agreement with a number of the actual remedies proposed: a different approach to the question of textual meaning, with a focus on both texts and interpreters; an emphasis on readers from around the globe, now in the process of gaining a voice for the first time; a commitment to postmodernism and its view of reality as fractured, especially in terms of class, ethnicity, and race; recourse to a broad range of methods and theories; a view of the texts as both religious and social.

However, I would point to some discrepancies as well:

- I would much prefer to talk in terms of going beyond the canon rather than broadening the canon itself. I would be in favor, therefore, of surveying the whole panorama or spectrum of expression at any period of time, past or present.
- I would eschew any type of formulation that would imply or suggest, no matter how lightly or unintentionally, the presence of a preexisting, independent, and stable meaning in the text, the mind of the author, or the world of the text—formulations along the lines of the meaning "back then," letting the text speak, being true to the past, or achieving a fuller meaning of the text.
- I would go beyond recourse to a broad range of methods and theories to an emphasis on metatheory, on the origins and developments of the different methods and theories as well as on the relationships between and among such methods and theories.

4. With regard to the goals and hopes undergirding such remedies for change, I would again distinguish between principle and concrete proposals. To begin with, I find myself in total agreement with the principle invoked: the need for the discipline to become less Western, more inclusive, and more global. In point of fact, I have argued consistently that the influx of outsiders into the discipline has radically changed its character for the better and that such developments will continue, inexorably, in the

future. I further find myself in agreement with some of the goals and hopes expressed: an awareness of Christianity as a global religion, presently undergoing a profound shift in numbers and vitality away from the West and toward the Two-Thirds World; dialogue among the different groups and cultures, now approaching the texts from such diverse locations and points of view; the vision of liberation.

At the same time, I would express the following reservations:

- I would not share any view of the Bible that would regard it, no matter how unintentionally, as non-ideological and thus as an ideal corrective for a fragmented reality, whether expressed along the lines of the Bible as a depository for the principles of human dignity, justice, and peace or as a magna carta for the liberation of all men and women.
- I would not favor the prospect of having the different groups and peoples engage in a recontextualization of the images and stories of the Bible in their own contexts.

With such preliminary observations and comparisons in mind, I should like to advance at this point, within the context of my own previous delineations of intercultural criticism as a reading strategy,[5] a constructive proposal for the teaching of the discipline in the face of a new century.

CULTURAL STUDIES AND PEDAGOGY: A PROPOSAL

The proposal has two basic frameworks or driving forces at its core, both derived from central components of intercultural criticism. First, it is a proposal that takes diversity to heart—diversity in texts, diversity in readings, and diversity in readers. In so doing, it follows closely my description of the path of recent biblical criticism as a movement of liberation—from hegemony of approach and practitioners, to diversity in approaches, to diversity in practitioners. The proposal sets out to incorporate such diversity into the discipline at every step of the way. Second, it is a proposal that takes the reality of empire, of imperialism and colonialism,

---

[5] See F. F. Segovia, "Toward Intercultural Criticism: A Reading Strategy from the Diaspora," in *Reading from This Place*, vol. 2: *Social Location and Biblical Interpretation in Global Perspective*, ed. F. F. Segovia and M. A. Tolbert (Minneapolis: Fortress Press, 1995), 303-30; see also "Toward a Hermeneutics of the Diaspora: A Hermeneutics of Otherness and Engagement," in *Reading from This Place*, vol. 1: *Social Location and Biblical Interpretation in the United States*, ed. F. F. Segovia and M. A. Tolbert (Minneapolis: Fortress Press, 1995), 57-73.

as an omnipresent, inescapable, and overwhelming reality in the world—the world of antiquity, the world of the Near East or of the Mediterranean Basin; the world of modernity, the world of Western hegemony and expansionism; and the world of today, of postmodernism and postliberalism, the world of postcolonialism on the part of the Two-Thirds World and of neocolonialism on the part of the West. As such, it follows closely my description of the course of recent biblical criticism as a movement of decolonization away from its Western moorings and toward an exercise of truly global dimensions. The proposal seeks to integrate this imperial/colonial dimension into the discipline at every step of the way—at the level of texts, readings of texts, and readers of texts.

The structural selection and deployment of these two driving forces or basic frameworks should be seen as by no means fortuitous but rather as deliberately reflecting specific, distinctive, and formative developments of a sociocultural and sociopolitical character at the turn of the twentieth century. That is to say, both liberation and decolonization, while certainly no strangers to the world of the nineteenth century—indeed, one should never forget in this regard the primordial and remarkable example of the Haitian Revolution (1790s-1804)[6]—and the early part of the twentieth, emerged as distinctive global battle cries in the later course of the century. I would add only that, while the element of diversity is pursued in full in what follows, that of imperialism/colonialism is introduced by way of anticipation, as a sign of things to come.[7]

Some further observations are in order. First, the proposal advances a modus operandi, a pedagogical agenda or program, that is still very much bipolar in nature and hence very much in process as well. On the one hand, the proposal does reflect actual practices and guiding principles in my own present exercise of the profession; on the other hand, I would readily acknowledge, the proposal also reflects certain goals and ideals that remain not only out of reach but also out of focus at this point. Second, the proposal represents an exercise in cultural studies: a self-conscious construction that takes as its point of departure the context of postmodernism and postliberalism and that has as its point of destination a postcolonial pedagogy within the academic context of religious and theological studies. Third, the proposal is made from the perspective of a

---

[6] A story often silenced not only by historians of the period but also by subsequent historians as well. See M.-R. Trouillot (*Silencing the Past: Power and the Production of History* [Boston: Beacon Press, 1995]), who sees Haiti as the first modern state of the Third World, subject to all the trials and tribulations of postcolonial nation-building, and who understands such silencing along the lines of the denial of the Holocaust in Europe and the debate over the Alamo in the United States.

[7] See chap. 5 in this volume.

Christian theologian and critic, a lay person from the Roman Catholic tradition.[8]

Diversity in Texts

Scope of Diversity

With regard to the ancient texts themselves, I would argue that diversity should be actively pursued at three different levels: (1) diversity of texts; (2) diversity within texts; and (3) diversity within cultures. All three elements have been pursued by practitioners of the discipline in the past, beginning with historical criticism itself, where the various critical impulses outlined below (metacanonical analysis of texts; focus on tensions within texts; and comparative studies of the history-of-religions variety) may be found at one time or another. The proposal gathers these various impulses together, in sustained and systematic fashion, as a first step in its programmatic pedagogical agenda.

By *diversity of texts* I have in mind a deliberate move away from any exclusively or highly canonical approach to the discipline, whereby the focus of inquiry is placed, solely or primarily, on a study of the "New Testament" or the "Old Testament," that is, on those texts collectively known, acknowledged, and revered as "Scripture" or "Word of God." The proposed collapse of the canonical boundary gives way to a study of ancient Judaism or early Christianity,[9] as the case may be, in terms of the

---

[8] First of all, as a "Christian" theologian and critic, I remain quite aware that the Christian Bible contains not only the Christian scriptures but also the Hebrew scriptures and thus the scriptures of another religious tradition, an independent and living tradition. Such a situation, needless to say, calls for special sensitivity as well as circumscribed claims: my proposal emerges out of a Christian context. Second, as a "Catholic" theologian and critic, I am also quite aware of the fact that, for me, historically or experientially, the Bible does not represent the sort of semantic and symbolic world that it does for the Protestant tradition in general. Such a situation calls for openness and sensitivity on all sides: my proposal emerges out of a Catholic context. Third, as a "lay" theologian and critic in the Catholic tradition, I am quite aware that I am in no way an official representative for the institutional and hierarchical church. Such a situation, much to my liking, involves rootedness as well as independence: my proposal emerges from the ranks of the educated lay people.

[9] The issue of nomenclature is problematic for anyone writing out of the Christian tradition, not so much from the point of view of Christianity but from the point of view of Judaism (see n. 8 above). With regard to Christianity, such appellations as "early Christianity," "texts of early Christianity," and "texts of Christian antiquity" are intended to refer, first and foremost, to the literary production of the first two centuries of the Christian movement, although such a designation could be readily expanded to include the pre-Constantinian period as a whole and even beyond. With regard to Judaism, the question is how to avoid supersessionism

[continued]

entire literary production of the period in question, with "canonical" texts set indistinguishably alongside "extracanonical" texts. As a result, each religious tradition is analyzed in its entirety, that is to say, in the light of all surviving voices from any particular period or angle of study. Thereby, no particular voice or group of voices is privileged a priori. Rather, emphasis is placed instead on the din of texts and authors as such, the cacophony of voices in the ancient agora or forum, coming from every direction and going every which way—voices drawing away from or intersecting one another, ignoring or engaging each other, supporting or clashing with one another.

The aim behind this metacanonical approach is not to move beyond the obviously theological element of canon in search of a more "objective" standpoint, for such an approach is in the end as theological as any canonical approach. The aim, rather, corresponds to a fundamental pedagogical imperative: the need to survey the totality of what was produced at any one time within either tradition—the spectrum of expression—with a corresponding emphasis on variety, interaction, relationships, contrasts, struggles. The aim, therefore, is not to highlight the canonical—what became authoritative and normative—but rather to jump into the thick of the discussion—to listen to its manifold voices, note the ceaseless give and take; observe the inevitable power plays—always with the realization in mind that what has survived must represent but a minimal part of the discussion at any one time.

By *diversity within texts* I mean not only the possibility that a text may contain within itself actual remnants of an earlier text (an earlier draft of itself or a different document altogether), as traditionally entertained by historical criticism in its quest for preexisting sources, but also that such other elements as dissenting voices, suppressed voices, or contradictory voices may be found within it as well. Thus, even when a text is judged to constitute a literary unity, a unified and coherent whole, ruling out thereby the presence of any disparate or conflicting literary layers, the possibility still has to be considered that such a text (1) achieves a unity that is, given the juxtaposition of irreconcilable voices, forced, illusory, and evanescent—voices that the "whole" simply cannot keep together; (2) preserves

---

in these matters, difficult as that is, given both the inclusion of the Hebrew scriptures as part of the Christian Bible and the view of Judaism as pointing to Christianity central to the foundational documents of the latter. Avoiding supersessionism thus means, on the one hand, moving beyond a historical classification of Judaism in terms of its relationship to Christianity and, on the other, taking into consideration the long history of Judaism itself, not only as preceding Christianity by an enormous period of time but also as an ongoing living tradition alongside its entire history. In the end, I have settled for the use of the terms "ancient Judaism," "texts of ancient Judaism," and "texts of Jewish antiquity" to refer to its literary production through the Second Jewish-Roman War (132-35 C.E.).

within itself, no matter how faintly, echoes or hints of different or discordant voices—suppressed voices now largely bypassed and present only as telling silences in the text; or (3) undertakes a direct repudiation of other voices—dissenting voices with which it finds itself in fundamental disagreement, if not outright struggle. In this view, therefore, a text may in itself embody a number of different texts whose voices also form part of and contribute to the overall din at work. A second pedagogical imperative is very much at work here as well: the need to bring all such voices to the fore.

By *diversity within culture* I have in mind the placement of all such texts, canonical and extracanonical alike, within the overall sociocultural framework of the period under consideration. In other words, the analysis of the full literary production of early Christianity or ancient Judaism is further undertaken in terms of the wider literary production, religious or otherwise, surviving from the period or angle of study in question, with the former texts as a subset of the latter. Thus, just as the first example of diversity in texts described above involved the breakdown of any canonical division, so does this final example represent a similar breakdown of any religious division, whether formulated along the lines of Jews/Gentiles or Christians/pagans.

The intention, once again, is not to leave behind the obviously theological element of a socioreligious tradition in quest of a more "neutral" vantage point, for no such vantage point is to be had. The proposed approach is as theological as any confessional approach. The intention, rather, corresponds to a third pedagogical imperative: the need to survey the totality of what was produced at any one time, the panorama of expression, whether in terms of religious texts from other traditions or texts of a different orientation altogether. The end result, of course, is a far greater din of texts and authors, a much louder cacophony of voices in the ancient agora or forum, within which the voices of either tradition, in themselves highly pluriform, constitute but one element or dimension of the overall din.

CONCLUDING COMMENTS. What such an approach entails by way of pedagogical practice is—taking my own field of study, early Christianity, as an example—a reading of the extant texts without reference to canonical status, as sundry expressions of early Christian life and thought; a reading of such texts as potential metaphorical palimpsests, possibly bearing within themselves sediments of other texts, whether by way of preexisting sources, contradictory positions, revealing silences, or open polemics; and a reading of such texts against the larger sociocultural background of the Mediterranean Basin. The goal would be as wide a presentation as possible of the din of voices emerging out of the early Christian experience, by way of open and hidden texts, within the much larger din of voices to be found in the area of the Circum-Mediterranean.

Diversity in Texts and Intercultural Criticism

In my exposition of intercultural criticism, in itself grounded in a hermeneutics of otherness and engagement, I argued for a consideration of the ancient texts as *others* (with italics signifying a positive sense of otherness—a self-defined and affirming otherness) rather than "others" (with quotation marks signifying a negative sense of otherness—an imposed and denigrating otherness)—as realities from a very different social and historical context that are to be acknowledged, respected, and engaged rather than overridden and overwhelmed. I went on to argue, therefore, for a threefold approach to the reading and interpretation of these texts, with a first movement involving a view of the texts as literary or artistic products, rhetorical or strategic products, and cultural or ideological products.

In other words, a text is to be seen as constructing, from a particular perspective and underlying social location, a multilayered or multifaceted reality—a poetic reality by way of its artistic architecture and texture; a rhetorical reality given the strategic concerns and aims behind such a poetic reality; and an ideological reality on account of both the view of the world and of life in that world conveyed by means of such a poetic and rhetorical reality. This approach calls, in turn, for a combination of formalist, practical, and cultural methods in order to interpret texts and *discover their reality as *others*.

A number of comments are in order regarding the relationship between the first pedagogical goal of diversity in texts and this first interpretive movement of texts as constructs:

1. For the pedagogical agenda, it is the din of authors and texts that is important; for the interpretive project, it is that reality constructed and advanced by texts that is important. As such, reality is seen as neither common nor universal but as a multitude of realities constructed by the different texts, all perspectival and contextualized in nature. It is this fluid, polyvalent, polyglot view of reality that ultimately informs and guides the pedagogical focus on the cacophony of voices in the ancient agora or forum. Each voice, whether canonical or noncanonical, is regarded as a poetic, strategic, and ideological product.

2. From the perspective of the interpretive project, the possibility is granted that the reality constructed by any one text may be diffuse rather than concordant due to the presence of preexisting, dissident, suppressed, or contradictory texts within it. Such texts would be seen as poetic, rhetorical, and ideological products of their own—even if presently filtered through the reality of the primary text within which they are contained, and thus available only as "others." From the perspective of the pedagogical agenda, such diffuseness in texts would add to the overall din of authors and texts at work at any one time.

3. For the pedagogical agenda, such a cacophony of voices would be situated within the far more extensive din of texts and authors present in

the broader sociocultural context. For the interpretive project, such a comprehensive sociocultural context would be seen in terms of a far more numerous multitude of realities created by its texts—an overall reality in which the texts of early Christianity or ancient Judaism would interact in ever so many ways with the texts of the Near East or the Mediterranean Basin.

4. Finally, I have argued that the goal behind this first movement of intercultural criticism lies not in antiquarian interest, even if that were theoretically possible, but rather in critical engagement with the texts—in dialogue and struggle in the light of one's own reality and experience. Similarly, I would argue that the goal of this first pedagogical emphasis on diversity in texts is not simply to jump into the thick of the discussion, marveling at its complexity and following its endless paths, but rather to take an active and critical part within it, thus adding one's own voice to that overall din of a very different time and a very different culture.

Imperial-Colonial Framework

For this first pedagogical goal of diversity in texts, I would argue further for an analysis of the texts of ancient Judaism and early Christianity that takes seriously into consideration their broader sociocultural contexts in the Near East and the Mediterranean Basin, respectively, in the light of the reality of empire, of imperialism and colonialism, as variously constituted and exercised during the long period in question. Thus, over and around the din of texts and authors of both religious traditions as well as the larger din of texts and authors from their respective social contexts, the shadow of empire is to be highlighted.

Diversity in Readings

Scope of Diversity

With respect to the readings of ancient texts, I would argue for diversity to be actively pursued, once again, at three different levels: (1) diversity of reading traditions; (2) diversity of disciplinary paradigms; and (3) diversity within paradigms. It is only in recent times, with the breakdown of the stranglehold of traditional historical criticism on biblical criticism and the emergence of alternative critical approaches in the discipline, that such considerations have begun to make their way into the discipline. The present proposal places such critical impulses at center stage, in sustained and systematic fashion, as a second step in its programmatic pedagogical agenda.

By *diversity of reading traditions* I refer to the existence of a variety of longstanding and overarching ways of interpretation: the academic or scholarly, the theological or churchly, the religious or devotional, the cultural or popular. To be sure, this first level of analysis does impinge upon the category of diversity in readers to follow, insofar as it begins to deal with the socioeducational and socioreligious identities of real readers. Nevertheless, quite aside from the fact that these categories are in themselves interrelated and porous, I include such a concern at this point in the discussion, under the category of diversity in readings, because of what I regard as a fundamental pedagogical imperative: the need to conceive of the discipline as discipline—that is, as an academic field of study, with its own area of inquiry and research and its own base in institutions of higher learning of whatever kind—and thus to look upon its academic or scholarly way of reading these ancient texts as one among several such modes.

To do so, it is necessary to distinguish the academic type of reading from the other traditions of reading—the theological or churchly, the religious or devotional, the cultural or popular. This can be readily accomplished by describing the different ways of reading available within each tradition. First, with regard to the churchly or institutional mode of reading, one must deal with the following spectrum of approaches: the dogmatic or traditionalist;[10] the fundamentalist or literalist;[11] the denominational or ecclesiastical;[12] and the liberationist or sociopolitical.[13] Second, with respect to the devotional or spiritual mode of reading, one needs to examine the many actual and enduring practices of reading observed in daily life: from the cover-to-cover, sequential reading of the text; to the flipping-of-pages, at-random reading for the message of the day or the moment; to the recurring, ad hoc reading of specific texts for edification

---

[10] I have in mind the historical ways of interpreting the Bible with the church and theology in mind: from the patristic, to the medieval, to the Reformation and Counter Reformation, to the nineteenth century and the rise of modernism (see, e.g., R. M. Grant and D. Tracy, *A Short History of the Interpretation of the Bible,* 2d ed., rev. and enl. [Minneapolis: Fortress Press, 1984]).

[11] See, e.g., J. Barr, "The Problem of Fundamentalism Today," in *The Scope and Authority of the Bible* (Philadelphia: Westminster Press, 1980), 65-90; N. Ammerman, "North American Protestant Fundamentalism," in *Fundamentalisms Observed,* ed. M. Marty and R. S. Appleby (Chicago: The University of Chicago Press, 1991), 1-65; G. M. Marsden, *Understanding Fundamentalism and Evangelicalism* (Grand Rapids, Mich.: William B. Eerdmans, 1991).

[12] I have in mind the different ways of interpreting the Bible with the church and theology from the modernist period—that is to say, alongside the academic reading—through contemporary times. See, e.g., Pontifical Biblical Commission, "The Interpretation of the Bible in the Church," *Origins* 23:29 (January 6, 1994): 498-524; C. E. Braaten and R. W. Jenson, eds., *Reclaiming the Bible for the Church* (Grand Rapids, Mich.: William B. Eerdmans, 1995).

[13] See, e.g., C. Boff, "Hermeneutics: Constitution of Theological Pertinence," in *Theology and Praxis: Epistemological Foundations* (Maryknoll, N.Y.: Orbis Books, 1987), 132-53; C. Rowland and M. Corner, *Liberating Exegesis: The Challenge of Liberation Theology to Biblical Studies* (Louisville: Westminster/John Knox Press, 1989).

at specific moments or occasions—to name but a few.[14] Third, with regard to the popular or intertextual mode of reading, one should look at the broad appropriation and deployment of biblical motifs, scenes, situations, and themes in such diverse fields as literature, film, art, music, and so forth.[15]

It has been my experience over many years of teaching that the vast majority of students who take up biblical criticism for the first time do so out of specific and cherished institutional, spiritual, and/or intertextual modes of reading. As such, it is essential to begin with a critical analysis of the different traditions of reading—their origins, contours, and claims—in order to allow students not only to bring to the surface and come to terms with their own already established mode(s) of reading but also to realize what the academic study of these texts implies and entails and how such reading contrasts with their own traditional and beloved practices.

By *diversity of disciplinary paradigms* I point to the fact that the academic or scholarly mode of reading is by no means monolingual. Thus, once such a mode of reading has been properly differentiated from the other major reading traditions, it is necessary to analyze its own origins, contours, and claims as well. This can be readily done in terms of the different paradigms or umbrella models of interpretation developed within the discipline, in the past as well as in the present. Three specific elements make such a task less daunting than it would otherwise seem: (1) the discipline as discipline is not that old, tracing its origins—as in the case of so many other disciplines—to the intellectual ferment that marked the aftermath of the French Revolution in the early nineteenth century;[16] (2) for a very long period of time, indeed close to a century and a half, the discipline remained under the tight control of one such paradigm, historical criticism;[17] and (3) all major paradigms in question can still be found at work, to one degree or another, in the discipline today.

---

[14] See, e.g., C. McDannell, "The Bible in the Victorian Home," in *Material Christianity: Religion and Popular Culture in America* (New Haven, Conn.: Yale University Press, 1995), 67-102.

[15] One should note in this regard the launching by Sheffield Academic Press of a new journal, *Biblicon*, with Alice Bach as general editor, to serve as a forum for the analysis of the cultural appropriation of the Bible as well as for crosscultural debates on the popular use of the Bible.

[16] On this point, see J. Appleby, L. Hunt, and M. Jacob, "Part I: Intellectual Absolutisms," in *Telling the Truth about History* (New York: W. W. Norton & Co., 1994), esp. 15-125; P. Novick, "Part I: Objectivity Enthroned," in *That Noble Dream: The "Objectivity Question" and the American Historical Profession* (Cambridge: Cambridge University Press, 1988), esp. 21-108.

[17] See R. A. Harrisville and W. Sundberg, eds., *The Bible in Modern Culture: Theology and Historical Critical Method from Spinoza to Käsemann* (Grand Rapids, Mich.: William B. Eerdmans, 1995).

Given my sustained analysis of these paradigms—historical criticism, literary criticism, cultural criticism, cultural studies—in the course of this project, I would only emphasize at this point a second pedagogical imperative: the need for an expansive and informed perspective regarding the grounding, tenor, and import—the presuppositions, language, and ramifications—of all such paradigms. Its aims would be as follows: to construct a comprehensive interpretive spectrum; to be able to situate within such a spectrum the different types of readings in question, including one's own; to be capable of establishing a sound critical dialogue with such ways of reading. In other words, the time is now past, irrevocably, when the discipline could be transmitted uniformly, when one paradigm could be conveyed as the sole paradigm of interpretation, often without any awareness regarding its own character as a paradigm, and when all students could be given essentially the same training in the academic reading of these texts. This means, of course, that scholarly training today must involve, from the first, a degree of sophistication in metatheory, that is, in the principles underlying the various paradigms as well as in the relationships among the paradigms themselves.

Such a task proves, more often than not, highly disconcerting to the student, whether coming to biblical criticism for the first time or having been previously taught within the confines of a single paradigm (invariably historical criticism). In effect, the student now faces, from quite early on, a series of difficult challenges: an unfamiliar array of critical approaches to a text, each with its own distinctive mode of discourse; modes of discourse whose technical terminology and conceptual apparatus require familiarity with other disciplines; and the growing realization that, sooner or later, a personal choice and rationale for such a choice are inevitable. Nevertheless, despite all such difficulties, there is no other way out of this quandary, since to opt for training within any one paradigm first often leads to the privileging of such an umbrella model and a corresponding view of other umbrella models as superfluous, if not altogether deficient. Under such circumstances, mastery of all paradigms is simply out of the question, for no individual—no matter how gifted, learned, or devoted—can possibly assimilate the range of materials in question. The aim behind such training, therefore, cannot be full control but rather informed awareness, a sort of working sophistication sufficient to follow and interact with a number of particular lines of argumentation, to engage in border crossings, so to speak.

By *diversity within paradigms* I refer to the fact that no paradigm or umbrella model of interpretation, despite the presence of a distinctive mode of discourse, is monolingual. Consequently, once the various paradigms at work in the discipline have been properly identified and described, it becomes necessary to examine in turn the variety of methods and theories, reading strategies and theoretical orientations, that make up each paradigm and account for its characteristic mode of discourse. This means, of course, that one must examine each paradigm in terms of its own origins, contours, and claims.[18]

Again, since in the course of this project I have had occasion to analyze the different paradigms in terms of their respective constitutive components, I limit myself at this point to a third pedagogical imperative, actually an extension of the second one mentioned above: the need for an expansive and informed perspective regarding the grounding, tenor, and import—the presuppositions, language, and ramifications—of the major lines of interpretation to be found within each paradigm. The basic aims behind such a proposed expertise remain the same: to delineate a series of concrete interpretive spectrums; to be able to situate within each spectrum the different types of reading in question, including one's own, should one choose to write in that vein; and to be capable of establishing a sound critical conversation with such readings.

Even when historical criticism functioned as the sole paradigm in the field, it was still necessary to become acquainted with its different lines of interpretation, from textual criticism to composition criticism. The situation has now changed drastically in two respects. On the one hand, with the proliferation in paradigms has come a corresponding multiplicity in constitutive components. On the other hand, such multiplicity within historical criticism always remained much closer, from both a linguistic and a conceptual point of view, than it ever does within the new paradigms. In other words, the differences in technical terminology and conceptual apparatus among the various lines of interpretation within each of the recent paradigms prove far more difficult to master and bridge than the differences within historical criticism itself. This means, of course, that scholarly training today must involve not only a measure of sophistication in metatheory at the level of paradigms but also at the level of their

---

[18] Recent times have witnessed the appearance of a new genre of scholarly literature in biblical criticism in which the variety of methods and theories, both within paradigms and across paradigms, is addressed by means of critical introductions on the part of a corresponding variety of scholars. See, e.g., S. L. McKenzie and S. R. Haynes, eds., *To Each Its Own Meaning: An Introduction to Biblical Criticisms and Their Application* (Louisville: Westminster/John Knox Press, 1993); F. Watson, ed., *The Open Text: New Directions for Biblical Studies?* (London: SCM Press Ltd., 1993); E. V. McKnight and E. Struthers Malbon, eds., *The New Literary Criticism and the New Testament* (Valley Forge, Pa.: Trinity Press International, 1994); J. B. Green, ed., *Hearing the New Testament* (Grand Rapids, Mich.: William B. Eerdmans,1995); The Bible and Culture Collective, *The Postmodernist Bible*; P. F. Esler, ed., *Modelling Early Christianity: Social-Scientific Studies of the New Testament in Its Context* (New York: Routledge, 1995). Clearly, the generic progenitor of and model for all such endeavors, present and to come, is Fortress Press's splendid series entitled Guides to Biblical Scholarship, ongoing.

respective components, in the principles underlying the various interpretive models and the relationships among the models themselves.

Such a task, of course, proves even more disconcerting to the student, now faced as well with a broad variety of methods and theories within any one paradigm: an array of different though related approaches to a text, each with its own particular mode of discourse; modes of discourse that demand familiarity with a number of specific movements both inside and outside the field; the further realization that beyond a choice of umbrella model lies a choice of working interpretive model as well. Again, there is simply no way out of this situation. At the same time, it should be clear as well that even mastery of a paradigm is out of the question, that the most one can aim for is a sort of informed awareness, a working sophistication, that enables one to follow and interact with a variety of interpretive models, to engage in border crossings.

CONCLUDING COMMENTS. I argued in the previous section that the goal behind the pedagogical emphasis on diversity in texts was to unfold as broadly as possible the din of texts and authors, the cacophony of voices in the ancient agora or forum, present in either ancient Judaism or early Christianity within the much larger din of texts and authors surviving from either the Near East or the Mediterranean Basin. The added emphasis on diversity in readings represents a significant extension of this goal. What such an approach entails by way of pedagogical practice is a reading of the extant texts—canonical or noncanonical, open or hidden—in terms of the many readings and interpretations—the panorama of expression—produced by different reading traditions, different paradigms within the academic tradition, and different methods and theories within each scholarly paradigm. The result is a deafening din of texts and authors, a more extensive as well as more pronounced cacophony of voices in the modern marketplace or *mercado*, as the ancient texts become refracted into endless readings and interpretations within the tradition of the West.

Diversity in Readings and Intercultural Criticism

Again, given its call for a consideration of the ancient texts as *others*—as realities from a very different social and historical context that are to be acknowledged, respected, and engaged, rather than overridden and overwhelmed—intercultural criticism calls in turn for a threefold approach to the reading and interpretation of these texts. The third movement within such an approach involves a view of all readings as literary or artistic products, rhetorical or strategic products, and cultural or ideological products. To begin with, for intercultural criticism, textual meaning is the result of interaction between texts and readers—socially and historically conditioned texts and socially and historically conditioned readers. As such, a text is always regarded as a "text"—as read and interpreted in a certain way by a certain reader or group of readers within a certain context (time and place). Consequently, each "text" or reading is also seen as constructing, from a particular perspective and social location, a multi-layered or multifaceted reality—an artistic reality, with a poetics of its own; a strategic reality, with a rhetoric of its own; and a cultural reality, with an ideology of its own.

Again, therefore, intercultural criticism calls for a similar combination of formalist, practical, and cultural methods in the analysis of "texts." The goal of such analysis is twofold: first, to help in dis-covering the reality of texts as *others*, given one's own reading of the text and production of a "text"; second, to assist in dis-covering the reality of these "texts" as *others* in their own right—as realities from different social and historical contexts than one's own. In other words, in foregrounding readings of the texts as it does, intercultural criticism seeks to prevent any overriding or overwhelming of texts by readers and to place any one reading or interpretation—any one "text," including one's own—within a full spectrum of expression.

Some observations are in order regarding the relationship between the second pedagogical goal of diversity in readings and this second interpretive movement of readings as constructs:

1. For the pedagogical agenda, it is the deafening din of "texts"—of readings and interpretations, in terms of major and overarching reading traditions, paradigms within the academic type of reading, and methods and theories within the various scholarly paradigms—that is important. For the interpretive project, it is that reality constructed and advanced by each and every "text" or reading that proves important. In effect, there is no meaning of the text out there, stable and extractable, preceding, guiding, and sanctioning interpretation; instead, what one finds is a multitude of "texts," of readings of the same text, all perspectival and contextualized in nature. It is such a fluid, polyvalent, polyglot view of meaning and text that ultimately informs and guides the pedagogical focus on the cacophony of voices in the modern marketplace or *mercado*. Each "text" is looked upon as a poetic, strategic, and cultural product.

2. Given the fact that for the interpretive project there is no final or definitive text or meaning as such, the unfolding of the din of readings and interpretations with regard to any one text as part of the pedagogical agenda is not intended to produce or aim for a final and definitive reading and interpretation of such a text, but rather to drive home the spectrum of opinion resulting from the choice of reading glasses available with which to approach the text, both outside and inside biblical criticism, that is to say, the academic or scholarly reading tradition. The point is to see in each reading of a text not only a "text," a version of that text and a rendition of its meaning, but also a text of its own, a product in its own right.

3. Finally, the goal behind this second movement of intercultural criticism is not intellectual curiosity per se but critical engagement with

"texts"—in dialogue and struggle in the light of one's reality and experience. Likewise, the goal of this second pedagogical emphasis on diversity in readings is not to become a mere spectator of the discussion, witnessing its goings-on and taking pleasure in its many twists and turns, but to fashion a "text" of one's own by taking an active and critical role within the discussion—to offer a version of the text and, in so doing, produce yet another "text" within the overall din of many different times and different cultures.

Imperial-Colonial Framework

For this second pedagogical goal of diversity in readings, I would argue as well for an analysis of the readings and interpretations of the texts of Jewish and Christian antiquity that takes seriously into account their broader sociocultural context in the West, whether by way of Europe or North America, in the light of the reality of empire, of imperialism and colonialism, now with regard to the Western imperial tradition of the last five hundred years. Consequently, over and around the deafening din of scholarly readings and interpretations emerging from the West, the shadow of empire should, once again, be underlined.

Diversity in Readers

Scope of Diversity

With regard to the readers of ancient texts, I would argue that diversity should be pursued at two different levels: (1) diversity of intratextual readers; and (2) diversity of extratextual readers. While the former consideration goes hand in hand with the emergence of alternative critical approaches in the discipline, the latter comes to the fore with the recent and ever-increasing influx of outsiders into the discipline. In effect, with the emergence of literary criticism and, above all, of reader-response criticism within literary criticism, one begins to find formal interest in the reader-constructs employed in the analysis of the ancient texts. Similarly, with the influx of outsiders, one begins to find formal interest as well in flesh-and-blood readers and on how the social location of such readers affects and influences their analysis of ancient texts.

Early stirrings in this direction can be detected in both feminist and liberation hermeneutics. On the one hand, the discourse of feminism arises within the West (Western women), brings the element of gender to critical consciousness, and is then simultaneously deconstructed and expanded through the irruption of non-Western women as well as ethnic/racial minority women in the West.[19] On the other hand, the discourse of liberation arises in Latin America, raises the element of social class (the poor

---

[19] On this, see "Feminist and Womanist Criticism," in *The Postmodernist Bible* (New Haven, Conn., and London: Yale University Press, 1995), 225-71.

and the oppressed) to critical consciousness, and is then simultaneously deconstructed and expanded through the intervention of African and Asian theologians, women theologians of all three continents, and diasporic theologians in the West.[20] In both cases real readers begin to raise their own voices as flesh-and-blood readers and become increasingly differentiated in the process. By the early 1990s, as the recent calls for change indicate, the discussion reached a crucial and sophisticated stage. The proposal places such critical concerns, in sustained and systematic fashion, at a climactic position, as a third and final step in its programmatic pedagogical agenda.

By *diversity of intratextual readers*, I understand readers "in the text," that is, the variety of reader-constructs developed and employed by flesh-and-blood readers for the reading and interpretation of texts, including the texts of Jewish and Christian antiquity. I have in mind such categories as implied reader, intended reader, naive reader, seasoned reader, and so on. This first level of analysis might be said to belong more properly within the previous category of diversity in readings, insofar as it deals with the different reader-constructs presupposed and activated by the various reading strategies adopted vis-à-vis the text. In other words, as interest and sophistication in reading strategies and theoretical orientations increases, so do interest and sophistication in the development and employment of reader-constructs. However, quite aside from the highly interrelated and porous nature of these categories, I have included this level of analysis at this point, under the category of diversity in readers, because of what I take to be a first pedagogical imperative: the need to be aware of the different reading "masks" or "personas" adopted by flesh-and-blood readers, including oneself, with regard to the texts.

Elsewhere I have characterized this distinction between intratextual readers and extratextual readers in terms of a universal-reader/real-reader axis.[21] Within such an axis, intratextual readers represent variations of a universal reader-construct, with the following characteristics in common: uncontextualized or without location, and hence neither historically situated nor culturally conditioned; perceptors and describers of reality; objective and value-free.

Such variations may be further classified in terms of three different analytical perspectives: the process of reading, the knowledge of the reader,

---

[20] On this, see "Ideological Criticism," in *The Postmodernist Bible*, 272-308.

[21] See F. F. Segovia, "Reading Readers of the Fourth Gospel and Their Readings: An Exercise in Intercultural Criticism," in *"What Is John?": Readers and Readings of the Fourth Gospel*, ed. F. F. Segovia (Atlanta: Scholars Press, 1996), 240-42. I would emphasize that the nomenclature used for this axis, as well as for all those to follow, although seemingly binomial in character, characterizes the opposite poles of the axis and thus presupposes a full spectrum of opinion between such poles.

and the experience of reading. First, the process of reading yields a first-time-reader/multiple-reader axis, depending on the degree of acquaintance with the text accorded to the reader. While the former construct possesses no previous familiarity whatsoever with the text, the latter has had extensive dealings with it. Second, with knowledge of the reader comes a historical-reader/textual-reader axis, depending on the sort of information relied upon by the reader. The former construct would read the text as if living in the same time and culture as those of the text, availing itself of all sorts of information external to the text, while the latter would read the text as if it were its implied reader, relying solely on the information provided by the text itself. Finally, the experience of reading yields a naive-reader/informed-reader axis, depending on the information granted the reader with regard to the subject matter of the text. While the former construct approaches the text with innocence, the latter does so with sophistication.

By *diversity in extratextual readers,* I understand readers "outside the text"; that is, the variety of flesh-and-blood readers who set out, for whatever reason, to read and interpret texts, including the ancient texts of ancient Judaism and early Christianity. While a focus on the flesh-and-blood readers themselves has not formed part of the discipline, I place such a consideration at this climactic position in the proposal because of what I regard as a second pedagogical imperative: the need to realize that behind all readings and interpretations of ancient texts, behind all reading "personas" or "masks" used to read such texts, stand real readers.

Within the universal-reader/real-reader axis, extratextual readers represent variations of the real-reader construct, with the following characteristics in common: thoroughly contextualized and located, and thus historically situated and culturally conditioned; constructors of "reality"; subjective and value-oriented. Such variations may be further classified according to two different analytical points of view: the identity of the reader and the reaction of the reader. First, with the question of the reader's identity emerges an individual-reader/social-reader axis, depending on whether the reader is approached as an individual subject or as a social subject, a member of distinct social groupings or communities. While the former construct emphasizes psychological location and the psychological issues of the individual in question, the latter emphasizes social location and the social issues of the grouping(s) or communities in question.

To be sure, both constructs admit of many variations. In the case of the individual-reader construct, such variations are theoretically countless, though limited in practice by the number of options available regarding psychological or psychoanalytic models to be used. In the case of the social-reader construct, such variations are numerous, depending on which dimension(s) of social identity is (are) highlighted (e.g., sociocultural, sociobiological [including gender and race], sociopolitical, socioreligious, socioeconomic, socioeducational, sociolinguistic, and so forth). Second, the question of the reader's reaction yields a compliant-reader/resistant-reader reaction, depending on the basic posture adopted by the reader vis-à-vis the perceived claims of the text as an ideological construct. While the former construct willingly submits without question or reserve to such claims, the latter has nothing to do with them and may even actively oppose them.

CONCLUDING COMMENTS. I argued in the previous section that the goal behind the pedagogical emphasis on diversity in readings—in itself an extension of the goal informing and guiding the pedagogical emphasis on diversity in texts—was to display as fully as possible what I referred to as the deafening din of texts and authors, the more extensive and more pronounced cacophony of voices in the modern marketplace resulting from the refraction of ancient texts into the endless readings and interpretations within the tradition of the West. This concluding emphasis on diversity in readers represents a further and substantial extension of such a goal.

What this approach entails by way of pedagogical practice is a reading of the flesh-and-blood readers who stand behind the reading and interpretations of the ancient texts (canonical or noncanonical, open or hidden) and hence behind the production of the many readings and interpretations of such texts (by way of different reading traditions, different paradigms within the academic tradition of reading, and different methods and theories within the scholarly paradigms themselves). Such a reading calls for attention to the various sorts of reading "masks" or "personas" (the intratextual readers) employed, implicitly or explicitly, by flesh-and-blood readers, as well as to the flesh-and-blood readers themselves (the extratextual readers), both as individual subjects and as social subjects.

Such a reading further involves, given present developments in the discipline, paying close attention to the new flesh-and-blood readers at work within the discipline for the first time in its history—female practitioners, both Western and non-Western; non-Western practitioners, both male and female, both at home and in the diaspora. The result is an incredible din of texts and authors, an even more extensive, indeed global, and more pronounced, indeed multilingual and multicentered, cacophony of voices in the contemporary marketplace or *mercado*, as all sorts of readers everywhere, now increasingly outside the West, refract the texts of ancient Judaism and early Christianity into countless readings and interpretations within their own respective contexts and traditions.

Diversity in Readers and Intercultural Criticism
Once again, in keeping with its call for a consideration of the ancient texts as *others*—as realities from a very different social and historical context, not to be overridden or overwhelmed but rather acknowledged, respected, and engaged—intercultural criticism also calls for a threefold

approach to the reading and interpretation of these texts. The third and final movement within such an approach involves a view of all readers as literary or artistic products, rhetorical or strategic products, and cultural or ideological products.

First of all, it should be recalled that for intercultural criticism all "texts," all readings and interpretations of the ancient texts, are the result of inter-action between socially and historically conditioned texts *and* socially and historically conditioned readers. In the end, therefore, there is as much of the reader as of the text, if not more, in any "text." From this theoreti-cal perspective it proves necessary to examine not just the many readings and interpretations of the ancient texts but also the readers behind such "texts" as well. As such, an analysis of flesh-and-blood readers becomes imperative, as one seeks to understand and explain how and why real readers, both as individual and social subjects, reach and produce certain readings and interpretations of these texts. In the process the flesh-and-blood readers come to be looked upon as "texts" themselves—constantly engaged as they are, whether implicitly or explicitly, in a process of "self"-construction. Consequently, real readers are approached in the same way as both the ancient texts and the readings and interpretations of such texts, that is, as constructing, from a particular social location and per-spective, a multilayered or multifaceted reality—an artistic reality, with a poetics of the "self"; a strategic reality, with a rhetoric of the "self"; and a cultural reality, with an ideology of the "self."

Once again, therefore, intercultural criticism deems a similar combina-tion of formalist, practical, and cultural methods as essential for its analy-sis of readers. The goal behind such analysis is twofold: First, to be of further help in establishing or dis-covering the reality of both texts and "texts" as *others*, given the emphasis placed on the otherness of the real readers who proceed to read such texts and produce such "texts." In other words, by highlighting the otherness of the flesh-and-blood readers, their provenance from very different social and historical contexts, the other-ness of both their readings of texts and of the ancient texts themselves is further reinforced as well. Second, to move beyond an analysis of readers in terms of their own readings of texts (their intratextual reader constructs) to an analysis on the basis of their own readings of them-"selves" (as extratextual constructs), thus bringing attention to bear on the complex relationship that exists between their construction of their own "selves" and their corresponding readings and interpretations of ancient texts. By foregrounding the real readers in this way intercultural criticism seeks to prevent, once again, any overriding or overwhelming of texts by readers, including oneself, and to explore the relationship between how readers read themselves and how they read the ancient texts.

A number of comments are in order regarding the relationship between the third pedagogical goal of diversity in readers and this third interpre-tive movement of readers as constructs:

1. For the pedagogical agenda, it is the incredible din of readers—both by way of readers in the text and readers outside the text—that proves important; for the interpretive project, it is that reality constructed and advanced by each reader that is regarded as important, again both in terms of the intratextual reader-construct adopted and the shape of the extratextual "self" assumed. In other words, there is no universal or objective reader out there, engaged in scientific and value-free interpretation, abstracted from all the social and historical circumstances of this world; on the contrary, what one finds is a host of flesh-and-blood readers, socially conditioned and historically situated, who construct their own "selves" in any number of ways, who approach the ancient texts from within such constructions, all perspectival and contextualized in nature, and who develop a variety of intratextual readers in so doing. It is such a fluid, polyvalent, polyglot view of the reader that ultimately informs and guides the pedagogical focus on the cacophony of voices in the contemporary marketplace or *mercado*. Each reader is looked upon, therefore, as a poetic, strategic, and cultural product.

2. Since for the interpretive project there exists no ultimate and definitive reader-construct as such, given the fact that all such constructs are contextualized and perspectival, the emphasizing of the din of the readers as part of the pedagogical agenda is not for the purpose of producing or aiming toward such a final construct, but rather of stressing the fact that all readers are "textual" constructions and that out of such constructions they proceed to approach the ancient texts and produce the readings and interpretations of such texts that they do. The point is that behind any reading or interpretation of a text stands not only a version of that text, a "text," but also a flesh-and-blood reader.

3. The goal behind this third movement of intercultural criticism is not intellectual curiosity per se but critical engagement with other readers—in dialogue and struggle in the light of one's own reality and experience, one's own construction of one-"self" as reader. Similarly, the goal of this third pedagogical emphasis on diversity in readers is not simply to stand in awe of the many and varied flesh-and-blood readers engaged in the discussion but to produce as a flesh-and-blood reader oneself a reading and interpretation of the ancient text, to be aware of the relationship between such a "text" and one's own construction of one-"self," and to introduce thereby one more reader, both individual and social, into the overall discussion.

Imperial-Colonial Framework

For this third pedagogical goal of diversity in readers, I would argue once more for an analysis of the readers of the texts of ancient Judaism and early Christianity. This analysis must take seriously into consideration their broader sociocultural contexts in the global sphere, whether in the West or outside the West, in the light of the reality of empire, of imperialism and colonialism, now in terms of the reaction against the Western imperial tradition from outside the West within the context of the postcolonial yet neocolonial world of the last half-century. Therefore, over and around the overwhelming din of flesh-and-blood readers from every corner of the globe, the shadow of empire must, yet again, be highlighted.

CONCLUDING REFLECTIONS

I should like to bring this discussion to a close with some reflections on various implications and ramifications of the proposal for the discipline:

1. It should be evident that the proposal itself is of a theoretical rather than practical sort; that is to say, it deals with pedagogical discourse and practices in general, in the abstract, rather than with concrete strategies for teaching the various courses of the curriculum. As such, the proposal calls for a considerable amount of creative work on the part of the professor in the academy—regardless of the level of instruction involved, whether graduate or professional or undergraduate/tertiary—regarding the translation of such general visions and directives into specific curricular visions and course designs.

Thus, each and every course—from the basic introduction to socio-historical context and subject matter, to the general introduction to a particular body of works, to the concentrated analysis of a particular writing, to the specialized seminar on a specific theme or problem or tradition—calls for a different application of the basic pedagogical principles and imperatives invoked. Similarly, the curriculum itself calls for the development of an overall personal vision to guide and inform not only those courses for which one is directly responsible but also the curriculum as a whole—its sense of unity and coherence, of sequence and teleology. In the end, the goal is not to develop a structuralist type of grid—a series of steps to be followed in proper sequence, with the instructor ultimately in control of the process. The goal, rather, is to provide a working framework: a set of general contours or parameters within which the various principles and imperatives in question can be applied in any variety of ways, innovative ways, with the instructor aiming throughout for freedom of space and freedom of imagination.

2. Mention of the academy serves as a reminder that the proposed pedagogical agenda has dealt primarily with the academic or scholarly tradition of reading and thus with the discipline of biblical criticism, with its base in higher institutions of higher learning, of whatever kind, means, and orientation. In this regard the academic reader or critic should always keep in mind that such a way of approaching the texts of ancient Judaism and Christianity is but one of several modes of reading, and a relatively recent one at that. This awareness should immediately bring to the fore as well a number of related issues and concerns.

a. While biblical criticism has openly and consistently looked down upon alternative modes of reading as subjective and deficient, it in turn has been accused, both traditionally and in recent times, of being decidedly rationalistic, elitist, and removed from the life of the church and the concerns of the world. In many respects such corresponding evaluations are the result of a failure on the part of all modes of reading, including biblical criticism itself, to see and understand themselves as *modes* of reading, socially and historically conditioned as well as perspectival in nature. Such self-awareness on the part of all modes of reading is not only salutary but also imperative in this day and age.

b. Academic readers must come to terms with the fact that they are highly privileged individuals, not so much from a socioeconomic perspective—although the economic social location of such readers, especially in the West, should by no means be downplayed—but certainly from a socioeducational point of view, insofar as they have attained a degree of educational expertise and sophistication that ranks them far beyond most other readers of these texts. Such privilege is not without responsibilities. Thus, for example, it is incumbent upon critics to analyze the other traditions of reading with as much zeal, seriousness, and thoroughness as they have used to examine the ancient texts as well as the traditions of interpretation within the discipline. Indeed, academic reading is better equipped, in principle, than the other traditions of reading to carry out such a task, given precisely the intellectual sophistication and expertise it has acquired in the academy. However, the spirit behind such analysis should be one of critical dialogue, with a vision of how the different modes of reading relate to and influence one another, both historically and in the present. In other words, the role of criticism in this regard should be not only to teach but also to learn.

c. Biblical critics should never forget, given the admittedly elite nature of their training, teaching, and writing, that the audience they reach is a very limited one indeed, more often than not consisting of fellow members of the academy. In other words, their influence and power is thoroughly circumscribed. Quite aside from a much-needed spirit of humility, such considerations should drive home the point that, while necessarily elite in nature, their mode of reading need not and should not be elitist, turning a cold shoulder to all other traditions of reading. In other words, critics need to wrestle with certain questions that have up to now been largely bypassed in the discipline: What is the proper role of the academic reader of these texts with regard to such other traditions of reading? to the academy? to the church? to society at large? Instead of living a life of leisure in an imagined past, critics must come to terms with the present, not only with the ramifications of their own reconstructions of the past for the present but also with the fact that it is in the present that they construct them-"selves" and the past.

d. Finally, in the light of their own highly circumscribed audience and influence, academic readers should come to terms with how they have tended to treat one another in the past: the frantic quest for academic renown and glory; the insatiable drive to provide the ultimate and definitive interpretation of any one text or even of antiquity itself; the untoward exaltation of one's self and one's work; the demolition and humiliation of others and their work; the desire for control of and devotion on the part of students, sometimes to the point of abuse and harassment; the subtle and sometimes not-so-subtle disdain for those who never had the means or ability to pursue higher studies of any kind. Surely, the times call for a different type of critical dialogue, with an emphasis on both "critical" and "dialogue."

3. It would be quite foolish to think, even for a moment, that the adoption of the proposed pedagogical agenda will be a largely painless exercise; quite to the contrary, its incorporation into the curriculum will inevitably face serious difficulties, both from within and from without. I shall mention but a few.

a. The question of metacanonical diversity is a hard one for many individuals and institutions to contemplate. There is so much invested in the canon, in "Scripture" or "Word of God"—whether socially or ecclesiastically, ideologically or theologically—that any attempt to set the canon as an indistinguishable or nondistinctive element within the wider scope of ancient Judaism and early Christianity, let alone within the more expansive scope of their broader sociocultural contexts, will often meet with enormous resistance, if not theological odium. I would recall in this regard that the aim behind such a pedagogical move is quite sound, ecclesiastically as well as socially, ideologically as well as theologically: to set forth and engage as fully as possible, in the past as well as in the present, the whole panorama of expression—to let all voices speak and to engage in critical dialogue with all voices. In other words, if one tends to look askance at canons today, why should one not do so with regard to canons of antiquity?

b. There is also the problem of the sheer volume of subject matter involved, not only at the level of texts but also at the level of readings and readers of such texts. I would only point out that what is important here is the principle, even if the praxis is perforce limited: to establish the din of voices and to be aware that such a din is always present.

c. Along the same lines, there is the problem of metatheory as well, the enormous range of methodological apparatuses and theoretical orientations present in the discipline today. I would emphasize again that it is the principle that is important above all, even if mastery of such various discourses and practices is beyond any one's grasp: to be aware of the din of voices and to establish, as much as possible, a working familiarity with such voices, in order to be able to understand and engage them.

d. The question of regarding all texts, readings, and readers as literary, rhetorical, and ideological products and constructions, highly contextualized and perspectival, represents a bitter pill for many to swallow, especially with regard to the last element. So much has been invested in the ideal of the objective reader—as well as in committed readers of various kinds—that to throw wide open the question of social location and perspective vis-à-vis readers is to shatter any number of sacred and beloved mythologies. I would respond in this regard that the proposal involves, no more and no less, than to do unto readers of the ancient texts what they themselves have not hesitated to do unto the texts themselves.

In the end, of course, as the history of any one discipline readily shows, it is good to keep in mind that any new proposal more often than not calls forth opposition from the powers that be. I would argue that such opposition is actually to be welcomed, even if oftentimes its tone is much to be regretted, insofar as it may serve as an opportunity for further reflection, correction, and development.

4. Academic readers should never, even for a moment, forget that they are social subjects and belong to any number of social groupings. In addition to the intellectual traditions and currents to which they subscribe as members of the academy, they should be conscious of their own inescapable relationship to the other theological disciplines, to religious communities, and to society at large.

First, critics should not see themselves as mere suppliers of raw data for the rest of the theological disciplines but as theologians or religious thinkers in their own right: their religious or theological visions (or lack thereof) are at work in the way they approach the data, reconstruct the past (its textual remains and physical remains), and expound it to the contemporary world.

Second, critics should not see themselves simply as members of the academic community but also as members, faithful or estranged, of religious communities. Such affiliations—faint or strong, favorable or hostile—not only find their way into their search for and representations of antiquity but also call for critical responses vis-à-vis the communities themselves, whether by way of sympathetic commitment or radical critique. In other words, membership in academic communities should be no excuse for abstention from contemporary issues and disputes in the socioreligious or theological sphere, although obviously the degree of involvement will differ from reader to reader, issue to issue, situation to situation.

Third, critics should not see themselves, much as they might like to be, as citizens of times long past and cultures far removed. They are very much citizens of their own times and cultures and should see themselves as such. The way they read and interpret ancient texts, as well as the way they read and construct them-"selves," not only reflects their social location and perspective but also has ramifications for such contexts and agendas. Criticism involves taking positions, implicitly or explicitly, at all times;

the past provides neither shelter nor escape from the present. Critics should, therefore, be constantly aware of both the presuppositions and the ramifications of their critical practices and discourses. Indeed, critics should be aware of their own location and stance in a world that is still under the shadow of empire—a postcolonial world, almost free of empire in the Two-Thirds World, yet a neocolonial world, in continuing subjection to Western imperial culture.

A final word would seem utterly unnecessary yet remains imperative. It would be most ironic for a proposal that has insisted so much on diversity and empire to present itself in any way as the one and only way for the future. I would only reiterate that this is a personal proposal, ultimately rooted in my own project of intercultural criticism and grounded in a postmodernist and postliberal, postcolonial and neocolonial, view of the world—the world at the turn of a century.

PART III

BIBLICAL STUDIES
AND POSTCOLONIAL STUDIES

5

Biblical Criticism and Postcolonial Studies

Toward a Postcolonial Optic

In the previous delineations of the paradigm of cultural studies in biblical criticism in chapters 1, 2, and 4, I have sought to bring to the fore the constellation of elements that I regard as fundamental to this most recent and still emerging umbrella model of interpretation in the discipline. Two of these I see as particularly relevant for the present study. The first involves a view of all interpretation, all recreations of meaning from texts, and all reconstructions of history as dependent upon reading strategies and theoretical models, with a further view of all such strategies and models and the resultant recreations and reconstructions as constructs on the part of real readers. The second concerns a view of real or flesh-and-blood readers as variously positioned and engaged within their respective social locations, with a further view of all such contextualizations and perspectives as constructs on the part of real readers as well. Such views regarding the character of interpretation and the role of critics bear immediate consequences for the dynamics and mechanics of the paradigm as a whole.

First, the task of interpretation is viewed in terms of the application of different reading strategies and theoretical models—whether produced or borrowed—by different real readers in different ways, at different times, and with different results (different readings and interpretations) in the light of their different and highly complex situations and perspectives.

Second, a critical analysis of real readers and their readings (their representations of themselves as well as their representations of the ancient texts and the ancient world) becomes as important and necessary as a critical analysis of the ancient texts themselves (the remains of the ancient world).

Third, all recreations of meaning and all reconstructions of history are in the end regarded as representations of the past—re-creations and reconstructions—on the part of readers who are themselves situated and interested to the core.

Finally, given the paradigm's overriding focus on contextualization and perspective, social location and agenda, and thus on the political character of all compositions and texts, all readings and interpretations, all readers and interpreters, its mode of discourse may be described as profoundly ideological.

In this chapter I should like to proceed a step further in the definition and analysis of my own stance within the paradigm of cultural studies. In effect, I should like to lay the basic foundations and contours for what I have come to regard as a most appropriate, most enlightening, and most fruitful approach to biblical criticism, as I presently envision and practice the discipline. I have in mind the model of postcolonial studies, currently in vogue across a number of academic fields and disciplines.[1] This is a model that I find both hermeneutically rewarding and personally satisfying. On the one hand, I find that the model can shed precious, concomitant light on the various dimensions that I have posited as constitutive for my own vision and exercise of the discipline. On the other hand, I find that the model speaks to me in a very direct way, not only as a contemporary biblical critic but also as a constructive theologian as well as a cultural critic.[2]

---

[1] There is no comprehensive—that is, cross-imperial and cross-colonial—study of postcolonial studies as such, no encompassing account of its origins, histories, and discourses across the various imperial/colonial experiences of Europe and the United States. There are, however, two very good readers. The first of these (P. Williams and L. Chrisman, eds., *Colonial Discourse and Post-Colonial Theory: A Reader* [New York: Columbia University Press, 1994]) focuses on theory, as a listing of its chapters readily reveals: "Theorizing Colonized Cultures and Anti-Colonial Resistance"; "Theorizing the West"; "Theorizing Gender"; "Theorizing Post-Coloniality: Intellectuals and Institutions"; "Theorizing Post-Coloniality: Discourse and Identity"; "Reading from Theory." The second (B. Ashcroft, G. Griffiths, and H. Tiffin, eds., *The Post-Colonial Studies Reader* [London: Routledge & Kegan Paul, 1995]) is organized according to themes, as again a listing of its chapters readily demonstrates: "Issues and Debates"; "Universality and Difference"; "Representation and Resistance"; "Postmodernism and Post-colonialism"; "Nationalism"; "Hybridity"; "Ethnicity and Indigeneity"; "Feminism and Post-colonialism"; "Language"; "The Body and Performance"; "History"; "Place"; "Education"; "Production and Consumption." There are also two excellent studies of literary production in the postcolonial context, both with an emphasis on the anglophone world of the former British Empire: B. Ashcroft, G. Griffiths, and H. Tiffin, eds., *The Empire Writes Back: Theory and Practice in Post-colonial Literatures* (London: Routledge & Kegan Paul, 1989); and E. Boehmer, *Colonial and Postcolonial Literature: Migrant Metaphors* (Oxford: Oxford University Press, 1995).

[2] I can no longer describe myself solely as a biblical critic, despite my specific hiring, assignment, and location in a department of New Testament and Early Christianity within the context of the highly compartmentalized academic divisions of a graduate department of religion based in a liberal Protestant divinity school. At the very least, I must now describe myself as a constructive theologian

[continued]

OPTION FOR A POSTCOLONIAL OPTIC

This is not the first time that I have had recourse to the language and concepts of postcolonial studies. Indeed, I have done so in the past both as a biblical critic and as a constructive theologian. I should like to recall such previous appeals as a point of departure for the present proposal regarding the adoption of a systematic and fully fledged postcolonial optic:[3]

First, from the point of view of my work in biblical criticism, I have described (see chapters 1 and 2) the development of biblical criticism from its beginning as an academic discipline in the early nineteenth century through to its formation at the end of the twentieth century as a process of "liberation" and "decolonization." The development itself involved the sequential emergence of four paradigms or umbrella models of interpretation: (1) the initial turn to and long reign of historical criticism, from early in the nineteenth century through the third quarter of the twentieth century; (2) the rapid rise and steady consolidation of literary criticism and cultural or social criticism, beginning in the mid-1970s and continuing right through the present; (3) the recent irruption of cultural studies, beginning in the late 1980s and early 1990s. This development, I further argued, resulted in the present stage of competing modes of discourse within the discipline. Finally, such historical development and disciplinary

---

as well, not only because I presently regard the traditional distinction between critic and theologian as having altogether collapsed, but also because I see myself as engaged in the task of discoursing about the "this-world" and the "other-world" in the light of my own sociocultural and sociohistorical context in the diaspora, both as a child of the non-Western World and a child of a minority group within the West. Indeed, in the end, I would have to describe myself further as a cultural critic, insofar as I am also interested in these various dimensions of my social context quite aside from their socioreligious aspect. From this point of view, I am quite in agreement with the view that the call of the minority scholar is to engage in academic border crossings (see A. R. JanMohamed and D. Lloyd, "Introduction: Towards a Theory of Minority Discourse: What Is to Be Done?," in *The Nature and Context of Minority Discourse*, ed. A. R. JanMohamed and D. Lloyd [Oxford: Oxford University Press, 1990], 1-16).

[3] Within the model of postcolonial studies, terminology itself proves quite varied and thus problematic. Suffice it to say for now that by *postcolonial* I mean ideological reflection on the discourse and practice of imperialism and colonialism from the vantage point of a situation where imperialism and colonialism have come—by and large, though by no means altogether so—to a formal end, but remain very much at work, in practice, as neoimperialism and neocolonialism. Thus, the postcolonial optic is a field of vision forged in the wake of imperialism and colonialism but still very much conscious of their continuing, even if transformed, power.

dénouement I classified in terms of "liberation" and "decolonization" on two grounds.

First, with reference to a fundamental transformation in theoretical orientation and reading strategy. In the process, I pointed out, the long-dominant construct of the scientific reader—the universal, objective, and impartial reader, fully decontextualized and non-ideological—yielded slowly but surely to the construct of the real reader—the local, perspectival, and interested reader, always contextualized and ideological. Second, with reference to a fundamental transformation in the ranks of the discipline. In the process, I further pointed out, the male, clerical, and European/Euro-American faces and concerns of the traditional practitioners of biblical criticism gave way, again gradually but steadily, to a variety of faces and concerns previously unknown to the discipline: at first, a large infusion of women from the West; subsequently, a growing presence of women and men from outside the West as well as from non-Western minorities in the West.

The end result of such transformations was not only enormous diversity in method and theory but also enormous diversity in faces and concerns within the discipline. This combined explosion of disciplinary perspectives and interpretive voices, I concluded, could and should be seen as a veritable process of liberation and decolonization: a movement away from the European and Euro-American voices and perspectives that had dominated biblical criticism for so long toward a much more diversified and multicentered conception and exercise of the discipline. Biblical criticism, I observed, had become in the process but another example of a much more comprehensive process of liberation and decolonization at work in a number of different realms—from the political to the academic and, within the academy itself, across the entire disciplinary spectrum.

Second, from the point of view of my work in constructive theology, I have described the recent emergence of contextual theologies, both in the Two-Thirds World and among minorities of non-Western origin in the West, as an exercise in "liberation" and "decolonization."[4] Thus, in setting out to formulate, as a distinctive expression within the rich matrix of U.S. Hispanic American theology, a theology of the diaspora—a theology born and forged in exile, in displacement and relocation—I characterized it as both a liberation and a postcolonial theology.[5]

---

[4] F. F. Segovia, "Two Places and No Place on Which to Stand: Mixture and Otherness in Hispanic American Theology," in *Hispanic Americans in Theology and the Church*, ed. F. F. Segovia (Special issue of *Listening: Journal of Religion and Culture* 27 [1992]: 26-27).

[5] F. F. Segovia, "Aliens in the Promised Land: The Manifest Destiny of U. S. Hispanic American Theology" and "In the World but Not of It: Exile as a Locus for a Theology of the Diaspora," in *Hispanic/Latino Theology: Challenge and Promise*, ed. A. M. Isasi-Díaz and F. F. Segovia (Minneapolis: Fortress Press, 1996), 21-31 and 195-200, respectively.

Modern Christian theology, I argued, was a theology that emanated from the center, grounded as it was in Western civilization. As such, certain fundamental traits could be readily outlined. It was a systematic and universal theology, altogether reticent about its own social location and perspective; a theology of enlightenment and privilege, tacitly considered by nature superior to any theological production from outside the West—past, present, or future; a theology of hegemony and mission, with the effective control and progressive civilization of the margins in mind. In contrast, I further argued, diaspora theology—like any other contextual theology—was a theology that emerged from the margins, in this case from the margins within the West itself. Consequently, certain fundamental traits could be readily delineated as well. It was a self-consciously local and constructive theology, quite forthcoming about its own social location and perspective; a theology of diversity and pluralism, highlighting the dignity and value of all matrices and voices, including its own; a theology of engagement and dialogue, committed to critical conversation with other theological voices from both margins and center alike.

The rapid and widespread rise of contextual theologies, such as U.S. Hispanic American theology and my own theology of the diaspora, I concluded, could and should be seen as an undeniable process of "liberation" and "decolonization": a movement away from the longstanding control of theological production by European and Euro-American voices and perspectives toward the retrieval and revalorization of the full multiplicity of voices and perspectives in the margins. As in the case of biblical criticism, therefore, theological studies, I observed, had also become in the process yet another example of the much more extensive process of liberation and decolonization at work in the world and in the academy.

Such past appeals on my part to the linguistic and conceptual apparatus of postcolonial studies have been, though quite useful and revealing to be sure, much too limited and unsystematic as well. A more fundamental grounding and deployment of the model is in order, therefore, and it is precisely this task that I should like to undertake in the present chapter, with biblical criticism specifically in mind. I do so, once again, because of the rich hermeneutical and personal dividends that I see as accruing from an explicit and sustained use of the model.

On the one hand, as I indicated earlier, this is a model that lends itself eminently to simultaneous application across the various dimensions that I see as central to my own conception and exercise of the discipline: first, the level of texts—the analysis of the texts of ancient Judaism and early Christianity; second, the level of "texts"—the analysis of readings and interpretations of such texts in the modern, Western tradition; third, the level of readers—the analysis of the modern and contemporary real readers of these texts and producers of the "texts" both inside and outside the West. In other words, postcolonial studies can function thereby as an excellent model for crosscultural studies in the discipline, and, in what follows,

I shall show how such is the case in terms of these three major dimensions of the discipline.

On the other hand, as I also stated earlier, this is a model that proves extremely appealing to me personally. The reason, I would readily acknowledge, has to do with my own social location and agenda. I come from the margins, from the world of the colonized; I reside in the center, in the world of the colonizers; and I have devoted myself to the struggle for liberation and decolonization, for the sake of both the colonized and the colonizer. For me, therefore, postcolonial studies not only comes from the heart, so to speak, but it also refreshes and invigorates the heart. A colonial genealogy is in order.

The history of my own colonial mapping is quite complex. To begin with, I am a child of the Caribbean Basin, one of the most highly colonized and contested sites of the globe, as both the almost total absence of indigenous peoples and the presence of anglophone, francophone, and hispanophone populations readily attest. Here the project of imperialism and colonialism was so immensely successful and so radically effective that, in a relatively brief period of time, the original local populations had disappeared and the original local languages had been replaced. Indeed, in the Caribbean archipelago one has to go almost island by island to explain the imperial and colonial dynamics at work over the five centuries since the European "discovery." Then, with emigration and exile, a further distinguishing mark of the Caribbean Basin, I became a child of the diaspora, a part of the Hispanic American reality and experience in the United States, a context of internal colonialism not unlike that facing other groups from outside the West now residing in the West.[6]

In my own case, therefore, as a native of the island of Cuba and an exile-immigrant in the United States, such mapping entails four distinctive experiences of imperialism and colonialism: (1) the aftereffects of possession by the Spanish Empire, from the very beginning of its landfall in "the Americas" to the very demise of the empire itself—from the first voyage of Christopher Columbus to the Spanish-American War (1492-1898); (2) the continuing effects of occupation by the American Empire at the very apex of its period of manifest destiny (1898-1902), followed by the period of the republic (1902-59), a period of neocolonial dependency marked by the watchful supervision of the United States, a number of military interventions by U.S. forces, and a series of cruel and corrupt dictatorships—from the declaration of independence to the triumph of the Cuban Revolution; (3) the new effects from the implantation of a socialist-Leninist system of government at the very height of the Cold War, under the neocolonial aegis of the Soviet Empire (1959-89), followed by the continuation of such a system of government even after the total

---

[6] Segovia, "Two Places and No Place on Which to Stand," 27-33; idem, "Aliens in the Promised Land," 21-31.

collapse of the imperial center (1989–present); (4) the situation of internal colonialism affecting by and large the Hispanic American population as a whole in the United States.

In the light of such a long and distinguished pedigree, it should come as no surprise that I regard and construct myself as carrying imperialism and colonialism in my flesh and in my soul, as a human subject and as a real, flesh-and-blood reader—and hence as a biblical critic, as a constructive theologian, and as a cultural critic. For me, therefore, the reality of empire—of imperialism and colonialism—constitutes an omnipresent, inescapable, and overwhelming reality. My option for a postcolonial optic should thus be obvious: it is a model that I find most helpful, most revealing, and most liberating. In what follows, therefore, I proceed to unpack its particular importance and relevance for biblical criticism.

POSTCOLONIAL STUDIES AND BIBLICAL CRITICISM

Postcolonial studies is a model that takes the reality of empire—of imperialism and colonialism—as an omnipresent, inescapable, and overwhelming reality in the world: the world of antiquity, the world of the Near East or of the Mediterranean Basin; the world of modernity, the world of Western hegemony and expansionism; and the world of today, of postmodernity, the world of postcolonialism on the part of the Two-Thirds World and of neocolonialism on the part of the West.

Postcolonial Studies and Ancient Texts

A first dimension of a postcolonial optic in biblical criticism involves an analysis of the texts of ancient Judaism and early Christianity that takes seriously into consideration their broader sociocultural contexts in the Near East and the Mediterranean Basin, respectively, in the light of an omnipresent, inescapable, and overwhelming sociopolitical reality—the reality of empire, of imperialism and colonialism, as variously constituted and exercised during the long period in question. Some preliminary observations regarding this phenomenon of empire are in order.[7]

First, the reality of empire should be seen as a structural reality that is largely defined and practiced in terms of a primary binomial opposition:

---

[7] For good, concise introductions to the phenomenon of imperialism and colonialism in general, see E. Said, "Yeats and Decolonization," in *Nationalism, Colonialism, and Literature*, ed. S. Deane (Minneapolis: University of Minnesota Press, 1990), 69-95; idem, *Culture and Imperialism* (New York: Alfred A. Knopf, 1994), 3-61; S. Deane, "Imperialism and Nationalism," in *Critical Terms for Literary Study*, ed. F. L. Lentricchia and T. McLaughlin, 2d ed. enl. (Chicago: University of Chicago Press, 1994), 354-68.

on the one hand, a political, economic, and cultural center—more often than not symbolized by a city; on the other hand, any number of margins politically, economically, and culturally subordinated to the center. This grounding binomial entails and engenders, in turn, any number of secondary or subordinate binomials: civilized/uncivilized; advanced/primitive; cultured/barbarian; progressive/backward; developed/undeveloped-underdeveloped.

Second, such a structural reality, despite the many and profound similarities in common, should not be seen as uniform in every imperial context across time and culture—say, for example, from the world of Assyria and Babylon, to the world of Greece and Rome, to the world of Western Europe and the United States—but as differentiated in constitution and deployment, though again with many and profound similarities in common.

Third, this reality, I would argue, is of such reach and such power that it inevitably affects and colors, directly or indirectly, the entire artistic production of center and margins, of dominant and subaltern, including their respective literary productions.

From the point of view of ancient Judaism and its literature, it is necessary to speak not just of one empire but of a succession of empires involving, depending on the locality of the center in question, the Near East as well as the Mediterranean Basin: Assyria, Babylon, Persia, Greece, Rome. From the point of view of early Christianity and its literature, it is obviously the massive presence and might of the Roman Empire, master and lord of the entire Circum-Mediterranean, with its thoroughly accurate if enormously arrogant classification of the Mediterranean Sea as *mare nostrum*.

To begin with, therefore, the shadow of empire in the production of ancient texts is to be highlighted. A number of key questions come to the fore as a result: How do the margins look at the "world"—a world dominated by the reality of empire—and fashion life in such a world? How does the center regard and treat the margins in the light of its own view of the "world" and life in that world? What images and representations of the other-world arise from either side? How is history conceived and constructed by both sides? How is "the other" regarded and represented? What conceptions of oppression and justice are to be found? From the perspective of postcolonial studies, such questions—questions of culture, ideology, and power—emerge as crucial.

Postcolonial Studies and Modern Readings

A second dimension of the proposed postcolonial optic in biblical criticism involves an analysis of the readings and interpretations of the texts of Jewish and Christian antiquity that takes seriously into account their broader sociocultural context in the West, whether by way of Europe or

North America, in the light of the same omnipresent, inescapable, and overwhelming sociopolitical reality that surrounded the production of the texts of ancient Judaism and early Christianity—the reality of empire, of imperialism and colonialism, now with regard to the Western imperial tradition of the last five hundred years.

First, the imperial tradition of the West may be approached in terms of three different phases and periods:[8] (1) early imperialism, with reference to the initial, mercantile phase of European imperialism—from the fifteenth century through most of the nineteenth century, from the monarchical states of Portugal and Spain to the early modern states of England, France, and the Netherlands, among others; (2) high imperialism, involving monopoly capitalism with its integration of industrial and finance capital in the major capitalist nation-states—from the end of the nineteenth century through the middle of the twentieth century, with England as prime example; and (3) late imperialism, with reference to both the end of formal colonialism and the continued impact and power of imperial culture in the world—from the middle of the twentieth century to the present, with the United States as its prime example.

Second, this tradition of Western empire-building was accompanied by a very prominent socioreligious dimension as well. Thus, the Western missionary movement may be divided into two major waves and periods, represented by the highly symbolic dates of 1492 and 1792.[9] The first date stands, of course, for the first European landfall in the "New World." This first stage of the missions (1492-1792) was primarily Catholic in orientation, involved the massive evangelization of the Americas, and found itself near exhaustion by the end of the eighteenth century. The second date, not as well-known, recalls two different though related events: first, with regard to Asia (India), the publication of William Carey's *Enquiry into the Obligation of Christians to Use Means for the Propagation of the Gospel among the Heathens* and concomitant formation of his missionary society; second, with regard to Africa (Sierra Leone), the establishment of the first church in tropical Africa in modern times (interestingly enough, by people of African birth or descent from North America). This second stage (1792–present) was at first primarily Protestant in nature, concerned the massive evangelization of Africa, Asia, and remaining areas of the Americas, and remains quite vigorous today. Over the last five

---

[8] I find myself in agreement with the caution offered for postcolonial studies in general by M. Sprinker ("Introduction," in *Late Imperial Culture*, ed. R. de la Campa, E. A. Kaplan and M. Sprinkler [London: Verso, 1996], 1-10), who insists on the need to offer and follow a historical periodization of the different types of imperialism at work in the West over this period of five centuries.

[9] I follow here the thesis of A. Walls, "Christianity in the Non-Western World: A Study in the Serial Nature of Christian Expansion," *Studies in World Christianity* 1 (1995): 1-25.

centuries, therefore, the different phases of European imperialism and colonialism brought with them, wherever they turned, their respective religious beliefs and practices, whether Catholic or Protestant.

Third, a comparison of this twofold division of the missionary movement of the West with the previous threefold division of Western imperialism proves instructive. On the one hand, the first missionary wave of the fifteenth through the eighteenth centuries coincides with the first imperialist phase—the mercantile stage of early imperialism; on the other hand, the second missionary wave of the nineteenth and twentieth centuries coincides with the transition from the first to the second imperialist phase in the nineteenth century and its full bloom at the end of the nineteenth century and the beginning of the twentieth—the monopoly, capitalist stage of high imperialism.

As such, the structural binomial reality of empire should be seen as involving a strong socioreligious component as well. The political, economic, and cultural center also functions as a religious center; that is to say, the practices and beliefs of the center are invariably grounded on, sanctioned, and accompanied by a set of religious beliefs and practices. Consequently, the primary binomial of center and margins entails and engenders a further binomial in this sphere as well—believers/unbelievers-pagans—which in turn gives rise to a number of other secondary and subordinate binomials, such as godly/ungodly (worshipers of the true God/worshipers of false gods) and religious/idolatrous-superstitious. As a result, the margins politically, economically, and culturally subordinated to the center must be brought into religious submission as well: their religious beliefs must be corrected and uplifted; their gods attacked and destroyed; their practices ridiculed and replaced.

Finally, such a reality, I would argue once again, further colors and affects, directly or indirectly, the entire artistic production of both center and margins, the dominant and the subaltern, including their respective literary productions.

From the point of view of biblical criticism, therefore, it is clear that the academic study of the texts of ancient Judaism and early Christianity, given the formation and consolidation of the discipline in the course of the nineteenth century, parallels the second major wave of the Western missionary movement as well as the transition period to the second, high phase of Western imperialism and colonialism: first, as Europe turns to Africa and Asia, in a renewed and frantic scramble for territories and possessions; second, as the United States turns West and beyond, with its eyes increasingly set on the islands of the Caribbean, the heart of Mexico, and territories in the Pacific.

Consequently, the shadow of empire in the production of modern readings of the ancient texts should also be underlined. In the process, certain crucial questions again come to the surface, not unlike those raised earlier but now from a different angle: How do such readings and interpretations, coming from the metropolitan centers of the West as they do, address and present such issues in the ancient texts as empire and margins, oppression and justice; the world and life in the world as well as the other-world and its inhabitants; history and "the other," mission and conversion, followers and outsiders; salvation, election, and holiness? Once again, from the point of view of postcolonial studies, questions such as these—questions of culture, ideology, and power—prove all-important.

Postcolonial Studies and Readers

For this third dimension of the proposed postcolonial optic in biblical criticism, I would argue once more for an analysis of the readers of the texts of ancient Judaism and early Christianity that takes seriously into consideration their broader sociocultural contexts in the global sphere, whether in the West or outside the West, in the light of the same omnipresent, inescapable, and overwhelming sociopolitical reality that engulfed the texts of Jewish and Christian antiquity as well as the readings and interpretations of such texts in the West—the reality of empire, of imperialism and colonialism, now in terms of not only the Western imperial tradition of the last five centuries but also the reaction against such a tradition from outside the West within the context of the postcolonial yet neocolonial world of the last half-century. Some preliminary observations are once again in order.

First, despite what I have described as its omnipresent, inescapable, and overwhelming character, the structural binomial reality of imperialism and colonialism is never imposed or accepted in an atmosphere of absolute and undisturbed passivity. Always in the wake of the fundamental binomial of center/margins and ultimately deconstructing it as well, in principle if not in praxis, lies the inverted binomial of resistance/fear. I say inverted because this is the one binomial opposition where the margins actually take the initiative, while the center is forced into a reactive position.

In effect, there is always—sooner or later, major or minor, explicit or implicit—resistance to the center on the part of the politically, economically, culturally, and religiously subordinated margins, even when such resistance brings about, as it inevitably does, further measures of control on the part of the center, designed to instill fear into the minds and hearts of the margins. Such measures, to be sure, only serve to contribute to a further deconstruction of the binomial reality, as the civilized, advanced, cultured, progressive, developed, and believing center turns increasingly to measures of an uncivilized, primitive, barbarian, backward, undeveloped, and unbelieving order against the marginal groups. At some point, such resistance on the part of the margins may come to a climax, and this climax may involve in turn a variety of gradations: open challenge and defiance; widespread rebellion and anomie; actual overthrow and reorientation.

Second, I would argue that such resistance is precisely what has occurred in the discipline in the last quarter of the century, as more and more outsiders have joined its ranks. Such outsiders can be classified according to two groupings: women from the West; and men and women from outside the West as well as from ethnic and racial minorities in the West. In both cases a similar pattern of resistance can be observed: early stirrings in the 1970s—what could be called a situation of open challenge and defiance; maturation and solidification through the 1980s—a clear situation of widespread rebellion and anomie; sharpened sophistication in the 1990s—what could be compared to a situation of actual overthrow and reorientation.

Third, it should not go unobserved that such disciplinary changes took place not long after the commencement of the third major phase of Western imperialism and colonialism, marked by the end of formal colonialism, with wars of independence and the loss of colonies everywhere—the age of the postcolonial, and the continued impact of imperial culture everywhere—the age of the neocolonial. More specifically, such developments, one should recall, came soon after the crisis experienced by the West, both in Europe and North America, during the late 1960s and the early 1970s. Quite clearly, the upheaval in the world at large ultimately affects the discipline as well.

Finally, such a reality, I would argue yet again, does affect and color as well, directly or indirectly, the entire artistic production of center and margins, dominant and subaltern, including their respective literary productions.

From the point of view of biblical critics, then, it now becomes necessary to distinguish between two general groupings: On the one hand, those readers associated with the long imperial tradition of the West, especially from the time of transition to high imperialism to the present phase of neocolonialism within late imperialism—still the vast majority of critics; on the other hand, those critics associated with the colonies of the Western empires, what has come to be known as the Two-Thirds World, now raising their voices for the first time during the present phase of postcolonialism within late imperialism—a growing minority of critics.

Therefore, the shadow of empire in the lives of modern as well as contemporary readers must, yet again, be highlighted in biblical criticism. In so doing, a number of crucial questions come to the fore, similar to those outlined before but formulated from yet another angle of approach: How do traditional (male) critics, from the metropolitan centers of the West, stand—and construct them-"selves"—with regard to the relationship between empire and margins, the West and the rest, Christendom and outsiders; mission and conversion, oppression and justice, history and the other; salvation, election, and holiness; the this-world and life in the world as well as the other-world? What is the position of Western women in this regard, in their role as previous outsiders from the West itself? How do men and women from outside the West as well as from ethnic and racial minorities in the West respond to such issues? Such questions—questions of culture, ideology, and power—emerge as all-important from the point of view of postcolonial studies.

CONCLUDING COMMENTS

From the point of view of cultural studies, that paradigm within which I presently situate myself in the discipline, the model of postcolonial studies should be seen as one major line of approach, alongside others. Such a line of approach, furthermore, should also be seen as quite broad and quite rich—multidimensional, multicentered, multilingual. Not only is its theoretical apparatus immense and its range of reading strategies phenomenal, as reflected in the exploding corpus of critical literature, but also its scope and its reach prove to be radically global as well, drawing as it does on the discourses and practices of imperialism and colonialism across cultures and historical periods.

In the introduction I remarked that, as a model within cultural studies—an intermediate model within an umbrella model, as it were—postcolonial studies proves most appropriate, most enlightening, and most fruitful. The reasons should now be evident.

First, the model is not only thoroughly self-conscious of itself as a construct, dependent upon certain theoretical claims and reading strategies, but also calls for self-consciousness on the part of its would-be practitioners as constructs, dependent upon certain representations of themselves, of their own social locations and agendas, as real readers. Both with regard to interpretation and interpreters, therefore, the model presupposes and demands a specific optic with clear implications for both the representation of the past and the representation of the present.

Second, the model can address at one and the same time the various interrelated and interdependent dimensions of criticism: the analysis of texts—the world of antiquity; the analysis of "texts"—the world of modernity; the analysis of readers of texts and producers of "texts"—the world of postmodernity.

Finally, the model is profoundly ideological, for it looks upon the political experience of imperialism and colonialism as central to the task of criticism at all levels of inquiry.

In the end, however, as a model within cultural studies, postcolonial studies has no choice but to see itself and represent itself as *unus inter pares*; otherwise, it could easily turn into an imperial discourse of its own. It is an optic, not *the* optic, in full engagement and dialogue with a host of other models and other optics. Yet, even as one among equals, it proves most incisive and most telling, for it reminds us all, the children of the colonized and the children of the colonizer, that the discipline of biblical criticism as we know it and have known it must be seen and analyzed, like all other discourses of modernity, against the much broader geopolitical context of Western imperialism and colonialism. In so doing, furthermore, the goal is not merely one of analysis and description, but rather one of transformation: the struggle for "liberation" and "decolonization."

6

Notes toward Refining
the Postcolonial Optic

I should like to preface my remarks with a word of gratitude as well as a word of commendation to the members of the panel: gratitude, on the one hand, for their kind willingness to undertake the critical review of this volume, always a demanding and time-consuming task; commendation, on the other hand, for having done so in such a thorough, elegant, and well-meaning fashion.[1] It is from critique that one always stands to learn the most, and ever more so if such critique is formulated with care, decorum, and goodwill. This you have all done in eminent fashion, and, in so doing, you have forced me to think, both as contributor to the volume and as editor of the series, and for this I am always most grateful. Indeed, it is on the basis of such reflections that I have entitled these remarks of mine as I have, thereby picking up on the title of chapter 5 and signaling the need for ongoing refinement in the theorization and formulation of this interpretive project.

THE QUESTION OF NOMENCLATURE

I must begin with a critical comment of my own regarding the term "postcolonial" itself, as found, for example, in both the title of the volume *(The Postcolonial Bible)* and the field of studies in question (post-

---

[1] This chapter was a response to the review panel of *The Postcolonial Bible* (R. S. Sugirtharajah, ed., The Bible and Postcolonialism Series 1 [Sheffield: Sheffield Academic Press, 1998]) that took place at the 1998 AAR-SBL Annual Meeting in Orlando, Florida, in a featured session organized by the Bible in Africa, Asia, the Caribbean, and Latin America Section. The panel's reviews appeared in the *Journal for the Study of the New Testament* 74 (1999): 113-21.

colonial studies).[2] It is a designation that I have commonly used, but that I also find increasingly problematic. I have availed myself of it, within the context of ideological criticism and what I have come to call cultural studies,[3] to signify the realm of the geopolitical—the relationship between center and periphery, the imperial and the colonial, on a global political scale. This relationship I see as encompassing both social reality and cultural reality, that is, social formation as well as cultural production. At the same time, I find it no longer an altogether proper designation for all that the sphere of the geopolitical implies and entails. In other words, as a signifier I regard it as much too restrictive for all of the signified, all of the critical activity, that I see as falling within its compass.

To begin with, one can and should distinguish between "imperialism" and "colonialism," with their respective discourses.[4] One can and should further distinguish between these discourses and their corresponding counterparts, "anti-imperialism" and "anti-colonialism." Lastly, one can and should distinguish as well among different stages or periods within such discourses, with their resultant subdiscourses: "pre-imperialism" and "pre-colonialism"; "imperialism" and "colonialism" proper; "post-imperialism" and "post-colonialism"; "neo-imperialism" and "neo-colonialism." At this point, I readily confess, I have no substitute to offer with which I would find myself completely at ease, although I do find the expression "imperial-colonial" (as in imperial-colonial studies) more and more attractive. The hyphenated juxtaposition of these more abstract terms can, in my opinion, more accurately convey the various critical activities and subdiscourses at work, certainly far more so than "postcolonial," which in the end amounts to a not very helpful and perhaps even confusing example of synecdoche.

Even then, I would hasten to point out, in employing all such categories one continues to view the reality and experience of the periphery—as the various prefixes (pre-; post-; neo-) and qualifiers (proper) themselves make clear—with reference to the center and hence in terms of external intervention, domination, and oppression. As a result, the role of the center

---

[2] Actually, I would argue that the term as applied to the volume is not quite proper. My preference would have been to reserve such a designation to an actual commentary on the Bible from this perspective. Indeed, I would point out that this was not the original title intended for the volume. That was to have been, as specified in the original prospectus for the series, *The Bible and Post-colonial Criticism*, a far more acceptable description of its character and goal.

[3] See chap. 2 in this present volume.

[4] The question of nomenclature in this regard is extremely complex. I myself favor the use of "imperialism" to refer to all that pertains to the center and of "colonialism" to mark all that pertains to the periphery. For a similar position, see A. Loomba, *Colonialism/Postcolonialism*, The New Critical Idiom (New York: Routledge, 1998), 1-19.

continues to be privileged over that of the periphery. While this is perhaps inevitable given the highly unequal, long-lasting, and totalizing nature of the relationship in question, I should very much like to think otherwise. For now, however, I must limit myself to the question of nomenclature—whether the term "postcolonial" is appropriate and, if not, what is to be substituted in its place—and leave to another time the question of a more autochthonous definition on the part of the periphery. Nonetheless, given the still-tentative nature of my position on this point, I shall continue to employ the term "postcolonial" in what follows.

READING THE RESPONSES

With this reservation in mind, I turn to *The Postcolonial Bible* and the critical reviews. The volume itself is the first in a new series, The Bible and Postcolonialism, for which I have the honor of serving on the editorial board. As such, it represents an early attempt to bring together the fields of biblical studies and postcolonial studies.[5] A critique at this stage, therefore, is not only most welcome but also most useful, for such a critique can only serve to render the proposed dialogue between these two discourses more substantial, more sophisticated, and more fruitful. From this perspective, I see the responses as raising three main issues with regard to the project *as a whole*: (1) the question of pedagogy—teaching biblical studies in such a way that the postcolonial optic emerges as central rather than tangential to the enterprise; (2) the question of solidarity—doing postcolonial analysis in biblical studies without losing sight of its commonalities and links with other discourses of resistance and emancipation; (3) the question of applicability—deploying the postcolonial optic in biblical studies in a way that is keenly mindful of the differences between and among historical contexts and imperial/cultural formations.

Of these the most radical challenge to the project comes from the last point, raised by Professor David Jobling. Since it is the most fundamental, it is the one that requires the most attention, and so it is on this issue of applicability that I shall focus in my reflections. I begin with a reformulation of its basic premise, continue with a contextualization of this premise, and then turn to the beginnings of a response to the challenge in question. By way of conclusion, I deal briefly with the other two issues of solidarity and pedagogy.

---

[5] To the best of my knowledge, *Semeia* 73 represents the first such attempt (L. Donaldson, ed., *Postcolonialism and Scriptural Reading* [Atlanta: Scholars Press, 1998]).

Challenge of Applicability

Basic Premise

The premise for this challenge consists of a variation, formulated in the Marxist tradition, on the classic argument from historical distance, with reference to the "gulf" or "chasm" said to exist between the world of the past, the world of biblical antiquity, and the world of the present, the world of contemporary interpretation. Professor Jobling notes the crucial importance of the concept of mode of production in Marxist theory: not only does a mode of production frame all praxis and all theory in a society, but also a shift in mode of production changes all theory and all praxis, indeed, "down to the meaning of words." Such a phrase obviously comprehends the words of the Bible itself and raises immediately the problematic of interpretation. In effect, while the Bible was produced under one mode of production, that of tribute-slavery, we find ourselves at present under a very different mode of production, that of late capitalism. The question of applicability is sharply foregrounded as a result. In general terms, How can the Bible speak to our world? In specific terms, What can the Bible have to say to us with respect to matters of imperialism and colonialism? As Professor Jobling puts it, what sort of thing is the Bible in postcolonial analysis? A proper response, he argues, must go beyond simple links in the form of ahistorical analogues and must involve instead a complex process of historical comparison and translation. This sort of work, he concludes, is simply not to be found in this first volume of the Bible and Postcolonialism series, to its detriment.

Premise in Context

Two observations are in order with regard to this argument from historical distance. First, one should keep in mind that its theoretical framework is that of traditional Marxist theory, with its view of history in the grand style, as objective, comprehensive and teleological, and its distinction between material base and superstructure. Second, one should also keep in mind the raging debate between Marxist critics and postcolonial critics. From the Marxist perspective, postcolonial critics deal with the superstructure of imperialism while bypassing the question of its material base. In so doing, they argue, postcolonial critics remain throughout at the level of the cultural production of capitalism and fail in the process to affect its social formation in any significant way. From the postcolonial perspective, Marxist critics fail to recognize any social difference other than that of socioeconomic class (relationship to the mode of production). Thus, they argue, Marxist critics ignore altogether the highly negative stance of the West toward its "others," following the example of Marx himself, who affirmed the need for the primitive world outside the West to undergo development so that the worldwide revolution of the proletariat could ensue as envisioned. In the end, Marxist critics can and do accuse postcolonial critics of succumbing to the ideology of late capitalism, just as postcolonial critics can and do accuse Marxist critics of falling prey to the ideology of racism present at the heart of the West.

I see the challenge of applicability as raised by Professor Jobling as falling well within the parameters of this ongoing debate between Marxist critics and postcolonial critics. Thus, in the face of this beginning application of postcolonial analysis to biblical studies, Professor Jobling argues that postcolonial critics must take into account not just cultural production in the Bible but also the material base or social formation of the Bible, and must do so according to the grand-scale model of successive modes of production in history, if such dialogue is to be at all productive; this, he contends, they have failed to do thus far.

Notes toward a Response

Needless to say, this challenge to the postcolonial project in biblical studies as represented by *The Postcolonial Bible* deserves far more time and space than the present response allows. In fact, it deserves far more reflection than I can, from a theoretical point of view, devote to it at this time. What I can do, however, is to offer a set of "notes" toward such a response, with the theoretical refinement of this postcolonial project in mind, a task that I regard as both necessary and ongoing.

A first note concerns the force of the argument from distance as such, regardless of theoretical framework. I would respond in both the affirmative and the negative. I do so, moreover, from the point of view of postmodernist historiography.[6] On the one hand, I would argue that two "texts" of any length or sort, from across historical or cultural distances, can be brought together in dialogue to see what sparks are generated in the process. Such a view would rest on the postmodernist conception of all models of comparison as constructions and thus as arbitrary.[7] On the other hand, I would argue that one can proceed to compare "texts," again of any length or sort, by paying close attention to issues of historical and cultural distance. Such a view could rest on any number of theoretical frameworks, as in the present case of an appeal to Marxist historiography and its concept of mode of production, though again, from a postmodernist perspective, I would regard all such models as constructs. With regard to the classic argument from distance, therefore, I see myself as able to go in either direction, depending on the purpose for so doing at the time of the

---

[6] For an excellent analysis of the impact of postmodernism on historiography in general, both in terms of history as metanarrative and history as pointilist, see K. Jenkins, "Introduction: On Being Open about Our Closures," in *The Postmodern History Reader*, ed. K. Jenkins (New York: Routledge, 1997), 1-30.

[7] On this point, see A. K. M. Adam, *What Is Postmodernist Biblical Criticism?*, Guides to Biblical Scholarship: New Testament Series (Minneapolis: Fortress Press, 1995), 61-71.

exercise. For the most part, however, I confess that I favor a preservation of a sense of distance as a way of trying to safeguard what I call the otherness of the text.[8]

The second note has to do with the reach of the proposed postcolonial optic and thus with the particular insistence of the Marxist model on matters socioeconomic. I would hold that such an optic should encompass both social reality and cultural reality, and thus demands an analysis of the forces that shape social formation as well as of the representations that emerge in cultural production.

Two further observations are in order. First, while the ideal in such analysis would be to undertake both sorts of investigation at the same time and to the same degree, questions of expertise, time, or sheer preference may drive any one critic in one direction or the other. From this perspective, one pursuit emerges as important as the other. Second, such analysis involves, whether at the level of society or of culture, attention to a variety of dimensions, among which the socioeconomic is certainly most important but neither unique nor necessarily primary. Once again, however, questions of expertise, time, or sheer preference may lead the critic in one particular dimension or another. From this perspective one focus is as important as the other. I would only add that, from a postmodernist perspective, social formation and cultural production should by no means be seen as poles of a dichotomy, since in the end social formation can only be addressed and analyzed by way of representation in cultural production.

A third note addresses the possibility of comparative studies with regard to imperial and colonial formations from different times and/or different places and is thus related to the first note above. A spectrum of logical positions comes readily to mind:

At one end, one can argue that each imperial and colonial formation is utterly unique, so much so that no comparison is possible or valid across history and/or culture. From this point of view, one can no more compare, say, the British Empire of the twentieth century with its contemporary counterparts in Japan, France, or the United States, than one can compare it with the Spanish and Portuguese empires of the fifteenth and sixteenth centuries or the Roman Empire of the first centuries. At the other end, one can argue that all imperial and colonial formations are basically the same regardless of history and/or culture. From this point of view, one can proceed to the task of comparison with confidence, whether that task concerns the British Empire and the Japanese, French, or U.S. empires of the twentieth century, the Spanish or Portuguese empires of

---

[8] On this point, see F. F. Segovia, "Toward a Hermeneutics of the Diaspora: A Hermeneutics of Otherness and Engagement," in *Reading from This Place*, vol. 1: *Social Location and Biblical Interpretation in the United States*, ed. F. F. Segovia and M. A. Tolbert (Minneapolis: Fortress Press, 1995), 57-73.

the fifteenth and sixteenth centuries, or the Roman Empire of the first centuries. Between these two poles, then, one would find any number of positions advocating a comparison mindful of similarities and differences between and among imperial and cultural formations, with varying degrees of emphasis on similarities or differences.

From a postmodernist perspective, and in keeping with my remarks of the first note, I would situate myself within the comparative side of the spectrum, not objecting to wholesale comparison across time and/or culture but favoring attention to similarities and differences between or among the various formations in question.

The fourth and final note involves the character and provenance of the study of antiquity and comes back in a roundabout way to the argument from distance. I would propose that the study of ancient imperial and colonial formations, such as those to be found in biblical antiquity, is not that removed, historically or culturally, from the study of recent imperial and colonial formations, since the study of antiquity has been the almost exclusive preserve, until quite recently, of the West. As such, it has been carried on and produced at the heart of its various imperial and colonial formations. Consequently, the study of the Bible and the study of the West cannot be easily separated or differentiated from one another.

Let the socioeconomic model of Marxism serve as an example in this regard. The very recourse on the part of Marxist theory to the concept of mode of production as a critical tool is a construct of the nineteenth century, neither conveyed nor demanded by the "data" for proper interpretation, yet applied by Marxist historiography on a grand scale to the study of antiquity in general and regarded by Professor Jobling as indispensable for proper historical comparison and translation with regard to the Bible. Its use, I would argue, reveals as much about the West as about antiquity, if not more. Indeed, from a postmodernist point of view, I would further argue, all methods and models as well as all recreations of meaning and reconstructions of history are constructions—and this includes all approaches to and all views of biblical antiquity, and its variety of imperial and colonial formations. In the end, therefore, while the historical "gulf" in question is quite profound, its representation is not, since all models for and accounts of such a "chasm" are either of recent or contemporary vintage, and unavoidably so.

Summary

Postcolonial studies and biblical studies may be brought together in dialogue with either scant or abundant reference to historical and cultural boundaries, with neither option to be posited as inherently better than the other but with the latter as favored. In such dialogue, first of all, the postcolonial optic should examine with the same vigor and thoroughness both the sociology and the culture of imperial and colonial formations. In such dialogue, furthermore, the postcolonial optic should not refrain from comparisons of imperial and colonial formations across time or culture, with neither open nor restricted comparison as inherently better, but with the latter as preferred. In the end, such dialogue actually brings together two discourses that are not that far apart, insofar as the study of imperial and colonial formations in antiquity arises and develops at the heart of the imperial and colonial formations of the West and thus represents constructs of the West, with as much to say about the West as about the Bible, if not more. In a very real sense, therefore, postcolonial studies and biblical studies constitute thoroughly interrelated and interdependent fields and discourses.

Challenges of Solidarity and Pedagogy

Solidarity

The proposed postcolonial optic in biblical studies is obviously a discourse of resistance and emancipation. It takes as its reading lens the geopolitical relationship between center and periphery, the imperial and the colonial, not only at the level of the text but also at the level of interpretation, of readings and readers of the text. It does so, moreover, with decolonization and liberation in mind, as it proceeds to highlight the periphery over the center and the colonial over the imperial. As a result, the question of its relationship to other discourses of resistance and emancipation in biblical studies—such as socioeconomic (Marxist) or feminist criticism—is inevitably and variously raised, always with the hope in mind of a collective practice of oppositional reading. Behind such hope, it seems to me, lies an underlying fear that the new optic may serve to disperse rather than strengthen the envisioned oppositional front, hence the call from various and different quarters for it to be mindful of its similarities and links with these other discourses. This is what I would refer to as the ideal of a cosmopolitics, a most worthy and most attractive endeavor indeed.

But a most problematic one as well. The project of resistance and emancipation, I would argue, should be seen not as uniform and harmonious but as multifaceted and conflictive, given the varied nature of domination and oppression, and thus as a dialogue between a global ideal (cosmopolitics) and a broad number of local ideals (micropolitics). From this perspective, the differences among the various discourses of resistance and emancipation are to be emphasized as much as the similarities, so that no one voice or stance is silenced or subsumed by others. In this regard, the focus of postcolonial analysis is clear: the geopolitical relationship between center and periphery, the imperial and the colonial, whether in antiquity or modernity or postmodernity. From this perspective, for example, neither the project of Marxism nor the project of feminism suffices in and of itself, since they both reflect their own origins in the West.

On the one hand, the ideal of socialism, lofty as it is, has to be critically examined. After all, the experience and reality of "real" socialism has been not only Marxist but also Leninist-Stalinist in orientation. Its record is clear, despite a longstanding and continuing romanticization of it on the part of a good many Western intellectuals. This record shows: (1) the solidification of an imperial-colonial formation as interventionist, controlling, and totalizing as any other, if not more—the Soviet Empire with Russia at its center and with surrounding spheres of colonial influence in Eastern Europe and beyond; (2) a policy of massive and systematic violations against human and social rights. From a postcolonial perspective, the historical track of real socialism is as imperial as that of any other geopolitical formation in the West.

On the other hand, the ideal of feminism, exalted as it is, has to be critically reviewed as well. In effect, the experience and reality of the women's movement has been not only feminist but also racist in orientation. The record is clear as well, as non-Western feminists have consistently pointed out: (1) a systematic bypassing, undervaluing, or dismissal of the experience and reality of both women in the non-Western world and non-Western women in the West; (2) an underlying attitude of racism toward men in the non-Western world or non-Western men within the West. From a postcolonial perspective, the historical track of "real" feminism is as prejudiced as that of any other social movement in the West.

In the end, I would argue, there is no self-evident project of resistance and emancipation for all in the periphery, although there may be quite self-evident projects for the various groups that comprise the periphery. The ideal of a cosmopolitics, therefore, is not one that can be advanced or defined by any one group, but rather one that has to be forged by all groups in question—a most challenging and demanding task. From a postcolonial perspective, such an ideal cannot do without the question of the geopolitical relationship between center and periphery. At the same time, this geopolitical ideal cannot dispense with either the factor of gender or that of class; socioeconomic and feminist criticism impinge upon it as much as it impinges upon them. In this regard, a clearing space is absolutely necessary at this point in time in which non-Westerners can dialogue with one another away from the eyes of the West, including those of Western feminists and those of Western Marxists.

I would only add by way of conclusion that I regard this conception of resistance and emancipation as a multidimensional and conflicted phenomenon as not at all debilitating but rather as liberating, insofar as it brings the issue of diversity to the fore, in itself a tremendous victory in the struggle of resistance and emancipation. Indeed, there is nothing more feared or disliked in any context of domination and oppression than the very possibility of diversity, of thinking and/or acting differently, away from the norm.

Pedagogy

The proposed postcolonial optic in biblical studies clearly demands, I would agree, a pedagogical vision to go hand in hand with its interpretive vision. Such a vision further demands, I would also agree, that this optic be central rather than tangential to the project. I would make but one comment. For such an optic to be central, it should be applied to both texts and their interpretation, the readings and readers of texts.[9]

CONCLUDING COMMENTS

I would conclude by reiterating that these reflections of mine represent but notes on the way toward a more ample and substantial response on my part to the challenges brought to the project of postcolonial criticism in biblical studies. For such reflections, brief and undeveloped as they are, I can only express, once again, my profound gratitude to the panel and their critical reviews. In forcing me to think as you have, you have provided me with an excellent point of departure for the goal of refining the conceptualization and verbalization of this project; as both editor and contributor, I stand in your debt.

---

[9] For a first step in the formulation of such a vision, see chap. 4 in this present volume.

PART IV

VOICES FROM OUTSIDE

7

My Personal Voice

The Making of a Postcolonial Critic

From the perspective of cultural studies, that umbrella model of interpretation within which I presently situate myself both outside and within
the field of biblical studies, the question of the personal voice—the voice
and role of the critic behind criticism, the historian behind historiography, the scholar behind scholarship—lies at the very heart of the critical
enterprise. Thus, Fred Inglis, one of its major exponents and proponents,
describes cultural studies as creative or imaginative thought with a focus
on human values.[1] To understand the centrality assigned to the personal
voice within such a framework, one would do well to recall the origins,
aims, and methods of cultural studies, and for this I draw on the fine
work of Inglis himself. This review will serve, in turn, as the basis for my
own reflections on the personal voice in biblical studies.

To begin with, cultural studies emerged as the result of a generational
revolt—at the height of the Cold War and with the student demonstra-
tions of 1968 as symbolic point of departure—against the established beliefs and practices of the human sciences.[2] This was a reaction driven,
inter alia, by a new generation's consciousness of a profoundly pluralistic

---

[1] F. Inglis, *Cultural Studies* (Oxford and Cambridge, Mass.: Blackwell Publishers, 1993), 3-24, 227-48.

[2] In 1968 I found myself rather safely ensconced in a seminary, pursuing studies toward ordination in the Roman Catholic Church. Nevertheless, while we in
no way resembled what was happening at Columbia University or the University
of California at Berkeley, much less what was happening in the streets of Paris, in
our own way we too felt and expressed this sense of generational frustration and
revolt. After all, these were the years that followed the conclusion of Vatican
Council II, when its many reforms of *aggiornamento* were beginning to be imple-
mented across the universal church. Such reforms touched the world of theological and ministerial education and occasioned many a battle between the old generation and the new generation.

world, concern for the entire spectrum and messiness of everyday life, commitment to all those human actors excluded from consideration, and a penchant for uncertainty in the face of metanarratives or grand theories. As such, cultural studies set out to restore a balance between spontaneity and seriousness to all the human sciences, with an emphasis on vitality and solidarity, bringing theory face to face with the actuality of experience and assuming responsibility for others as well as for oneself.

To do so, cultural studies would insist on such governing principles as honoring the plurality of perspectives, relishing the varieties of intellectual experience, and acknowledging the location and uncertainty of knowledge. They would insist as well on the interested character of all knowledge: on the one hand, because "knowledge" itself was regarded as the product of the human interest that had made it so; on the other hand, because "human interest" was regarded as broken and refracted by nature, given its emergence in different human groups (classes, nations, races, genders). Consequently, in the absence of a truly external stance or truly supernal view, cultural studies would turn such variables of knowledge into an object of study and proceed to study them from the inside.

For Inglis, in the end, cultural studies represents the critical study of human values. It is a study that takes into account the enormous diversity and refraction of such values, that looks upon such values as a mixture of fact (the way the world is) and commitment (the way human subjects see the world), and that seeks to do good in so doing, as reflected in its own values as an academic subject. In their concern for diversity and pluralism, for the quotidian and the plebeian, for the excluded and the marginalized, and, above all, for the location and interested character of all knowledge, a fundamental concern for the personal voice is evident as well.

This concern comes across most tellingly perhaps in Inglis's own preference for narrative in general and biography in particular as a way of doing cultural studies. Thus, he argues, one should always look for historical narrative wherever possible and should let such stories intertwine as theories, framing actions and making them intelligible. Further, he continues, there is no story more ready or more useful than a life history that throws light on a historical moment and reveals its basic parameters on the historical map. For Inglis, therefore, biography and autobiography bring about an ideal combination of observer and observed, subject and object, the way of the world and the way of seeing the world, insofar as the human subject is thrust thereby as an actor into the world and the world is read in and through the life of this human actor.

In this chapter I should like to pursue the question of the personal voice in biblical studies, and, as a subscriber to cultural studies, I should like to do so by inserting myself, in autobiographical fashion, into the world of biblical studies. I shall weave a story about that world in terms of my own life and experience as a critic within it, tracing both the emergence of the personal voice as such in the recent history of the discipline and the emergence of my own personal voice as a postcolonial critic in that world. A preliminary comment is in order, however, with regard to this self-description of myself as a postcolonial critic. A postcolonial critic such as I is both born and made. In other words, the adoption of a postcolonial optic is not a given, even if the individual in question happens to be a child of imperialism and colonialism or of neocolonialism and postcolonialism, as I am, and in multilayered fashion. It is an optic that requires a choice and hence a process of conscientization and construction as well. In the story that follows I proceed to recount the emergence of such a voice and the decision for such an option by way of a personal journey in and with the discipline, a journey involving three major stages.

HISTORICAL CRITICISM: SUPPRESSION OF THE PERSONAL VOICE

At the beginning of my academic and professional career in the late 1970s, I submitted an article for publication to one of the major journals of the discipline. At some point in this article, I wrote something to the effect that I discerned or perceived—I no longer recall the actual formulation—a particular structure in the passage under consideration. The article, which was accepted for publication, was returned with a request for a few minor changes, as suggested by the editorial readers. One of these changes, however, was phrased in a very different tone altogether, best described perhaps as a mixture of unbelief and exasperation. The reviewer thundered: The structure of a passage lies in the passage itself, not in the eyes of the exegete, and care should be taken to make sure that the language employed reflects such a critical given. This change I incorporated willingly and without hesitation, although the tone of the comment continued to strike me as most peculiar for years to come.

Little did I know at the time of the momentous implications and ramifications involved in such a directive. Indeed, it is only with the benefit of twenty years of critical hindsight that I am able to see such a seemingly minor disciplinary transaction as a significant cultural text in its own right. At the end of the 1970s, precisely as my own study was under evaluation, the discipline found itself in an incipient state of ferment and on the verge of fundamental change. The first voices of protest against the hegemony of historical criticism—the much-beloved scientific method that held sway in academic circles from the early nineteenth century to the third quarter of the twentieth—had already been raised, with accompanying calls for reform along two divergent paths: redirection, by way of literary criticism; recasting, by way of cultural criticism.[3]

Now, it would make for a wonderful story were I to lay claim to the heroic mantle of the avant-garde visionary at that time, striking quixotically at the ever-spinning wheels of tradition. The truth of the matter, however, is much more prosaic. The study in question happened to be a quite traditional piece, deeply steeped in historical criticism. After all, that is how I, like so many others before me, had been trained—not only thoroughly ignorant of the broader tradition of criticism in the academy, its manifold movements and developments, but also quite oblivious to ongoing and profound changes within the field of historiography itself.

The last thing on my mind would have been to argue that structure should not be seen as residing in the text itself, for readers to uncover and expose, but rather in the interchange between text and reader, or that structure should not be approached as fixed and stable but rather as variable and dependent on readers. My ready compliance with the change requested in no way represented, therefore, a strategic move on my part with publication in mind but actually an honest attempt to sharpen the language as requested, so that it did come to reflect as accurately as possible this view of structure as inherent in the text—determinate and determining. That had been, after all, my intent all along; yet, there was something about the militant tone of the comment that bothered me.

Not that I think, even for a moment, that my reviewer was aware of the profound critical issues involved—not in that journal and not at that time. Rather, I tend to see his comment as a gut reaction on his part—I use the masculine advisedly, for there were no female associate editors at the time. It was but the perceived appearance or hint of a subjective dimension in interpretation, in the exercise of biblical exegesis, that had caused his academic persona to go into convulsion and provoked such a heartfelt eruption. This was no encounter, therefore, between the old and the new, no battle between the traditional and the *dernier cri*—not at the surface anyway. Yet, in retrospect, the episode can be seen as profoundly symptomatic of things to come, already well under way at the time.

To understand the power of the reaction, it is necessary to recall the world and ideology of traditional historical criticism. Within the framework of such criticism, to raise the issue of the personal voice in interpretation was to commit *the* unthinkable and unforgivable sin. It was the very point of historical criticism to submerge, to bypass, to transcend the personal, the subjective, the contextual—to engage in exegesis, not eisegesis, as it was incessantly recited.[4] In its struggle against the dark forces of

---

[3] On the story of the discipline, see chaps. 1 and 2 in this volume.

[4] The letter of invitation for the project (Ingrid Rosa Kitzberger, April 22, 1996) made this point quite clearly, as it sought to define "personal voice criticism": "In contrast to the traditional historical-critical paradigm with its claim for objectivity and the strict separation of the critical task and the critic's person."

tradition and dogmatism, subjectivism and emotionalism, historical criticism purportedly brought the modern light of reason and science to bear on the study of ancient texts and antiquity itself. This was a light at once highly rewarding and highly demanding.

It was a light firmly grounded in positivism; both the meaning of the ancient text and the path of history were regarded as objective and univocal. As such, it was a light that called for a scientific approach in the study of such realities; textual meaning and historical development were retrievable, to the extent made possible by the sources, through the proper exercise of the right methodological tools. Such a light further required a universal and informed type of reader, a reader who aimed at objectivity and impartiality in interpretation through the rigorous and patient acquisition of the scientific method under the trained and watchful eyes of a master scholar.

A first and sacred goal of historical criticism was, therefore, the divestiture—through a combination of self-conscious exposé and methodological expertise—of all presuppositions and preconceptions, mostly framed in theological terms but also extending in principle to all matters sociocultural or ideological. The purpose behind such decontextualization was to lay open, for the first time in the history of interpretation, as it was claimed, the meaning of the ancient texts and the course of ancient history "in their own terms." Only then could such meaning and such history serve as a proper point of departure for any type of hermeneutical translation, reflection, or application.

Nowhere is this agenda of historical criticism more evident than in an article that proved quite influential, certainly in U.S. circles, for many years after its appearance. I am referring to the long entry on biblical theology authored by Krister Stendahl in the early 1960s for *The Interpreter's Dictionary of the Bible*.[5] The classic program of historical criticism at its very best was to be found here.

Biblical theology, Stendahl argued, encompasses three distinct movements: at one end, the "descriptive" task focused on the historical meaning of the biblical text—"what it meant"; at the other end, the "theological" task centered on the contemporary meaning of the biblical text—"what it means"; in the middle, the task of "translation," which presupposes extensive as well as intensive competence in the field of hermeneutics. The task of description, the realm of historical criticism, was sharply defined: the original meaning of the text—what the words meant when uttered or written—was to be spelled out "with the highest degree of perception" *in its own terms*, with the material itself providing the means to

---

[5] K. Stendahl, "Biblical Theology, Contemporary," in *The Interpreter's Dictionary of the Bible*, 4 vols., ed. G. A. Buttrick (Nashville: Abingdon Press, 1962), 1:418-32.

check whether the interpretation was correct or not.[6] In retrospect, the enormous self-confidence of the whole enterprise proves as astounding as its blessed innocence.

Within such a framework, one can readily understand how any consideration of the personal voice, any possibility of admission of its role and influence in interpretation, was looked upon as an unpardonable transgression of the ultimate epistemic taboo—a reading of the past in terms of the present. I would contend that it was precisely from such a context and such a world that the gut reaction of that reviewer of mine emanated. He perceived in my choice of expression, though quite unintended, an unacceptable hint of subjectivism and proceeded to rebuke me accordingly. Little did we both know at the time how things would change in the years to come.

CULTURAL STUDIES:
IRRUPTION OF THE PERSONAL VOICE

In the mid-1990s I had a chance encounter, at one or another of the annual meetings of the profession, with a colleague from the United States, approximately my age, with whom I share an area of specialization and whom I have known for a number of years. We had both been trained in the 1970s and had witnessed the development of our respective academic careers through the 1980s. In the course of our exchange, as we touched casually upon our recent work in our mutual field of interest, this individual suddenly began to chide me for abandoning the path of historical criticism, engaging in a quite unfair critique of its foundations and goals, and turning to other approaches that were patently political in character. Growing increasingly agitated, he brought this unexpected tirade to an end by proclaiming ex cathedra that historical criticism, as a scientific method, possessed no ideology. When I retorted, quite ironically I confess, what a blessing it must be to have surmounted all values and agendas, the exchange, such as it was, came to a rather abrupt silence, finally interrupted only by the departure of my interlocutor in obvious displeasure.

---

[6] To be sure, Stendahl (422) was not unaware of the obstacles involved in the descriptive task: the subjectivity of the historian in the selection of material; the paucity of sources, which does not allow for certainty in all areas; the appeal to some comparative material while neglecting other such material. In the end, however, such obstacles were not considered overwhelming; not only would the material itself serve as a proper corrective, but also the task could be carried out by believer and agnostic alike, even in unison. All that was required, Stendahl argued, was "description in the terms indicated by the texts themselves."

By this time a good fifteen years had elapsed since the first anecdote above. The tone of the reaction no longer proved surprising or disconcerting, although its vehemence was certainly striking, especially coming as it did from a younger scholar who had presumably lived through the very same disciplinary developments I had. By then, of course, those early voices of protest from the mid-1970s had not only congealed into full-fledged critical movements, quite diverse as well as quite sophisticated, but had also displaced historical criticism from its position of preeminence, turning the discipline into a veritable arena for competing paradigms. Clearly, as I described the changes in question, what for me had meant the liberation and decolonization of the discipline, for him amounted to a decline in standards and the anarchy of partisanship. In the process, needless to say, such transformations served to bring about as well a critical reconsideration of the personal voice in biblical scholarship.

In effect, with the flowering of literary criticism and cultural criticism, increasing attention began to be paid to the role of "the reader" in interpretation. An initial focus on formal reader-constructs, along the lines of the universal reader type, eventually gave way to a concern for "the real reader" as such, and with that came the inevitable realization that real or flesh-and-blood readers could only be approached and analyzed in terms of the manifold and highly complex dimensions of human identity. As a result, a fourth critical movement, cultural studies, began to claim its voice and fight for space in the disciplinary arena. It was from out of this movement, after fruitful sojourns in both literary and social criticism, that I proceeded to formulate my own rationale for the introduction of the personal voice in biblical criticism.[7]

First, I came to realize that there was no such thing as a neutral and disinterested reader, and that the proposed decontextualization aimed at the formation of the universal and informed reader was but the universalization of a bracketed identity. Readers, I argued, were always and inevitably positioned and interested, culturally and historically conditioned and engaged.

Second, I further realized that a text has no meaning and history has no path without an interpreter. I argued, therefore, that all reading strategies and theoretical models as well as all recuperations of meaning and reconstructions of history were constructs on the part of such real readers.

---

[7] See F. F. Segovia, "Toward a Hermeneutics of the Diaspora: A Hermeneutics of Otherness and Engagement," in *Reading from This Place*, vol. 1: *Social Location and Biblical Interpretation in the United States*, ed. F. F. Segovia and M. A. Tolbert (Minneapolis: Fortress Press, 1995), 57-73; idem, "Toward Intercultural Criticism: A Reading Strategy from the Diaspora," in *Reading from This Place*, vol. 2: *Social Location and Biblical Interpretation in Global Perspective*, ed. F. F. Segovia and M. A. Tolbert (Minneapolis: Fortress Press, 1995), 303-30.

Third, I clearly realized that I had to incorporate such insights into my own critical apparatus and practice. I thus argued for a reading strategy, intercultural criticism, that would regard and analyze all texts, readings of texts, and readers of texts as literary or aesthetic, rhetorical or strategic, and ideological or political constructs in their own right. I further based this method on a theoretical model, a hermeneutics of otherness and engagement, that sought not only to acknowledge and respect these others as others but also to engage such others in critical dialogue.

Finally, I fully realized, as reflected in the pivotal role attached to contextualization and perspective within this approach, the profoundly political character of the interpretive task. I argued, therefore, that the fundamental mode of discourse within cultural studies as a whole, and thus within both intercultural criticism and the hermeneutics of otherness and engagement, was neither historical nor literary nor cultural but rather ideological in nature.

In the light of these critical wanderings of mine—which in the end led me to affirm that the longstanding and much-beloved distinction between exegesis and eisegesis had altogether collapsed and that all exegesis was ultimately eisegesis—the charges of my interlocutor were, to a large extent, quite to the point, even if the scolding itself was out of order. From the point of view of his adherence to and espousal of historical criticism, its model and agenda, he had correctly perceived that I had abandoned the parameters of historical criticism, that I had mounted a fundamental critique of it, and that I had turned to a variety of other methods in my critical practice.

In so doing, I had come to adopt a point of view radically opposite to that which had at one time united us: there is no objective and impartial reader; all views of the past are contemporary constructions; all interpretation is contextual and ideological. Only such an antinomian position, such an open violation of the epistemic taboo, could provoke such a chiding. I stood guilty, not only plainly so but self-admittedly so, of espousing subjectivism in interpretation. Of course, so did many others by that time, and the riposte involving charges of an unfair critique and affirmations of objectivity appeared ever more fragile and obsolete, especially when devoid of any substantial theoretical foundations. The personal voice was here to stay in biblical scholarship, and our own parting of the ways in silence and discord captured accurately, as another significant cultural text in its own right, the pulse of the discipline as a whole.

POSTCOLONIAL STUDIES:
ENTRENCHMENT OF THE PERSONAL VOICE

Quite recently, at dinner at a committee meeting of one of the various professional societies to which I belong, I happened to sit next to a well-known and established scholar. This was a gentleman, many years my senior, perfectly cast in the social mold of the traditional learned scholar—the homo eruditus *oblivious to and distrustful of matters theoretical, with a view of all theory as outside the realm of history; largely unaware of as well as unconcerned by any major shifts in either discipline or academy; thoroughly self-absorbed in his own work. After speaking at length on his most recent accomplishments, he asked unexpectedly about my own research interests. When I explained my growing interest in the competing ideologies of the early Christian texts in the face of the Roman imperial situation that they faced and within which they had been produced, he asked politely whether I thought such a connection was really important. When I responded that I thought the connection was not only important for the ancient world but also for both the modern world and the contemporary world, since the development of criticism had paralleled the imperial expansion, contraction, and transformation of Europe and the United States, he discreetly dropped any further inquiries about my work and proceeded to outline at considerable length his own research agenda for the future.*

Now, coming as it did a couple of years after the second anecdote above, the nature of this brief exchange could hardly prove unexpected or baffling. Even its friendly tone, with no visible signs of exasperation or frustration, was fairly predictable. I had by then come to learn that in dealing with individuals committed to the more traditional methods and agendas of the discipline, especially of the older, erudite type, the best strategy to follow was that of polite give and take; in effect, harmless banter designed to pass the time in amicable fashion, while skirting issues of a controversial or problematic nature having to do with the discipline or the academy, even though such a policy might lead, as it did in this case, to interminable curriculum vitae recitations.

This is a strategy born of social grace and professional wisdom, a strategic realization that any type of serious critical exchange is not only bound to disrupt a culturally preferred ambience of bonhomie but also go absolutely nowhere, given the discursive and theoretical gulf involved. To be sure, on this particular occasion I did depart from such a strategy, but only as a result of questions addressed to me, and even then I proceeded to answer in as pithy and global a fashion as possible. Such brevity proved effective; my own interests were so remote from those of my interlocutor that he rapidly moved on to the much more familiar territory of his own work.

By then I had begun to move into postcolonial studies.[8] While turned to cultural studies, I had argued for the preeminence of the political or

---

[8] See chap. 5 in this volume.

ideological element in biblical criticism. In my formulation of intercultural criticism and the hermeneutics of otherness and engagement, I had set out to introduce this element at all levels of the interpretive task—at the level of texts, readings of texts, and readers of texts. At the same time, I had continued to struggle with the question of how best to engage in ideological analysis—in effect, with the question of theory and method. By that time, there were others engaged in ideological criticism from a number of different perspectives, but I wanted to do so specifically at a geopolitical level.

Certainly, I had already called upon key terms and concepts of postcolonial studies to describe developments in the discipline in terms of liberation and decolonization. I had also explained that such developments were due in large part to the infusion of outside voices heretofore absent from the study of religion, including voices from outside the West and voices from non-Western minorities residing in the West. I had further argued that the diversity now present in the discipline, methodological and theoretical as well as sociocultural, was the inevitable result of a postcolonial world. What I still lacked was a more expansive and systematic conceptual framework and practice with which to pursue the ideological dimension from a geopolitical perspective and at all levels of interpretation.

By the time of this conversation, I had come to realize that the phenomenon of imperial reality, of imperialism and colonialism, lay at the very heart of the discipline, across all levels of analysis: across the world of antiquity, the world of the Roman Empire—the world of the texts; across the world of modernity, the world of Western expansionism—the world of modern biblical criticism, its readers and readings; and across the world of postmodernity, the world of Western imperial contraction and transformation, of postcolonialism and neocolonialism—the world of contemporary biblical criticism, its readers and readings. I had also come to realize that it was proper, indeed imperative, to examine not only what the texts had to say about imperial reality but also how what they had to say had been interpreted in the modern Western tradition as well as in the contemporary Western and non-Western traditions. I looked upon such a multidimensional, interrelated, geopolitical approach as an ideal way of coming to terms with the political and ideological dimension of the discipline at all of its various levels of analysis.

After "subjectivism," there is perhaps no term more objectionable for any universal reader-construct, such as that behind the *homo eruditus,* than "ideology." To insist on the political character of the biblical texts, alongside or even over its religious or theological, literary or cultural, dimensions, by situating them within the geopolitical context of Roman imperialism and colonialism is already a rather daring move. To insist on the political character of all biblical criticism, modern as well as contemporary, by situating interpretations and interpreters within the geopolitical context of Western imperialism and colonialism goes beyond daring.

While such linkage at the level of the ancient texts may come across as quizzical, the proposed connection at the level of interpretation is beyond comprehension—in effect, how can any universal reader-construct be construed as profoundly ideological, thoroughly enmeshed in matters political and geopolitical, whether consciously or unconsciously so?

By arguing that the discourse and practices of the discipline had to be seen against the broader discourse and practices of modern imperialism and colonialism as well as postmodern neocolonialism and postcolonialism, I had politicized the discipline to an unacceptable level. The response could only have been wrathful indignation or silent dismissal. My interlocutor in this case opted for the latter alternative, in part because of my own conversational strategy and in part because of the seeming outlandishness of the claim. Yet, ideological criticism, in all of its various forms, was here to stay, as was my own geopolitical approach to the personal voice. And thus, the silence of politeness and insouciance that greeted my remarks can be readily taken as yet another significant cultural text in its own right.

CONCLUDING COMMENTS

This is by no means the first time that I have dealt with the question of the personal voice in my work. At a fundamental level I have used my life story as a foundation for my work as a critic in biblical studies, as a theologian in theological studies, and as a critic in cultural studies. In more specific studies I have used that story as point of departure for reflections on the life and role of racial and ethnic minorities in theological education and scholarship in general, as well as in biblical studies in particular.[9] In the present study I have had recourse to that story once again to trace both the emergence of the question itself within biblical studies and the development of my own option for postcolonial criticism. In so doing, I have relied on both the individual and the social dimensions of that story, depending on the context and aims of each writing in question, but always with a view of such dimensions not as binary oppositions but as interrelated and interdependent.

In the present chapter I have concentrated on the social dimension, focused on the personal voice within the discipline as such. Thus, I proposed to show how the emergence of my own postcolonial voice within the academy paralleled the emergence of the question of the personal voice in the academy. It is a focus that could be described as socioeducational or socioacademic. Certainly, I could have underlined instead the personal

---

[9] F. F. Segovia, "Theological Education and Scholarship as Struggle: The Life of Racial/Ethnic Minorities in the Profession," *Journal of Hispanic/Latino Theology* 2 (1994): 5-25; see also, chap. 8 in this volume.

dimension or highlighted both at the same time. I would have related then how the development of my postcolonial optic was also the result of struggle—the unceasing and unrelenting *lucha* (literally, "fight") of a child of the colonized against the forces of imperialism and colonialism.

Here the option for a postcolonial optic goes hand in hand with a process of conscientization and construction, of decolonization and liberation, as life in a variety of imperial and colonial contexts caused layers of ideology to fall one by one from my eyes. Climactic in this regard was my intense experience as an outsider, as "the other," within that quintessential institution of the dominant culture, the divinity school.[10] It was within such a context—at the very heart of theological liberalism itself, with its much-vaunted message of openness and freedom—that I finally came to the marvelously energizing realization that the emperor had no clothes, just as I was beginning to deal with real readers and cultural studies in the discipline. Indeed, it should not go unsaid that all three interlocutors alluded to in my personal anecdotes were exemplary specimens of liberal culture and theology. However, the story of this *lucha*, this concomitant personal struggle behind the making of this postcolonial critic, must be left for now, alas, to another time and place.

---

[10] On this point, see the fine cultural study of divinity schools as cultural indicators of the path of liberal theology: C. Cherry, *Hurrying toward Zion: Universities, Divinity Schools, and American Protestantism* (Bloomington, Ind.: Indiana University Press, 1995).

8

Racial and Ethnic Minorities
in Biblical Studies

According to the rationale that accompanied the invitation to contribute to this project,[1] the volume *Ethnicity and the Bible* was conceived with two primary factors in mind: the eruption of the issue of ethnicity on the global scene in recent years, and the perceived and corresponding responsibility on the part of biblical scholars to address the subject on an explicit and sustained basis. The rationale further identified two specific goals for the project: in pursuing the issue of ethnicity, the volume would also serve to highlight the diversity in method and theory presently to be found in the discipline as well as to offer a new model for doing biblical theology in the contemporary scene, a model based on a broadly conceived theological reflection on the Bible in the light of the new methodological and theoretical pluralism in the discipline. Both aims are clearly reflected in the structure of the volume. While a first part brings together a variety of different approaches to ethnicity in the Bible, with corresponding sections on the Hebrew Bible and the Christian Scriptures, a second part focuses on ethnicity in the contemporary world, with sections on the relationship between the Bible and present-day ethnic issues as well as the politics of biblical interpretation. Thus, the rationale argued

---

[1] This chapter is a revised version of a presentation given at the 1994 Annual Meeting of the Society of Biblical Literature in Chicago, Illinois, in a session sponsored by the Committee on Underrepresented Racial and Ethnic Minority Persons in the Profession. I should like to express my gratitude hereby to all of my colleagues on the committee for their very kind invitation to serve as the keynote speaker for the session as well as to all the members of the panel who responded to my presentation out of their own particular histories and experiences (Professors V. P. Furnish, Southern Methodist University, Dallas, Texas; G. A. Yee, University of St. Thomas, St. Paul, Minnesota; C. S. Moon, San Francisco Theological Seminary, San Anselmo, California; and R. J. Weems, Vanderbilt University, Nashville, Tennessee).

157

for an approach to the new and pressing question of ethnicity from the point of view of both the text (ethnicity in the Bible) and the readers of the text (ethnicity in the interpretation of the Bible).[2]

My own contribution to the project belongs decidedly within the second part of the volume. Indeed, I see my task in this study as that of providing an overall critical view of the life and role of ethnic and racial minorities[3] in biblical studies, by which I mean both the discipline and the profession, especially in the light of the profound and radical changes at work at the end of the twentieth century, hence the rather broad title for the essay. As such, I am not interested here in the construction of ethnicity or race in the Bible or even in the relationship between ethnicity or race and biblical interpretation; rather, my particular concern is with ethnicity and race within the field and the guild of biblical studies and thus with the politics of interpretation from both disciplinary and professional perspectives.

I should like to begin, therefore, with an analysis of a number of factors that I see as constitutive for our situation at the turn of the century

---

[2] On both counts the rationale for the volume closely parallels the earlier rationale for the journal itself, as outlined in the Editorial Statement of the first issue (*Biblical Interpretation* 1 [1993]: i-ii). With regard to motivating factors, the editorial statement cited the recent burgeoning of new approaches to textual interpretation as well as the need for biblical studies to become more public and pluralistic. With regard to goals in mind, the statement presented the journal as both a forum for the fresh interpretation of texts through the use of the new critical approaches and a forum for theoretical debate regarding the theological and political implications of such new developments. Thus, the boldness behind the new journal—with its open criticism of the leading journals in the field for their failure to reflect the new pluralism within the discipline—was reflected in the boldness behind the proposed volume: in effect, given the rise of ethnicity as a global and public critical issue, it was imperative for biblical scholars to take an open and systematic stand on the topic, with particular attention to be given to the diversity of reading strategies in the discipline as well as broad theological reflection in the light of such pluralism.

[3] The expression "ethnic and racial minorities" represents a combination of the terms "ethnic group" and "racial group" as well as the term "minority group," all of which are basic concepts in the study of intergroup relations (see, e.g., J. R. Fegin, *Racial and Ethnic Relations*, 3d ed. [Englewood Cliffs, N.J.: Prentice-Hall, 1989], esp. 4-19). A word of explanation is in order. With regard to the first two terms, "ethnic group" and "racial group," these are concepts whose definitions vary widely not only in terms of historical usage but also with regard to perspective and ideology. In other words, neither "ethnicity" nor "race" is a self-evident and fixed concept grounded in nature or genetics; they are social constructs with an underlying historical and ideological base. My own use of these terms is social in nature and follows that of Fegin: ethnic and racial groups as social groups, singled out as such for social interest, whether good or bad, either from inside or outside the differentiated groups, on the basis of certain cultural or physical characteristics,

[continued]

and then conclude with a description of the life and role of ethnic and racial minorities in the light of such a context.[4] It is my firm belief that

---

respectively. With regard to the third term, "minority group," this is a concept that is often used of both ethnic and racial groups and that implies the existence of a majority group and the presence of ethnic or racial stratification. In other words, the term "minority group" is not just a descriptive classification but also an evaluative category. At times, the terms "dominant group" and "subordinate group" are preferred in the literature, in order to reflect the fact that a minority group in terms of stratification may actually be a majority group with regard to numbers. My own use of the term in this study implies both numbers and stratification.

In sum, I employ the expression "ethnic and racial minorities" to mean individuals from social groups, whether culturally (ethnic) or physically (racial) identified as such, who have traditionally been considered inferior within a scale of stratification set up by the West and operative in all the theological disciplines, including biblical criticism. In effect, such individuals may be described as critics of non-Western origins or descent who either live in their respective countries or reside within the West itself. Moreover, while they invariably represent, as a whole, a numerical majority in the world in terms of their own socioreligious affiliation, they represent a minority both in terms of stratification and numbers within the theological disciplines in general and biblical criticism in particular.

[4] As my use of the first person plural adjective indicates, my approach to the question is from an emic rather than etic perspective—the perspective of the insider, a representative of ethnic and racial minorities in the field and the guild. It is a perspective with a number of interrelated and interdependent layers of meaning, which I would describe as that of (a) a critic of non-Western origins; (b) with birth and primary socialization outside the West (in Latin American culture and, more specifically, within its Caribbean variant); (c) with secondary socialization and permanent residence, indeed citizenship, in the West (the United States); (d) and hence, a member of an ethnic minority group within the United States, the Hispanic Americans, constituting at present approximately 9 percent of the population (close to twenty-two million people) and widely recognized and differentiated as such both by the group itself and the majority culture. (Note: The 2000 Census is projected to show a U.S. Hispanic American population of well over thirty million people, constituting over 12 percent of the population.) I would define the group as follows: people of Hispanic descent, associated in one way or another with the Americas, who now live permanently, for whatever reason, in the United States.

Such a perspective I have characterized in terms of the diaspora. For a sharper delineation, see (a) regarding its hermeneutics: "Toward a Hermeneutics of the Diaspora: A Hermeneutics of Otherness and Engagement," in *Reading from This Place*, vol. 1: *Social Location and Biblical Interpretation in the United States*, ed. F. F. Segovia and M. A. Tolbert (Minneapolis: Fortress Press, 1994), 57-73; and "Toward Intercultural Criticism: A Reading Strategy from the Diaspora," in *Reading from This Place*, vol. 2: *Social Location and Biblical Interpretation in the Global Scene*, ed. F. F. Segovia and M. A. Tolbert (Minneapolis: Fortress Press, 1995), 303-30; (b) regarding its theological locus and mode: "Two Places and No Place on Which to Stand: Mixture and Otherness in Hispanic American Theology," *Listening: A Journal of Religion and Culture* 27 (1992): 26-40; and "In the World but Not of It: Exile as Locus for a Theology of the Diaspora," in *Aliens in the Promised Land: Voices of Hispanic American Theology*, ed. A. M. Isasi-Díaz and F. F. Segovia (Minneapolis: Fortress Press, 1996), 195-217.

ethnic and racial minorities have a fundamental role to play in the future direction of the discipline and the profession in what I would describe as the post-Western, postcolonial world of religious studies and theological studies in general and biblical criticism in particular. It is also my firm belief, however, that such a role is not at all an easy one to play; in fact, it involves and calls for struggle as a way of life. In the end, however, I would argue that such struggle is for life, and a very promising life indeed.

RACIAL AND ETHNIC MINORITIES IN BIBLICAL STUDIES AT THE TURN OF THE CENTURY

There are three factors at work in the contemporary scene that I regard as fundamental for the life and role of ethnic and racial minorities in biblical studies at the turn of the century—that pregnant period of time, which has come to be known in intellectual history as the *fin de siècle* and which we have already properly entered as such, marking the close of one century and the beginning of another, and so laden with meaning of all sorts, both before and after the fact. One such dimension of meaning that I would associate with the present *fin de siècle* has to do with the drastically changed nature of doing theology or criticism in a postcolonial, post-Western world. The first factor concerns the world of global affairs—the geopolitical context; the second, the world of biblical criticism—the disciplinary context; the third, the world of the biblical guild—the professional context.

Geopolitical Context: The World of Global Affairs

To begin with, a few remarks are necessary with regard to the geopolitical scene at large. In a much-debated article on world politics, Samuel Huntington, Eaton Professor of the Science of Government and Director of the John M. Olin Institute for Strategic Studies at Harvard University, has argued that global politics is presently entering a new and different phase of development altogether.[5] It is an argument that I find,

---

[5] S. P. Huntington, "The Clash of Civilizations?" *Foreign Affairs* 72 (Summer 1993): 22-49. The ensuing discussion may be traced as follows. First, a number of responses appeared in the very next issue of *Foreign Affairs* 73 (September-October 1993): F. Adjami, "The Summoning" (2-9); K. Mahbubani, "The Dangers of Decadence: What the Rest Can Teach the West" (10-14); R. L. Bartley, "The Case for Optimism" (15-18); Liu Bynian, "Civilization Grafting" (19-21); and J. J. Kirkpatrick et al., "The Modernizing Imperative" (22-26). Then, Huntington himself responded in a second article: "If Not Civilizations, What?" *Foreign Affairs* 74 (November/ December 1993): 186-94. Since then, a number of studies have contributed further to the discussion, e.g., R. D. Kaplan, "The Coming Anarchy," *The Atlantic Monthly* 273:4 (February 1994): 44-76; and M. Connelly and P. Kennedy, "Must It Be the Rest against the West?" *Atlantic Monthly* 274:6 (December 1994): 61-84.

on the whole, insightful as well as persuasive and reproduce here in its essentials as an appropriate preamble to, and overall framework for, my own reflections regarding the state of affairs in the discipline and the profession.

For Huntington, this new phase in question is marked not so much by the end of history, the return of traditional rivalries among nation-states, or the decline of the nation-state in the face of tribalism and globalism—as many would have it—but rather by a new source of conflict in the world, neither economic nor ideological but *cultural*. As such, nation-states will neither disappear nor go into a period of decline; to the contrary, they shall continue to function as the most powerful actors in world affairs. At the same time, however, global conflict will be increasingly defined not by conflicts among nation-states—a development that would signify a return in principle to a previous phase of evolution, as outlined below—but rather by conflicts between nations and groups of different *civilizations*, with the "fault lines" between such civilizations as the "battle lines" of the future.[6]

This new phase, moreover, represents the fourth and latest stage in the evolution of conflict in the modern political world. Thus, while in the past conflict has been by and large the result of conflicts *within* Western civilization, with all non-Western peoples and governments as objects of history, from this point on conflict will be driven by conflicts *between* civilizations. The earlier development of conflict, encompassing the last three hundred and fifty years of Western history (1640s-1990s), Huntington traces in terms of the following three stages:

---

[6] Huntington ("Clash of Civilizations," 23-25) defines a "civilization" as (a) a cultural entity—not unlike villages, regions, ethnic groups, nationalities, and religious groups, all of which are said to have distinct cultures at different levels of cultural heterogeneity; (b) of the most comprehensive sort—involving the highest cultural grouping of people and the broadest level of cultural identity on the part of people. The concept carries a number of other connotations as well. First, civilizations include objective elements (language, history, religion, customs, institutions) as well as subjective elements (the self-identification of people). Second, civilizations are fluid rather than fixed concepts, insofar as people can and do redefine their identities with a resulting change in the composition and boundaries of civilizations. Third, civilizations may involve large numbers of people (e.g., China) or a very small number of people (e.g., the Anglophone Caribbean). Fourth, civilizations may include several nation-states (e.g., Islam, Latin America, and the West) or one (e.g., Japan). Fifth, civilizations blend and overlap and thus may include subcivilizations. Here, the example of the West is very much to the point, with its two major variants (Europe and the United States), although there are other examples as well (as in the case of Islam, with its Arab, Malay, and Turkic variants). Finally, civilizations are dynamic, not only dividing and merging but also rising and falling.

1. To begin with, for about a century and a half after the Peace of Westphalia (1648-1789)—that is to say, from the end of the Thirty Years War and the emergence of the modern international system in 1648 to the outbreak of the French Revolution in 1789—conflict in the West consisted largely of conflicts among princes: emperors, absolute monarchs, and constitutional monarchs, all attempting to expand their bureaucracies, armies, mercantilist economies, and territories.

2. Subsequently, for the next one hundred and twenty-five years (1789-1914/18)—namely, from the aftermath of the French Revolution (1789) to the conclusion of the First World War in 1918—conflict in the Western world took the form of conflicts between or among nation-states; as princes expanded the territories over which they ruled, nation-states came into being and clashed with one another over the long course of the nineteenth century and right into the first decades of the twentieth century.

3. Then, for the next seventy years, and hence the greater part of the twentieth century (1918-1989)—in effect, from the aftermath of World War I (1918), especially in terms of the Russian Revolution and the reaction against it, until the implosion of the Soviet Empire and the end of the Cold War in 1989—conflict in the West consisted of conflicts involving ideologies. Such conflict involved two distinct stages: first, prior to the Second World War (1918-1939), among communism, fascism-nazism, and liberal democracy; subsequently, during the Cold War (1945-1989), between communism and liberal democracy, as embodied in the struggle between the two superpowers, the Soviet Union and the United States, neither of which was a nation-state in the classical sense and each of which defined its identity in terms of its ideology.

Again, all such conflicts amounted to conflicts within Western civilization, Western civil wars as it were. However, with the collapse of the Union of Soviet Socialist Republics and the end of the Cold War, Huntington sees international politics as moving beyond its long Western phase, with enormous and radical consequences for the world at large, including the West. On the one hand, non-Western peoples and governments begin to move thereby from a position as objects of history—or, perhaps more accurately, its targets—to a position as movers and shapers of history alongside the West, as "subjects of history," as liberation theology has so often and so aptly put it.[7] On the other hand, conflict takes on as a result the form of

---

[7] This, however, is an aspect of the discussion that, in my opinion, Huntington does not engage or pursue in adequate fashion. While quick to draw numerous implications for the West, both short-term and long-term, of this tectonic change in international politics and fully cognizant of how the global discussion has been controlled for centuries by the West with its own fundamental interests in mind, he fails to give sufficient attention to the grave responsibility borne by the West for the present state of affairs. After all, the legacy of the West in this regard—an often bypassed but intrinsic part of Western civilization and culture—is a most

[continued]

conflicts involving civilizations.[8] On one level, such conflict involves the different civilizations, with eight identified as major in this regard—African, Confucian, Hindu, Islamic, Japanese, Latin American, Slavic-Orthodox, and Western.[9] On another level, such conflict also involves "the West and the Rest," given not only the undisputed primacy of Western civilization but also its long history of imperialism and colonialism.[10]

---

heavy burden indeed: from the centuries of colonialism, involving the widescale domination, exploitation, and extermination of other peoples; to the technological perfection of displacement, forced labor, and genocide by Germany, in the name of a *Herrenvolk*, in the course of the twentieth century; to the ongoing and unchecked ethnic cleansing at work in the Balkans and the growing resentment of and hostility toward immigrants and refugees in the West, especially those from the non-Western world. In other words, the magnificent legacy of the West—its great "creed" (for which see n. 11 below)—extended only so far and was accompanied throughout by political domination and economic exploitation, social and cultural disdain, ethnic and racial prejudice and discrimination, ultimately leading to the slavery and extermination of millions upon millions of peoples. Indeed, it was the failure of the West to extend its "creed" to the rest, to see the other in the light of its own "creed," that is largely responsible for the situation faced by the world as it begins to move into the twenty-first century.

[8] Huntington ("Clash of Civilizations," 25-29) sees such a coming state of affairs as inevitable for a variety of reasons: (a) Differences among civilizations are real and basic, the product of centuries. (b) As the world becomes a smaller place, the increasing interactions between peoples of different civilizations intensify civilization-consciousness, both in terms of similarities within civilizations and differences between civilizations. (c) The processes of economic modernization and social change separate people from their local identities, not only weakening thereby the nation-state as a source of identity but also giving rise to fundamentalist religious movements across the globe, which rush in to fill the void. (d) The dual role of the West, a West at the peak of its power, but also a West that no longer calls forth imitation but rather a return-to-the-roots movement in the non-West. (e) Cultural characteristics and differences are less mutable and less easily compromised than political or economic ones. (f) There is an increase in economic regionalism, both grounded in and reinforcing civilization-consciousness. The end result is an overall growth in an "us *vs.* them" relationship among civilizations.

[9] From the point of view of the "us *vs.* them" mentality, such conflicts take place at both a micro and a macro level. At the micro level, adjacent groups along the "fault lines" struggle for control of territory and each other. At the macro level, states from different civilizations compete for relative military and economic power, struggle over the control of international institutions, and promote their own political and religious values.

[10] The phrase is borrowed from an earlier piece by K. Mahbubani ("The West and the Rest," *The National Interest* [Summer 1992]: 3-13). From the point of view of the "us *vs.* them" mentality, the efforts of the West to promote democracy and liberalism as universal values, maintain its military predominance, and advance its economic interests are met with countering responses from other civilizations, with an increasing appeal to common religion and civilization-identity in this regard.

From a geopolitical point of view, therefore, ethnic and racial minorities in biblical studies, whether based in their respective countries and cultures or in the West itself, represent by and large the children of cultures (1) formerly controlled by the West during its long period of global hegemony and as a result of its extensive process of colonial expansionism and domination in the world at large; (2) trapped until very recently as pawns within the dualistic struggle between the free world or First World and the communist world or Second World; and (3) only now beginning to attain a measure of self-identity, self-consciousness, and self-determination, cultural and otherwise. Those living in the West—mostly by way of its North American variant (the United States) and including individuals of African, Asian, Caribbean, and Latin American descent—further represent a significant and increasingly unwelcome presence of non-Western cultures at the very heart of the West, no matter how inscribed in the West they may be or how devoted to its foundational creed and principles.[11] In the end, the broad geopolitical shift outlined by Hun-

---

[11] In the past few years the backlash against immigrants and immigration from outside the West into the West has increased sharply, in Europe as well as in the United States. It is a presence that is seen as harmful to the West, its culture and way of life, and even as ultimately leading to its demise. For the European scene, with an informative breakdown of the numbers and countries of origin involved, see F. Monteira, "Ser extranjero en Europa, algo poco recomendable," *El País* (July 30, 1990), int. ed.: 4. In the United States, in particular, the projections of the Census Bureau have thrown fear into the heart of the majority and dominant culture with its estimates that by the year 2050, given the continuation of present levels of immigration, the American population will be 23 percent Hispanic-American, 16 percent African American, and 10 percent Asian-American—in effect, just under 50 percent of the population will be of non-European origin. See, e.g., W. A. Henry III, "Beyond the Melting Pot," *Time* (April 9, 1990): 28. The question raised by commentators from the dominant culture is posed in explicit ethnic and racial terms: whether such immigrants will espouse the "twin bedrocks" of the country—European culture and the "American Creed" of liberty, equality, individualism, and democracy. See, e.g., B. D. Porter, "Can American Democracy Survive?" *Commentary* (November 1993): 37-40; and Huntington, "If Not Civilizations," esp. 189-190, from whom I have borrowed the terms in quotation marks above.

See also the recent book by P. Brimelow, which takes the argument to a new and alarming level of discourse (*Alien Nation: Common Sense about America's Immigration Disaster* [New York: Random House, 1995]). Brimelow, himself an immigrant from England, argues for a drastic curtailment of present immigration policy on the part of the United States, in effect since the Immigration and Naturalization Act of 1965, which opened the doors widely to immigrants from outside the European continent. This clarion call for a respite in immigration again reveals strong and stereotypical ethnic and racial connotations: a focus on the reunification of families has turned immigration into a kind of civil right for in-

[continued]

tington will have a further and inevitable effect on ethnic and racial minorities in all the theological disciplines, including biblical criticism, as these individuals and groups proceed to reflect more and more on what it means to do theology from their own social locations and to read and interpret the Bible from their own places.

Disciplinary Context: The World of Biblical Criticism

Some remarks are in order as well with regard to the present state of affairs in the discipline we practice, what I call biblical criticism, for lack of a better name, given the inevitable but unintended canonical connotations of such a designation.[12] It is a discipline that finds itself at present in a situation of seemingly stable anomie or liminality, due in part to a number of theoretical and methodological developments within the discipline itself in the course of the last twenty-five years or so, but also in part to certain important sociocultural developments.[13] It is this latter aspect that I should like to highlight in the present context.

---

habitants of third-world countries; the new immigrants are disproportionately prone to poverty, crime, and welfare dependency; and new racial minorities, such as Asians and Hispanics, will alter the very nature of the American nation-state, traditionally white in character.

In the end, such arguments reflect the traditional position of the Protestant Anglo-Saxon dominant culture of the country and were being voiced not too long ago, during the last great wave of immigration into the country from the 1890s to the 1920s, against such "races" as the Jews and other ethnic groups of southern and eastern European extraction, Catholic and Orthodox to boot. Nowadays, the face of the enemy has changed; it is no longer the Jew, the Greek, the Slav, or the Italian, but the non-European or non-Westerner who has become the target of suspicion, fear, and even hatred. That too, I am afraid, is part of the legacy of Western civilization—a profound and persistent contradiction at the heart of its "creed" of liberty, equality, individualism, and democracy.

[12] By "biblical criticism" I mean, from my Christian perspective, the study not only of the canonical texts of the Bible as such—however defined, whether one follows the Catholic tradition or the Protestant tradition—but also of all the other extant texts of ancient Judaism and earliest Christianity. I mean as well not only the study of literary texts and other cultural artifacts but also the study of the interpretation of such "texts." I readily acknowledge the need for a more comprehensive term for the discipline, a term that would include but not privilege the "canon" as such, that would place the canon within the wider framework of the socioreligious world in question; I also confess that so far I have found none to my satisfaction.

[13] For a personal plotting of the course of the discipline in the present century in terms of four paradigms or umbrella models of interpretation (historical criticism, literary criticism, cultural criticism, and cultural studies), see chap. 1 in this volume. For a delineation of the fourth and most recent paradigm, what I call cultural studies, see chap. 2.

In effect, following a pattern at work not only across a broad disciplinary spectrum but also within religious and theological studies in general, biblical criticism, which had remained since its inception as a discipline, in the aftermath of the French Revolution, exclusively the preserve of Western males—Western male clerics, to be more precise—has witnessed during the last twenty years or so an influx of outsiders into the discipline, individuals who had never formed part of the field before and who were now making their voices heard for the first time: Western women; non-Western theologians and critics; ethnic and racial minorities from non-Western civilizations in the West.[14]

These individuals began to question the character and agenda of biblical criticism, especially with respect to the unquestioned and unquestionable construct of the scientific researcher, objective and impartial—the universal and informed reader—operative in one form or another not only in historical criticism but also in the other two emerging paradigms of literary and cultural criticism and to raise instead the radical question of contextualization and perspective. This growing insistence on the situated and interested nature of all reading and interpretation brought additional, pointed, and unrelenting pressure on biblical criticism—already in serious turmoil as a result of internal methodological and theoretical challenges—to come to terms with the question of real readers, the flesh-and-blood readers.

From a disciplinary point of view, ethnic and racial minorities in biblical studies, whether outside the West or within the West, have resisted and continue to resist, given their cultural origins outside the West, any view of criticism as timeless and value-free, seeing it instead as thoroughly enmeshed in the public arena and thus as irretrievably political in character and ramifications, both from the point of view of the narrower meaning of

---

[14] On the globalization of the discipline, see the section on "Reading the Field" in the first issue of *Biblical Interpretation* 1 (1993): 34-114, esp. D. A. J. Clines, "Possibilities and Priorities of Biblical Interpretation in an International Perspective," 67-87; and D. Jobling, "Globalization in Biblical Studies/Biblical Studies in Globalization," 96-110. See also J. R. Levison and P. Pope-Levison, "Global Perspectives on New Testament Interpretation," in *Hearing the New Testament: Strategies for Interpretation,* ed. J. B. Green (Grand Rapids, Mich.: William B. Eerdmans, 1995), 329-48. For similar though earlier developments in other fields and their consequences, see (a) from the point of view of historical studies: J. Appleby, L. Hunt, and M. Jacob, *Telling the Truth about History* (New York: W. W. Norton, 1994), 126-59; and P. Novick, *That Noble Dream: The "Objectivity Question" and the American Historical Profession* (Cambridge: Cambridge University Press, 1988), 469-521; (b) from the point of view of literary studies: V. B. Leitch, *Cultural Criticism, Literary Theory, Poststructuralism* (New York: Columbia University Press, 1992), 83-103; (c) from the point of view of social studies: S. Seidman, *Contested Knowledge: Social Theory in the Postmodern Era* (Cambridge, Mass.: Blackwell, 1994), 234-80.

this term (the realm of politics within the sphere of the sociopolitical) and its broader meaning (the realm of power within the sphere of the ideological). In other words, ethnic and racial minorities insist on reading with their own eyes and making their own voices heard, while challenging their colleagues in the West to do the same, in an explicit and public fashion. In this regard, the profound geopolitical transformation at work outlined above will only magnify this twofold resistance on the part of ethnic and racial minorities against the construct of the universal and learned reader, with its corresponding vision of a non-ideological reading, and insistence on the construct of the flesh-and-blood reader, with its corresponding vision of all reading as ideological to the core.

Professional Context: The World of the Biblical Guild

Finally, some remarks are in order with regard to the profession and its guilds, that is to say, its network of learned organizations. There is a wide range of such groups in existence; while some have a distinctly local, national, or regional focus, others are more international in scope. Among the latter, some focus on the study of either the Christian scriptures (e.g., the Society for the Study of the New Testament) or the Hebrew Bible (e.g., the International Organization for the Study of the Old Testament), while others encompass both areas of specialization (e.g., the Catholic Biblical Association and the Society of Biblical Literature). All of these international organizations have, quite understandably from both a historical and an economic point of view, their origins in the West. Moreover, although their membership is open in principle to non-Western critics, their overall character and orientation, as well as actual attendance at the annual meetings, remain overwhelmingly Western in character. Consequently, at a time when the number of biblical critics from outside the West is clearly on the rise, there is still no international organization in the field with a primary base outside the West; no occasion when non-Western critics from across the globe can meet on their own, as the West so often does; no meeting in the West where non-Western critics ever represent more than a handful of participants; and no gathering anywhere where the West and the non-West, the colonizers and the colonized, can come together on a regular basis for dialogue in sufficient numbers from both sides.

Yet, an exception may be in the making, by way of the Society of Biblical Literature. First, the Society is beginning to hold its annual international meetings outside Europe on a regular basis, with a first such meeting held in Australia in 1993 and a second in South Africa in 2000. Second, as part of its Challenge Campaign, a multi-year drive for funds and endowment, the Society has established as one of its primary goals for the future the expansion of the circle of voices participating in biblical studies, with increased contacts and interaction between the West and the non-West as a concrete desideratum.[15] Third, the makeup of the Society within the United States, its home base, is also beginning to change. Such changes should come as no surprise, given the broader demographic currents at work in U.S. society at large. Two recent sets of statistics should be especially noted in this regard.

First, not long after the national census of 1990, the U.S. Census Bureau reported a profound shift at work in the society: while in 1980 U.S. citizens of non-European descent represented one-fifth or 20 percent of the nation's population, by 1990 they accounted for one-fourth or 25 percent of the population—a development of unbelievable proportions.[16] Second, in 1987, a few years before the census, the Hudson Institute published a report entitled "Workforce 2000," which has turned out to be quite influential in the national discussion.[17] The report predicted, among other things, that the labor force of the not-too-distant future would be increasingly diverse, more and more composed of women, members of minority groups, and other alternatives to the traditional white, male breadwinner. Thus, what the Hudson Institute report of 1987 had anticipated for the year 2000, the census findings of 1990 had begun to confirm in no uncertain way.

Such demographic changes and projections, involving a rapidly growing presence of individuals of non-Western origins or descent, were bound to have, sooner or later, an impact on the academic profession, its graduate programs, and its guilds. Neither biblical criticism nor the Society of Biblical Literature has been an exception in this regard. Indeed, a look at program offerings and institutional structures shows that the Society has gradually begun to reflect such larger societal changes as well. For example, for some time now two such groups have been hard at work: the African American Theology and Biblical Hermeneutics Section and the Bible in Africa, Asia, and Latin America Section (BAALA). Subsequently, two more groups have emerged: the Asian and Asian-American Biblical Studies Section and the Bible in Caribbean Culture and Tradition Consultation, which merged with BAALA to create the Bible in Africa, Asia, the

---

[15] For the scope and goals of the Challenge Campaign, see the news release and report of the executive director in *Religious Studies News* 10 (February 1995), 15-18. The report indicates that SBL members come from eighty countries and that 10 percent of the membership resides outside North America.

[16] See, e.g., F. Barringer, "Census Shows Profound Change in Racial Makeup of the Nation," *The New York Times* (March 11, 1991), nat. ed.: A1. It is this trend that is reflected in the Census Bureau's long-range projections for the year 2050, when the percentage of the non-European population of the nation is expected to reach just under 50 percent. It is also this trend that is causing increasing concern among U.S. citizens of European descent (see n. 11 above).

[17] W. B. Johnston, *Workforce 2000: Work and Workers for the Twenty-first Century* (Indianapolis, Ind.: The Hudson Institute; Washington: U.S. Department of Labor, 1987).

Caribbean, and Latin America Section (BAACLA). Later, another group was formed: the New Testament Studies and Postcolonial Studies Consultation. Similarly, for a good number of years now, the Committee on Underrepresented Racial and Ethnic Minority Persons in the Profession has endeavored to provide leadership, community, and advocacy within the Society for minority concerns and issues.

Given such developments within the SBL in the United States, the Society could very well become, if it were to reach out and incorporate—in keeping with its stated goals—the ever-growing number of scholars from outside the West in biblical criticism, the first truly international organization in the profession, with enormous and healthy ramifications for both Western and non-Western critics alike. Indeed, there is no other group on the horizon that could even come close to such a reality—or would want to, for that matter. To be sure, even within such a transformed vision of the Society, the West would continue to predominate, not only by way of governance and numbers but also in terms of discourse and practice; at the same time, however, a vital space would be open for dialogue between the West and the rest, with sufficient numbers in attendance from both camps to ensure a balanced discussion and engagement.

From a professional point of view, ethnic and racial minorities in biblical studies have begun to see their numbers increase and their concerns and interests expand both inside and outside the West. Such a presence will continue to grow as our numbers in theological education and graduate programs continue to expand, and expand they will: outside the West, not only because of the fundamental geopolitical changes taking place in the world but also because of the continuing power and impact of liberation theology in all of its various forms, with its clear call for conscientization—for a sense of self-identity, self-consciousness, and self-determination; inside the West, on account of the continuing factors of high immigration, a relatively young population, and a high birthrate among ethnic and racial minorities, alongside a similar impact on the part of liberation theology.

Concluding Comments

Such, then, is my assessment of our overall situation as ethnic and racial minorities in biblical studies at the turn of the century. To summarize: (1) From the perspective of world affairs, we represent, whether at home or in the diaspora, the children of non-Western cultures at a defining time in international politics, a time when the long era of Western global domination begins to draw to a close and "the rest" begin to regard and exert themselves as subjects of history. The impact of such geopolitical developments on all academic disciplines, including religious studies and the classical theological disciplines, is bound to increase as this process continues to unfold, gradually but inexorably. (2) From the perspective of the discipline, we call into question the dominant Western and modernist myth of the impartial and objective observer, the ideal and universal reader, and call instead for an explicit focus on real readers, on place and ideology. In so doing, we argue for a different approach to the discipline, involving critical analysis of contextualization and perspective at all levels of inquiry, as well as a different approach to pedagogy. (3) From the perspective of the profession, we witness our presence in the guild—our numbers and influence, our concerns and interests—very much on the rise. Highly conscious of the fact that we are no longer solely inscribed in the West, we begin to look toward our own cultures and histories for grounding and inspiration. With this general context in mind, therefore, I should like to turn at this point to an analysis of our life and role in the discipline and the profession.

LIFE AND ROLE OF ETHNIC AND RACIAL MINORITIES IN BIBLICAL STUDIES

Such a state of affairs, while seemingly quite promising and attractive on the surface, is, to say the least, not without untoward consequences. In an earlier analysis of the life and role of ethnic and racial minorities in theological education and scholarship I described our situation in terms of struggle, as a *lucha*, constant and unrelenting but also worth fighting.[18] I am afraid I cannot but describe our situation in biblical studies, whether with reference to the discipline or the profession, in similar terms of struggle, unremitting and ever-present but worth engaging as well. In what follows, then, I begin with a few observations regarding the nature of this struggle, with recourse to the same three factors invoked above, as a point of departure for a final reflection on the need to take up the struggle.

Life as Struggle

A Geopolitical Perspective

From a geopolitical perspective biblical criticism is perceived as both alien and alienating by ethnic and racial minorities. On the one hand, the roots and moorings of our discipline and profession have been profoundly and understandably Western. As such, the canon of works and authors to be read, the issues and concerns in question, the historical contexts and perspectives to be studied, and the interpretive frameworks and traditions

---

[18] F. F. Segovia, "Theological Education and Scholarship as Struggle: The Life of Racial/Ethnic Minorities in the Profession," *Journal of Hispanic/Latino Theology* 2 (1994): 5-25. In so doing, I borrowed from the popular religion of my cultural group as filtered through the prism of my own family, the focal vocabulary of life as both struggle and counterstruggle.

to be used in the analysis of such works, issues, and perspectives have been those of the West. As ethnic and racial minorities enter the discipline and the profession from outside the West, they find that neither the content nor the mode of discourse is their own. The situation proves to be in many ways, therefore, an alien one. Such individuals find themselves—their works and authors, their issues and concerns, their contexts and perspectives, their interpretive frameworks and traditions—not only out of place but also out of sight.[19] For such individuals, therefore, to pursue biblical studies is to enter yet another dimension of the Western world and to see the biblical world as re-constructed and re-presented by the West.

On the other hand, the problem is not only one of different contents and modes of discourse but also one of sociocultural perception and attitude. At this point one must keep in mind the dynamics of hegemony and colonialism—the relationship between the center and the margins, the dominant group and the subordinate groups, the majority group and the minority groups. Colonial discourse and practice function largely in terms of binary oppositions: a primary opposition of center/margins engendering and supporting a number of other oppositions, such as superior/inferior, civilized/savage, advanced/primitive—all coalescing in the end in the traditional geopolitical opposition of the West/the rest. Consequently, ethnic and racial minorities, coming as they do from non-Western cultures, enter not only an alien context in biblical studies but also an alienating context, a context where the content and mode of their discourse are not acknowledged, much less accepted or respected, as an equal though different or alternative vision of reality. For such individuals, therefore, to pursue biblical studies is to enter further into the world of social stratification set up by the West vis-à-vis "the other."[20]

---

[19] For a constantly expanding discussion, see, e.g., I. J. Mosala, *Biblical Hermeneutics and Black Theology in South Africa* (Grand Rapids, Mich.: William B. Eerdmans, 1989), esp. 1-42; C. H. Felder, *Troubling Biblical Waters: Race, Class, and Family* (Maryknoll, N.Y.: Orbis Books, 1990), esp. 3-21; C. H. Felder, ed., *Stony the Road We Trod: African American Biblical Interpretation* (Minneapolis: Fortress Press, 1991); R. S. Sugirtharajah, ed., *Voices from the Margins: Interpreting the Bible in the Third World* (Maryknoll, N.Y.: Orbis Books, 1991), esp. 1-6 and 434-44; P. J. Hartin, *Third World Challenges in the Teaching of Biblical Studies*, Occasional Papers 25 (Claremont, Calif.: The Institute for Antiquity and Christianity, 1993); K. O'Brien Wicker, "Teaching Feminist Biblical Studies in a Postcolonial Context," in *Searching the Scriptures*, vol. 2: *A Feminist Introduction*, ed. E. Schüssler Fiorenza (New York: Crossroad, 1993), 367-80; R. S. Sugirtharajah, "The Bible and Its Asian Readers," *Biblical Interpretation* 1 (1993): 54-66; and R. S. Sugirtharajah, ed., *Commitment, Context and Text: Examples of Asian Hermeneutics*, spec. issue of *Biblical Interpretation* 2 (1993): 251-376.

[20] On prejudice and discrimination from the point of view of intergroup relations, see Fegin, *Racial and Ethnic Relations*, 15-17.

To be sure, what is true of biblical studies is true of all other theological disciplines as well. I should like to recount in this regard a personal story that Gustavo Gutiérrez, the Peruvian theologian, shared with me some time ago in the course of a conversation on theological studies from an international perspective. I do so not only because it is truly a classic, a perfect example of the sense of struggle I am striving to convey, but also because of the individual in question. Gutiérrez recalled how, during his days as a doctoral student in theology at the University of Lyon, a fellow student of his from Europe told him how hard he found it to accept that he (Gutiérrez) *could have anything to teach him at all.* This is a story with which all ethnic and racial minorities can readily identify, a situation that we have all faced at one time or another in the course of our socioeducational journey in the West, whether in England, France, Germany, or the United States; it is a story that I hear in endless variations not only from graduate students but also from seasoned scholars on a fairly regular basis. In fact, as one such scholar once put it, one is often made to feel like the man born blind of John 9, as he is told by the powers that be, "You were born in utter sin and you dare to teach us!"

From the point of view of biblical studies in particular, I should like to share one such close encounter of my own, which took place some years ago at an international meeting of the discipline. It involved a young German scholar who, having heard a presentation of mine partially grounded in a hermeneutics of liberation, asked, in a tone of arrogance and disdain such as I have seldom heard in the whole of my professional life, what all this had to do with him. This reaction was what I would call a variation of the center-of-the-world syndrome: a thoroughly uncritical acceptance of European concerns and hermeneutics as pivotal for the world at large, with a corresponding dismissal of all other hermeneutics and concerns as inferior and irrelevant. To such individuals, it would come as a complete and unfathomable surprise for any of us to answer the question, as well we could, with the counter question, what does anything you do have to do with us? Except that our sense of dialogue, of being inscribed in various discourses and practices at one and the same time, theoretically prevents us from doing so, since in fact we see all hermeneutics and concerns as ultimately interrelated.

I could go on and on recounting stories that either I myself have experienced or that others have shared with me over the years. The point is clear, however: it is very difficult for the West to enter into serious dialogue with the non-West, given the enduring psychological and cultural dynamics of hegemony and colonialism. In fact, it is well-nigh impossible for the West to listen to the critique from the non-West, radical and severe as it often is and must be, in the light of the intervening historical and political relationship. This is quite understandable. How can a position that has been dominant for so long accept the worth, let alone the critique, of the subordinate? How can insubordination be tolerated, much less engaged?

A Disciplinary Perspective

From a disciplinary perspective, ethnic and racial minorities tend to be quite conscious and open about their agenda and social location, while Westerners still hold on, by and large, in practice if not in theory, to the construct of the impartial and objective observer. Their own perspective and contextualization are not acknowledged, much less analyzed, because the construct of a universal and disinterested gaze prevents them from doing so. From such a normative gaze, therefore, what ethnic and racial minorities do, especially since it is foregrounded as such, is seen as contextual and limited; what they themselves do, however, is seen as world-encompassing and significant. As a result, a historical experience and cultural reality as particularized and contextualized as any other is bracketed and universalized as normative human experience and reality—the reality and experience of the center—with the rest unable to transcend their own social locations—the realities and experiences of the margins.

Again, let me offer a personal story by way of illustration. This one has to do with a young English scholar and a conversation, in the course of another international meeting, on the character and aims of traditional historical criticism. Visibly angry and turning surprisingly emotional, this individual protested that the method had no agenda as such, that its goals of impartiality and objectivity were solid, and that the basic problem was that people such as I were trying to politicize the discipline and derail it from its established scientific path. This reaction reflects what I would call a variation of the innocence syndrome: a belief to the effect that interpretation of the Bible is beyond any and all agendas and thus entirely removed from the political realm. For such individuals it is impossible to see that the myth of innocence is in itself a highly political agenda.

A Professional Perspective

From a professional point of view it should also be kept in mind that Western institutions having to do with religion, and thus including academic guilds and graduate programs, function by and large out of a liberal-humanist paradigm and thus presuppose a structuralist-functionalist model of society and religious groupings. As such, they replicate the profound contradictions at work in the paradigm: on the one hand, one finds within such institutions an open and heartfelt commitment to openness and tolerance; on the other hand, one also finds a much more subtle but equally forceful emphasis on consensus and conformity. Thus, while harmony and cohesion are much loved and emphasized, conflict is greatly feared and studiously avoided, with solutions to conflict generally sought behind the scenes rather than face to face.

When conflict originates with those who are not only outsiders—expected to be grateful, happy, and compliant for their very admission into such circles of privilege—but also outsiders who are by nature, as children of the colonized, perceived as marginal and inferior, the situation becomes especially problematic, almost intolerable, above all if such conflict has to do, as it usually does, with issues of justice and representation. The paradigm finds it very hard, if not altogether impossible, to deal with such a situation, and paternalism usually kicks in as a result: How could those for whom we have done so much react in such a way? The charges that follow are well-known: malcontents, ungrateful, difficult, and—my favorite—politicized.

Again, a personal story will serve to illustrate this aspect of the struggle. It concerns a young Belgian scholar and involves a conversation, during yet another international meeting, on the relationship between colonialism and hermeneutics. While quite aware of the historical consequences of Western religious expansionism in the world, involving an onslaught on all native religious beliefs and traditions as primitive or idolatrous, this individual held on for dear life to the belief that in the end the West had done far more good than evil for its colonies throughout the world. This reaction represents what I would call a variation of the all-we-have-done-for-you syndrome: failure to realize that the rest of the world never had much of a choice regarding this Western program of doing good unto others and its offer of salvation. For such individuals, it proves impossible to deal, theologically and otherwise, with that other and highly destructive side of Western civilization.

In sum, it is not difficult to see why the discipline and the profession of biblical studies should prove a struggle for so many ethnic and racial minorities. It is very difficult to deal with a discourse and practice that are not one's own, that do not regard one's discourse and practice as on a par with those of the reigning paradigm, that refuse to see themselves, like others, particularized and contextualized, and that have a visceral or structural aversion to conflict and confrontation. Within such a paradigm, ethnic and racial minorities are constantly reminded, whether actively or passively, of their marginal status and role in both discipline and profession. Such conditions give rise to and enthrone that sense of struggle that so distinguishes our life in biblical criticism. I would argue that there should be no illusions in this regard. It is a way of life that must be accepted as inevitable, not only for the time being but also, as the stories above indicate, for the foreseeable future, given the age of the interlocutors in question. At the same time, I believe it is a way of life that is very much worth fighting and engaging, insofar as it is a struggle for life.

Struggle for Life

It seems to me that ethnic and racial minorities in biblical studies, as in religious studies or the other classical theological disciplines, embody a profound contradiction at the turn of the century. There is a very real sense in which, from any number of perspectives, the course of events favors us greatly: our recent and irreversible emergence as subjects of history on the world stage; the utter demise of the modernist construct of the ideal observer and narrator and its replacement with the postmodernist construct of the always situated and engaged narrator and observer; our growing presence in the profession, both outside and inside the West, with a corresponding focus on our own concerns and interests, our own readings and interpretations. At the same time, and precisely because of such reasons, our life and role in the discipline and the profession will continue to be one of struggle. Times of change are never easy, especially for those used to power. It is very hard, even traumatic, for the center to come to terms with the loss of center; to have to admit that the center has not only shifted but actually disintegrated, giving rise to a multiplicity of voices; and to engage all such other voices in dialogue as one among many.

In the end, however, I would also argue that our future is a most promising one. Several factors compel me to argue in this direction. First, postmodernism is unstoppable, as more and more new faces join the discussion and reclaim their voices, especially when attempts are made to squash or derail such developments. Second, our numbers and our coalitions, which are crucial, will continue to push the movement forward and make it ever stronger and more sophisticated. Finally, we do have many well-meaning friends among our Western colleagues. Here I have in mind not those whom I would call cultural transvestites, who not only love to be one of us but also wish to show us, as our leaders, the way to the promised land, but rather those who are willing to listen and perhaps even follow, for a change.[21] I am convinced that the future of biblical studies—like the future of religious and theological studies in general—is a postcolonial, post-Western future, and in that future racial and ethnic minorities will have a fundamental and decisive role to play, whether outside the West or in the trenches in the West. It is a future in which the reading and interpretation of the Bible will be pursued and analyzed from any number of different contexts and perspectives, social locations and agendas, places and ideologies. It is a future with such tasks as the following before us:

---

[21] For the same problematic from the perspective of gender, see E. Showalter, "Critical Cross-Dressing: Male Feminists and the Women of the Year," *Raritan* 3 (1983): 130-49. I will never forget in this regard a planning conference for a biblical project with global pretensions to which a number of ethnic and racial minorities, including myself, had been invited. It gradually emerged in the course of the discussions that no minority had taken part in the planning stages of the project; that an extensive charter document had already been drafted for the project, to which we were expected to react; and that we would not benefit at all from the large funding in question, despite the fact that our ideas and our names would serve as the backbone for the revised draft of the document. Needless to say, all of us left the conference with a rather bitter taste in our mouths, the taste of having been used yet again. This is something against which we must be constantly on the watch, putting our hermeneutics of suspicion to good use over and over again.

1. First and foremost, a re-reading and re-interpretation of the biblical texts from outside the Western context, with a focus on such issues as the following: the self-construction of the early Christian groups; their construction of the "other"—of all those outside the boundaries of the group—and of their relationship vis-à-vis such "others"; their construction of the political realm and of their relationship to this realm, whether at the imperial level or at the local level; their visions of a different world, a world in which peace and justice prevail.

2. A critical reading of the re-construction and re-presentation of early Christianity on the part of the West, with a focus on such questions as how it was presented, or the poetics of construction; why it was presented in the way it was presented, or the rhetoric of the construction; and for whose benefit or detriment it was presented as presented, or the ideology of the construction.

3. A thorough analysis of the relationship between biblical interpretation and Western hegemony and colonialism, especially in the course of the nineteenth and early twentieth centuries, when both the formation of the discipline and the process of expansionism found themselves at their respective peaks.

4. Beyond a re-reading of the texts, a critical dialogue and engagement with the texts, their constructions and ideologies, in the light of one's own contextualization and perspective. In this regard, I believe there is an urgent need to engage the Bible not so much in the light of events in Europe in the twentieth century—what is often referred to as the post-Holocaust context—but rather in the light of events outside the West, in its colonies and territories, in the course of the last five hundred years—what I referred to earlier as the other face of Western culture and civilization. In other words, there is a need to address the wider question of how to read and interpret the Bible in the aftermath of centuries of domination, discrimination, exploitation, and the wholesale displacement and extermination of countless "others" who stood in the path of Western progress. While the question of doing theology in the light of the Holocaust could hardly be ignored by the West, given its occurrence at the very heart of Europe, the question of doing theology in the light of colonialism has not received as much attention or sympathy on the part of the West, no doubt given the removed nature of such policies and events.

5. The pursuit of a new kind of dialogue among the colonized themselves, that is, a dialogue between and among the different non-Western groups and cultures in the absence of the West. This is not to say that the dialogue between the West and the rest must come to an end, but rather that the dialogue must be expanded to cover a variety of axes without necessary inclusion of the West at every step of the way.

It is in the light of tasks such as these that I describe the future of biblical studies as a future that is very much worth the struggle, a future full of life and, as I said at the beginning, a very promising life indeed. As a product of the diaspora and thus as someone deeply inscribed in the West, I would further describe it as a future in which the admirable "creed" of the West—and admirable it is indeed—is carried forward one step further and extended to all human beings, regardless of ethnicity or race.

Asian Biblical Hermeneutics and Postcolonialism
Contesting the Interpretations
R.S. Sugirtharajah
ISBN 1-57075-205-2

"A most recent and most powerful critical approach in
Biblical Studies has been that of Postcolonial Studies. In this
volume, Dr. R.S. Sugirtharajah, one of its foremost theorists
and exponents, pursues this type of criticism from the point
of view of Asian Biblical Hermeneutics. The result is an
excellent introduction to and exposition of this new and
exciting approach. It receives my highest recommendation."
—*Fernando F. Segovia*

Dictionary of Third World Theologies
Virginia Fabella, M.M., and R.S. Sugirtharajah, editors
ISBN 1-57075-234-6

This essential reference work makes available in one
volume the breadth and richness of the theological
contributions of the peoples of Africa, Asia, the Caribbean,
Latin America, the Pacific, and the minority and indigenous
peoples of the world. With over 150 entries by Third World
theologians from around the world, this is a unique and
historic contribution. Contributors include Fernando
Segovia, Mercy Amba Oduyoye, Gustavo Gutiérrez, Virgilio
Elizondo, María Pilar Aquino, Leonardo Boff, Tissa
Balasuriya, James H. Cone, and many others.

Please support your local bookstore, or call 1-800-258-5838.
For a free catalog, please write us at
Orbis Books, Box 308
Maryknoll, NY 10545-0308
Or visit our website at www.maryknoll.org/orbis
Thank you for reading *Decolonizing Biblical Studies*.
We hope you enjoyed it.